MAINTAINING SEGREGATION

Making the Modern South

David Goldfield, Series Editor

MAINTAINING

CHILDREN AND RACIAL INSTRUCTION IN THE SOUTH 1920–1955

SEGREGATION

LEEANN G. REYNOLDS

LOUISIANA STATE UNIVERSITY PRESS

Baton Rouge

Published by Louisiana State University Press

DESIGNER: Mandy McDonald Scallan
TYPEFACE: Whitman
PRINTER AND BINDER: McNaughton & Gunn, Inc.

Library of Congress Cataloging-in-Publication Data
Names: Reynolds, LeeAnn Garrison, author.
Title: Maintaining segregation : children and racial instruction in the
   South, 1920–1955 / LeeAnn G. Reynolds.
Other titles: Making the modern South.
Description: Baton Rouge : Louisiana State University Press, [2017] | Series:
   Making the modern South | Includes bibliographical references and index. |
   Based on the author's thesis (Ph. D.)—Vanderbilt University, 2007.
Identifiers: LCCN 2016042878| ISBN 978-0-8071-6564-5 (cloth : alk. paper) | ISBN
   978-0-8071-6565-2 (pdf) | ISBN 978-0-8071-6566-9 (epub) | ISBN 978-0-8071-6567-6 (mobi)
Subjects: LCSH: Southern States—Race relations. | Segregation—Southern
   States. | Race awareness in children—Southern States. | Segregation in
   education—Southern States. | Southern States—Race relations—Religious
   aspects.
Classification: LCC E185.61 .R478 2017 | DDC 305.800975—dc23
LC record available at https://lccn.loc.gov/2016042878

For Clara, Lois, and Lila

CONTENTS

ACKNOWLEDGMENTS

The idea for this project began at Vanderbilt University in two courses with sociologist Larry Griffin. Memory studies were all the rage at the time, and for the first time I read autobiographies by southerners such as Lillian Smith, Anne Moody, and Carl Rowan. Although Larry and I have not always seen eye to eye on this project, he exposed me to sources and helped me frame questions that led me to a discovery: both black and white southerners remembered that silence—the unwillingness of parents to discuss segregation with their children—helped maintain the system. These autobiographies and others like them, along with John Cell's analysis of segregation in the American South and South Africa, inspired me to explore segregation as an institution.

My interest in studying history began even earlier, when I took a U.S. history survey course with Bruce Wheeler at the University of Tennessee. Dr. Wheeler turned my amateur interest in southern history into a major, and he served as my advisor and mentor throughout my undergraduate career. I later studied African and South African history with Catherine Higgs. Dr. Higgs's demand for excellence forced me to work harder, especially on my writing, and she convinced me that I might be able to pursue history as a career. In retrospect the coalescing of these areas of geographical focus likely laid the groundwork for my interest in segregation.

At Vanderbilt I encountered professors and graduate students who pushed me to develop as a historian but also to interrogate my worldview. I am indebted to all those who made my time at Vanderbilt so rewarding. My advisor, David Carlton, and I forged a warm and productive working relationship over the years, and I appreciate him letting me go my own way. Dennis C. Dickerson taught me African American and civil rights history and continues to serve as a source of encouragement. Others who assisted me, including Michael Kreyling, Devin Fergus, Chase Lesane-Brown, and Marjorie Spruill, provided invaluable advice, and Jim Epstein and Michael Bess offered friendship and reassurance throughout my graduate career. My graduate colleagues at Vanderbilt sustained me over the course of seven years, and their critiques made this project better. In particular I would like to thank Sue Marasco, Tim Boyd, Beth Sensing, Mark Vertuli, Steven P. Miller, Barry Robinson, Rachel Donaldson, Peter Kuryla, and Nicholas Beasley. Vanderbilt's Department of History, American Studies Program, Center for Teaching, and

Robert Penn Warren Center for the Humanities provided funding that helped me complete an earlier version of the project. The year I spent as a graduate fellow at the Warren Center was especially productive, in large part thanks to the feedback and support offered by the other fellows and director Mona Frederick.

After leaving Vanderbilt, I had the privilege of spending a year as a Franklin Postdoctoral Teaching Fellow at the University of Georgia, where the faculty and graduate students made me feel welcome. John Inscoe was kind enough to send me his extensive list of southern autobiographies early in my research process, and he took an interest in me and my work. Steve Berry also served as a source of friendship and wise counsel. During my years at Samford University, I have introduced many of my students to the same autobiographies that did so much to shape my thinking on southern history, and I have gained fresh perspective from seeing those narratives through their eyes. I am deeply grateful to my colleagues in the History Department, along with David Chapman, for giving me the time and space I needed to finish the book.

A number of institutions and individuals have provided crucial assistance that helped me complete this project. Grants from the Presbyterian Historical Society, the Southern Baptist Historical Library and Archives, and the General Commission on Archives and History of the United Methodist Church enabled me to spend extended time in their archives and find the sources I needed to expand my analysis of racial instruction in southern churches. Numerous archivists and librarians assisted me with finding documents, checking citations, and retrieving sources. My work would not have been possible without their skills and their willingness to help. Mark Smith took an early interest in this project and gave me valuable source suggestions. David Goldfield, my series editor at Louisiana State University Press, also expressed an interest in the project early on, and I am grateful for both his patience and his feedback as the book came to fruition. Rand Dotson and the rest of the editorial staff at the press have shepherded the project through the publication process, and the book is stronger for each person who took the time and care to work on it. My copyeditor, Elizabeth Gratch, saved me from numerous errors.

My personal debts are many. My faith has given me strength and resilience. My friends and family have worked with me to maintain close relationships despite the distance. They have cheered my successes and comforted me through setbacks and times of sadness, and I could not have persevered without them. My brother, Ross Reynolds, has encouraged me throughout my life, and he provided me with a place to stay on several research trips to North Carolina. My parents, Lois and

Arlin Reynolds, have given me unfailing love and support. Knowing that they are always there to help me if I need them has given me the courage to take each new step in my life.

I met my husband, Zac Smith, at the University of Georgia. Together we have built a happy and fulfilling life with our daughter, Lila. Our life proves that for all of the challenges of an academic marriage, the rewards are so much greater. He has assisted with this project in countless ways, from bringing me library books and playing with Lila while I worked to keeping me company late into the night while I tried to finish a chapter or check one more citation.

This book is dedicated to three generations of "Garrison girls" in my family. My grandmother Clara Lois Lee Garrison was a lifelong educator who passed away during the early stages of this project. The standards she set and the values she instilled continue to guide me every day of my life. My mother, Lois Ann Garrison Reynolds, is my best friend and primary editor, and her efforts have improved every page of this book. Finally, my daughter, Lila Garrison Smith, has been the source of tremendous joy and considerable stress, and her arrival gave me the discipline I needed to finish the book.

MAINTAINING SEGREGATION

INTRODUCTION

I n 1915 Katharine Du Pre Lumpkin—inspired by the "new social Christianity" during her years at Brenau College in Georgia—attended a Young Women's Christian Association (YWCA) conference in North Carolina, where the white women in attendance faced a provocative proposal: a "Miss Arthur," an African American woman on the YWCA staff, wished to speak to them about "Christianity and the race problem."[1] Lumpkin remembered the conflicting emotions that surfaced among the young women as they contemplated participating in this "unheard of transgression." Guilt at breaking the "unwritten and written law of our heritage" conflicted with guilt at violating their new commitment to the Social Gospel. The knowledge that parents and church leaders at home would disapprove competed with the need to make their own choices. Finally, the notion that a "*Miss* Arthur" would be speaking to them and not a "Mary" or a "Jane" was perplexing in itself. In the end they acquiesced, and aside from feeling their hearts beat a little faster, they "found the heavens had not fallen, nor the earth parted asunder to swallow us up."[2] In her memoir, *The Making of a Southerner*, Lumpkin compared this encounter to the troubling Old Testament story of Uzzah, who touched the Ark of the Covenant as it threatened to slip from an ox cart and was immediately struck dead, not for his well-meaning concern for the ark but for his violation of the precise regulations for its handling.[3] Lumpkin observed that for white children in the South the "tabernacle of our sacred racial beliefs" was "untouchable" and that it had been "ingrained" in her that "to touch it would bring direst consequences." Despite such warnings, Lumpkin wrote, "I had reached out my hand for an instant and let my finger-tips brush it . . . and nothing, not the slightest thing had happened."[4]

James Farmer, who grew up two decades later in Mississippi, recalled a moment of reflection about his status in the segregated South inspired by his own college experience. When Farmer was a freshman at Wiley College in Texas, one of his professors criticized him for condemning segregation yet still sitting in the balcony of a segregated movie theater. His professor challenged him not to cooperate with the system he denounced and suggested he read Henry David Thoreau's

"Civil Disobedience." Farmer responded to this criticism by contemplating the daily compromises he had made with segregation since he first became conscious of it. For Farmer this awareness had come as a child when his mother told him he could not buy a Coke at a drugstore, as he had seen a white boy do, because he was "colored."[5] Farmer questioned, "How do people, how do I, go on day after day doing things that dehumanize—without burning up inside? Eleven years ago a Coca-Cola that I did not drink cut my heart out; but now almost daily I walk by places with invisible 'WHITE ONLY' signs without a thought, with no pain. I climb those back stairs and it doesn't hurt. Each time I do it, it comes more naturally." He sought to understand his own response to the daily indignities he faced, asking, "What keeps me from a constant state of fury? It should hurt more each time I do it—till I finally explode. How can I climb those stairs, laughing and joking with friends, unaware?" He concluded of his reaction to segregation, "The nerves must become calloused to protect themselves from too much pain. It forces us to accept what is and become what they think we are—contented inferiors."[6] While Farmer would never accept this notion of inferiority and would devote his life to destroying segregation, he understood the process of conditioning that confronted every black child in the South.

Although the lives of these two southerners, growing up decades and states apart and on opposite sides of the color line, were vastly different, both Lumpkin and Farmer highlighted the way in which they were conditioned to accept segregation. Lumpkin grew up believing disastrous consequences would accompany any violation of the segregated code. Farmer, after initially experiencing a child's sense of the system's unfairness, had adjusted himself to segregation by the time he entered college to the extent that he no longer took conscious note of its routine humiliations. The racial instruction experienced by both black and white southerners in the region's homes, schools, and churches made possible the responses to segregation remembered by Lumpkin and Farmer. Such racial conditioning and the impact it had on black and white southerners are the subjects of this study. How did white children come to believe the sky would fall if segregation were violated? How, despite daily encounters with the injustice of the system, did black children learn to adhere to the code without experiencing "a constant state of fury"?

While the type of racial instruction remembered by Lumpkin and Farmer occurred to some extent from the time southerners who had lived through the Civil War first taught their children conflicting stories about slavery, the war, and Reconstruction, this instruction was most effective as a means of maintaining segregation in the years between 1920 and 1955. Violence had served as the primary means of establishing and maintaining the system before 1920, when lynching and other forms of public violence and intimidation were common. Yet after a surge in the number of reported lynchings in 1919 in the wake of post–World War I racial tensions, this most visible and violent expression of the ideology of white supremacy declined steadily over the next decade.[7] Violence in the form of bombings, beatings, and murders would later serve as a highly visible means of defense for the system during the era of massive resistance, starting in the mid-1950s. Although the threat and reality of violence would continue to play a significant role in ensuring adherence to segregation, overt, public forms of violence played a less prominent role in maintaining segregation during the period from 1920 to 1955.[8]

Segregation was maintained in large part during the years after 1920 through the creation of a culture of silence surrounding the institution. The accumulated individual choices and actions of millions of white and black adults and children throughout the region created this culture of silence. Adults discouraged children from asking questions about the system, and the white community punished and isolated blacks and whites who engaged in individual acts of dissent. Southerners who grew up during this era had never known life without signs designating "white" or "colored." In his classic study of segregation in South Africa and the American South, John W. Cell explained, "To those whose lives it regulates, segregation may appear to be normal and natural. It is neither."[9] Likewise, Jason Sokol observed that in the South segregation "was simply a part of one's daily life. . . . Like the lakes or the trees, racial separation came to possess the feel of something natural."[10] Many southerners raised during these years considered segregated life to be "normal" because they had no basis of comparison with either an earlier era or conditions outside the region. African American journalist Carl Rowan, writing about segregation in the early 1950s, explained, "People, especially the young, are conditioned to any long-existing way of life, and this compels them to look askance at any other system." He remembered of his childhood in Tennessee, "All my own years in the South were years of conditioning. The process started for me—as it starts for any child, black or white—almost with the day I was born."[11] As a result of their early racial conditioning, young black and white southerners could envision few alternatives to the way of life in which they had been raised, and they were largely unaware of the challenges to segregation emerging from significant quarters during this period.

Little in their experience had taught young southerners that they could challenge segregation. John Egerton, writing of the 1930s, observed that "every member of the society—man and woman, white and black—knew his or her place, and it was an unusual (not to say foolhardy) person who showed a flagrant disregard for the assigned boundaries and conventions." Outspoken dissent by African Americans was "known to be reckless, even suicidal." Dissent by white southerners was "almost as difficult—though not as dangerous." Egerton surmised that it took "a special kind of courage—or madness" to speak out against segregation. During these years the issue of whether segregation would remain intact "was effectively closed almost everywhere in the South." Even among southern liberals—white reformers who promoted gradual improvement in race relations through education and communication across the color line—the message during these years was, in Egerton's words: "For the foreseeable future, segregation is non-negotiable."[12] Other firsthand observers of segregation described the South before the 1950s in similar terms. Eugene Patterson, who won a Pulitzer Prize for his editorials on civil rights, recalled, "To know that period of the South is to know that it was frozen in silence. People were not discussing the issue. Neighbor and neighbor were afraid of each other. Conformity was established by precedent. And for a man who might doubt the wisdom of segregation to sit down with his neighbor and say, 'Hey, I'm not sure we're right' could have ruined that man in most Southern states."[13] Lillian Smith, perhaps the most outspoken white critic of segregation, likewise described "the hard frozen sterile quality of those times."[14]

The culture of silence surrounding the institution could not stifle all questions about segregation. Smith observed that the question "Why?" in regard to the racial situation in the South was "as old as the white man's and Negro's life together" and as "young as each new South-born child."[15] Questions about segregation repeatedly arose when children observed that the rules they were learning about the world did not apply in all situations or to all people. Many white and black adults responded to this initial period of questioning on the part of their children by discouraging them from discussing the system. White parents knew their way of life depended on unquestioned loyalty to segregation, and they were aware of the potential social consequences for themselves and their children of thinking or acting differently from their neighbors. Black parents knew the best way to ensure their children's safety—and the family's economic well-being—was to steer clear of the attention of whites. Thus, many black parents taught their children to avoid asking questions about segregation and meet the system's demands. Black parents who chose this strategy did so not because they preferred the physical separation and ritual humiliation characteristic of the system nor because they believed the fiction that African Americans were not entitled to first-class accommodations; they did so because they sought to protect their most vital interests: their children. Both white and black adults thus had strong motivation for silencing their children's questions about segregation.

Segregation was maintained during this period through a series of safeguards. First, the culture of silence discouraged young southerners from thinking about the system—that is, from consciously examining why it had been put in place, whose interests it served, and why one was required to participate in it. Second, adults instructed young people not to talk about segregation, its contradictions, or its impact on themselves and others, thus helping to cultivate the idea that segregation was an unquestioned, immutable reality of southern life. If one did happen to "see through" one's conditioning and begin to develop a critique of the system, the threat of violence or other consequences worked to prevent active dissent. If one did choose to challenge segregation openly, the reality of those consequences isolated dissent so long as it was undertaken on an individual basis. For white southerners social ostracism was the primary consequence of dissent. Black southerners faced economic reprisals, violence, and ultimately death if they challenged the system. While the threat and reality of consequences played an ongoing role in maintaining segregation between 1920 and 1955, the culture of silence—preventing conscious examination and public discussion of the system— played a primary role in maintaining segregation during this period.

The May 17, 1954, *Brown v. Board of Education* Supreme Court decision, which established the legal apparatus through which activists pursued desegregation of southern schools, was the first in a series of events in the mid-1950s that opened up the issue of segregation's future for national debate. The following year, in the wake of discussions inspired by *Brown* about the supposed immutability of long-established customs, C. Vann Woodward published his now classic study, *The Strange Career of Jim Crow,* in which he wrote, "Southerners and other Americans of middle age or even older are contemporaries of Jim Crow. They grew up along with the system. Unable to remember a time when segregation was not the general rule or practice, they have naturally assumed that things have 'always been that way.'"[16] Woodward argued that segregation, far from being an ancient and therefore ineradicable tradition, was actually a creation of the 1890s. Although Woodward's work has since faced considerable scrutiny, his underlying argument—that because segregation had been made, it could be unmade—had a significant impact on the debate about segregation in the period immediately following the *Brown* decision.[17]

In May 1955 the Supreme Court issued the so-called *Brown II* implementation decree, which mandated that compliance with *Brown* be undertaken with "all deliberate speed" and that desegregation be overseen by federal district courts in the various southern states. Such vague language along with localized implementation gave hope to those white southerners willing to defend segregation at all costs that an effective strategy might still be launched. In August of that year Emmett Till, a fourteen-year-old African American boy from Chicago who was visiting family in Mississippi, was lynched by two white men after an encounter with the wife of one of the men at a local store. Because Till was not raised in the South, he had not been subject to the kind of racial conditioning that might have warned him of the potentially dangerous consequences of interacting with a white woman.[18] Although the two men were eventually acquitted, Till's story became nationally known when his mother insisted on a public, open-casket funeral in Chicago and pictures of his bloated and mutilated face appeared in *Jet* magazine. Till's murder has long been viewed as a key impetus for the civil rights movement because of the jarring impact that the pictures and the story had on many who later became activists.[19] Finally, the Montgomery bus boycott, which has traditionally been seen as the start of the direct action phase of the movement, began in December 1955. Taken together, these events reveal the mid-1950s as a time when the issue of segregation was unavoidable. The notion that segregation could not be questioned was no longer sustainable. Champions of segregation would henceforth resort to more aggressive measures to defend—rather than simply maintain—the system.

Thinking of segregation as having been maintained through a culture of silence and a series of safeguards helps to explain how the system continued to function even as it faced mounting opposition in the decades before the civil rights movement as traditionally understood. John Cell argued, "Segregation triumphed for the very reason that it *was* flexible and sophisticated. . . . It enabled white supremacy to survive in an increasingly threatening, hostile world." He explained, "Time and again segregation was demystified. Time and again the ideology rebounded." The "toughness and resilience" of the institution, in Cell's estimation, dictate that "segregation must be recognized as one of the most successful political ideologies of the past century," if success can be defined by the ability of an ideological system to hold individuals in its grasp.[20] The sophistication and resilience of the system account for the persistence of segregation despite the activism that scholars now refer to as the "long civil rights movement." Closely identified with historians such as Jacquelyn Dowd Hall and Glenda Gilmore, the long civil rights movement invokes both opposition to segregation in the decades before the 1950s and the continuing struggles after the 1960s for economic justice and against institutional racism.[21] The search for antecedents to the nonviolent direct action campaigns of the 1950s and 1960s is important historiographical work, and skepticism about the success of the "short" civil rights movement, given the enduring structural inequalities in American society, is well-founded.[22] Much of the activism undertaken before the 1950s, however, was not widely known to the public, often by design, or involved activities such as institution building that were seen as nonthreatening.[23] The system could absorb such opposition and keep functioning.[24]

Many black southerners themselves did not recognize the existence of a *movement* prior to the 1950s and early 1960s; that is, they did not recognize outlets for broad-based, public opposition to segregation.[25] Mississippi farmer and activist Hartman Turnbow asserted that if he had been told about the changes that came to race relations in his community before they happened, he "just wouldn't have believed it." He explained, "I didn't dream of it. I didn't see no way."[26] Like Turnbow, many black southerners could not envision an effective means of challenging segregation, and they could only dream of a world where their children could grow up without the restrictions and humiliations of the system. The need to prepare black children for the reality of the life they had to lead served to blunt the potential impact of activism associated with the long civil rights movement narrative. Black parents did not learn from those efforts that it was practical to mount a public challenge to segregation or worth the risks involved to teach their children to do so. They learned those lessons instead from the activists of the 1950s and 1960s, though it should be noted that many black parents continued to express concern over their children's safety. The racial conditioning experienced by both black and white children in the South helps to explain why opposition to segregation before the mid-1950s—though vital to building the institutional apparatus and activist networks upon which the civil rights movement would draw—did not effectively undermine the system. Such conditioning prevented critiques of segregation from permeating popular perceptions and effecting change.

A historiographical counterpart to the long civil rights movement is the emphasis on "everyday forms of resistance."[27] Robin D. G. Kelley made an influential argument about the extent and nature of black southerners' opposition to segregation. Drawing on political anthropologist James C. Scott's work on "infrapolitics," Kelley examined how black working-class southerners resisted segregation, not so much through organizations such as labor unions or the National Association for the Advancement of Colored People (NAACP) but through everyday actions that served to challenge the system.[28] He wrote, "The appearance of silence and accommodation was not only deceiving but frequently intended to deceive. Beneath the veil of consent lies a hidden history of unorganized, everyday conflict waged by African-American working people." Kelley argued that working-class African Americans "always resisted, but often in a manner intended to cover their tracks." He distinguished between such infrapolitics and "organized resistance" or "collective, open engagement" as a means of challenging the system, though he asserted that "they are two sides of the same coin that make up the history of working-class self-activity." In his analysis African Americans need not have been aware that their actions constituted "resistance" for those actions to have "shaped" the segregated system.[29] Kelley's argument that black southerners shaped the system that was intended to control them is well taken. When black parents made choices about how to teach their children about segregation, when black teachers introduced supplementary lessons about black history, and when black Sunday school teachers taught young people they had value as children of God, they shaped the segregated world in which black children lived. Often, however, the lessons children learned in their homes, schools, and churches had the outcome of encouraging them to meet the demands of segregation.

Historiographical trends that privilege a long civil rights movement and everyday forms of resistance risk neglecting the voices of those black southerners who remembered having come to terms with segregation in light of the overwhelming opposition they faced. John Volter, who was interviewed by the Behind the Veil project at Duke University, explained of his childhood in the 1930s, "Segregation was an accepted thing. I'm not saying that people liked it but then, you know, you either accept something or you fight it, and so at that time there was no NAACP or nothing, so you accepted the role, praying that things would get better and they did."[30] Likewise, Gladys Austin, interviewed by the Mississippi Oral History Project, recalled of her childhood in the late 1920s and early 1930s, "Everything was separate and unequal. We believed it should be like that, and we accepted it." She explained, "We lived in the days when they said colored and white. This was a common practice. We just went to the colored fountain and didn't think anything about it. We knew [we] couldn't sit at a lunch counter and we didn't go there. OK? We knew that at some of these places, they did have a back door for the colored. And you know, we went in the back door, and this was no big deal." She concluded of her response to segregation, "We just didn't even think about it. I guess we thought that was the way it was supposed to be."[31] These voices and others like them do not support the prevailing historiographical trends, but they must be taken into account. Overstating the extent of active, intentional, effective resistance to segregation in the decades before the 1950s downplays the strength of the system with which African Americans had to contend and undermines the rare accomplishment that was the mobilization of a mass movement in the 1950s and 1960s.

Ultimately, black southerners responded to segregation in a variety of ways. Some resisted it either overtly or covertly, while others learned to accept life within its limits. Charles S. Johnson, an African American sociologist writing in 1943, believed the extent and nature of acceptance depended on factors such as class, education, and geography, and he drew a distinction between "unconscious conditioning to acceptance, which is an aspect of socialization in this environment" and "rational acceptance of a role as a measure essential to survival in the environment."[32] While it is imperative to chronicle the efforts of those black southerners who challenged segregation during the decades that preceded the mass movement, it is also vital to understanding segregation to acknowledge the voices of those who saw no outlets for protest or believed the risks of opposition to be too high. The accomplishments of those who challenged the system both before and during the civil rights movement cannot be fully understood without an appreciation for the obstacles they faced.

Another key historiographical development is the increasing focus on the role of children in the segregated South. Two notable studies that explore this issue are Jennifer Ritterhouse's *Growing Up Jim Crow: How Black and White Southern Children Learned Race* and Kristina DuRocher's *Raising Racists: The Socialization of White Children in the Jim Crow South*. Taken together, these two studies, along with my own, establish children as a pivotal point of entry for understanding southern race relations.[33] As Ritterhouse explained, "Race was something that each generation of southerners had to *learn*."[34] These studies also delineate key points of debate regarding the role of children in establishing and maintaining the racial order. One debate involves chronology. Ritterhouse covered the period from the end of the Civil War until World War II; DuRocher studied the years from 1890 to 1939; and my work focuses on the period from 1920 to 1955.[35] DuRocher's chronological focus and to a lesser extent that of Ritterhouse are informed by the long civil rights movement narrative, versions of which view World War II as a central plot point, if not as *the* beginning of the movement. A second debate involves whether white parents intentionally taught their children racial lessons with the primary goal of maintaining the social order. Although Ritterhouse hedged somewhat on this issue, at one point characterizing white parents' lessons as "reactive" rather than "part of a self-conscious plan of instruction," she also used words such as *effort, vigilance,* and *collusion* to describe white parents' approach to teaching their children about race.[36] Such terms imply intentional instruction on the part of white adults. DuRocher, for her part, argued that white parents engaged in deliberate "indoctrination" of their children—often by exposing them to lynchings—as a means of maintaining white supremacy.[37]

The debates surrounding chronology and the nature of white parents' racial lessons are linked. The way children learned about segregation in the late nineteenth century, as the system was being established, was very different from the way they learned about it as the system matured in the decades after 1920. As the system was being created, white southerners devised justifications for segregation and disfranchisement: the "tragedy" of Reconstruction revealed that freed slaves were not ready for equal participation in society; separate accommodations would lead to less friction between the races; and the presence of African Americans in politics led to violence and corruption that could only be eliminated through disfranchisement. White southerners intentionally taught such rationalizations to young people as the system was being crafted. As new generations of southerners were born who had no knowledge of life before the "white" and "colored" signs went up, racial instruction focused less on deliberate teaching of such justifications and more on discouraging the troubling questions inspired by the signs and the rituals that accompanied them. The old rationalizations were now lessons learned by rote, and white southerners' attachment to segregation came to be based less on intellectual justifications and more on unexamined emotional connections.[38]

As for racial violence, it played a crucial role in establishing and maintaining segregation, particularly in the decades around the turn of the twentieth century. Photographic evidence presented by both Ritterhouse and DuRocher reveals that some white children were taken to witness lynchings and to view the victims afterward.[39] Yet the "mass mob," or "spectacle," lynchings that DuRocher, in particular, described were much more characteristic of the period from 1890 to 1920 than they were of the 1920s and beyond.[40] DuRocher conceded, "By the 1920s, the number of reported lynchings had declined," in part because "white communities increasingly concealed evidence of lynching" in the face of mounting national criticism.[41] Over time lynching became a covert rather than a spectacle affair, which significantly reduced its efficacy as a tool of socialization.

While DuRocher placed violence at the center of her narrative, Ritterhouse focused on "racial etiquette" as a means of communicating racial lessons. She distinguished between segregation—whether de jure or de facto—and racial etiquette, which she saw as being rooted in the vertical racial domination of slavery rather than the horizontal racial order of segregation.[42] She consistently characterized segregation as involving only "physical separation," and she correctly argued that in domestic settings, for example, physical proximity was actually required in order for African Americans to perform the work for which they had been hired.[43] In contrast, my study explores the nature of segregation as an institution, and I define segregation as having involved both physical separation and ritual humiliation; thus, one could be subject to the indignity of segregation even while working alongside a white employer in the kitchen or in the fields. I also conceptualize instruction about segregation as having addressed both legal and customary means of social control.

Although all three studies recognize the home as a significant site for racial instruction, they diverge in their focus on additional venues for socialization. Ritterhouse devoted considerable attention to children's interactions within their "own social worlds," apart from the direct supervision of adults.[44] DuRocher explored socialization in the region's schools, through popular culture, and around the lynching pyre. I focus on institutions, examining how black and white children learned about race and segregation in the region's public schools and, notably, in its churches. While DuRocher focused exclusively on white children, I join Ritterhouse in examining the racial lessons learned by children of both races. Ritterhouse and I agree that white parents' lessons were more uniform than those of black parents, who faced a more complex dilemma about what to teach their children about race and segregation. We agree that much of black parents' instruction focused on building up their children's sense of self-worth, though I question the efficacy of the socialization strategy focused on "respectability." We disagree on the overall impact of racial instruction on black children. Influenced by James Scott and by the concept of everyday forms of resistance, Ritterhouse emphasized "self-conscious performance" as central to African Americans' response to segregation.[45] I explore, instead, the extent to which black children came to view segregation as an immutable fact of life in the South, "just the way things were," as there were few viable options for challenging it at the time.[46]

Finally, all three studies grapple with issues of memory. In the wake of scholarship on the limitations of memory and autobiography, historians have become more skeptical of both. Jacquelyn Dowd Hall noted, "When we speak and write *as historians,* we tend to position ourselves above and beyond memory, which we devalue as self-serving and inexact." Suspicious of personal memory, "historians take it upon themselves to piece together a plausible narrative from scattered, surviving shards."[47] The historian's method of piecing together the "shards" of the past is actually not all that different from the way an autobiographer pieces fragments of memory together to shape a coherent narrative of a life. In his groundbreaking work on autobiography, Georges Gusdorf explained, "The author of an autobiography gives himself the job of narrating his own history; what he sets out to do is to reassemble the scattered elements of his individual life and to regroup them in a comprehensive sketch."[48] Such sketches provide vital internal perspective on past events. Another pioneer of autobiographical studies, Roy Pascal, observed, "Autobiography has to give that unique truth of life as it is seen from inside, and in this respect it has no substitute or rival."[49] Likewise, autobiographical observations of segregation offer invaluable, firsthand accounts of how the system worked. In her study of segregation and southern memoir, Jennifer Jensen Wallach observed that an autobiographer "always functions as a cultural anthropologist of sorts" because autobiographers are "participant-observers" in the lives they lead.[50] The autobiographers whose works inform this study constitute an indispensable resource through which to understand segregation's theoretical basis.[51]

A recognition of the value of autobiography as a source for understanding segregation should not suggest a blindness to the genre's shortcomings. Memory, the "evidence" out of which autobiography is fashioned, is widely understood to be faulty and shaped as much by what is forgotten as what is remembered. Autobiography, in turn, depends on a process of selecting memories based on some organizing principle. Pascal explained, "Autobiography means therefore discrimination and selection in face of the endless complexity of life, selection of facts, distribution of emphases, choice of expression."[52] He believed historians are wary of autobiography not so much because they doubt the accuracy of particular facts but because they are suspicious of the practice of organizing a life story around a principle of selection that only becomes clear with the later perspective of having lived that life.[53] Yet this selection process is not always a liability. In the case of autobiographers who were conditioned not to attach meaning to troubling racial encounters, only the perspective of adulthood and an organizing principle that sought to re-create the experience of growing up in the segregated South could render those experiences visible. Efforts to recover the impact of these incidents at the time offer limited insight because the segregated system operated to ensure that little significance would be attached to such encounters. When a troubling racial incident occurred that did not match the narrative young southerners had learned about why their society was organized as it was, they dismissed it as anomalous. An accumulation of such encounters or an emotionally jarring event that allowed one to see through one's racial conditioning brought these earlier incidents to mind, giving them new meaning, and they became the raw material out of which a new narrative, a critique of segregation, was constructed. Accounts of growing up in the segregated South are written versions of those critiques.

Misgivings about the use of autobiography as historical source material have also involved the extent to which the genre is a form of "imaginative literature." In *Telling Lies in Modern American Autobiography* Timothy Dow Adams embraced this aspect of autobiography and questioned, "Is it important to be true or to ring true? How could any autobiographer, particularly a fiction writer, resist inventing telling episodes that present a life story more truthfully than what actually happened?"[54] Autobiographers use techniques of fiction—such as re-creating detailed conversations from the past—to enhance their narratives. In *Confessions of a White Racist* Larry L. King explained, "Man's memory is not infallible; neither are his interpretations. Sometimes problems of story structure encourage the convoluting of time. Or the blurring of scenes or people becomes necessary. In short, pure unadulterated truth does not automatically leap from pen to page."[55] Adams concluded that autobiographies are not meant to be taken as "historically accurate" but, rather, as "metaphorically authentic."[56] While autobiographers may not be able to tell a story that is altogether factually accurate, they are able—through their imaginative use of language—to capture the sense of having lived through an experience. Recognizing the necessarily constructed nature of the genre, one scholar nonetheless found most autobiographers to be honest and asserted that "an honest autobiography puts its illusion of the past forward in good faith."[57]

Many of the autobiographers featured in this study made a good faith effort to overcome the genre's limitations. King issued a compelling expression of good faith, writing that to distort his recollections "would be to defeat my larger purpose of attempting accurately to reflect my time, my place, and my condition as it related to the most explosive social issue of my day."[58] Other autobiographers checked their own memories against those of parents and siblings or against archival records. Finally, writers who were particularly sensitive to the drawbacks of autobiography found innovative ways to corroborate their accounts. Benjamin Mays had over one hundred interviews conducted with other African Americans who grew up in the South at the same time he did and compared those accounts to his own.[59] Paul Hemphill, aware that his white, blue-collar Birmingham, Alabama, upbringing gave him an incomplete perspective on life in the city, incorporated memories about segregation from John Porter, an African American man, and Mimi Tynes, an elite white woman, to round out his analysis.[60] Through such strategies authors sought to minimize the limitations of autobiography.

The ultimate value of autobiography for studying segregation can be found in the motivations that southerners cited for recording their experiences. Pat Watters, a white journalist who covered civil rights, described how the movement "struck at the roots of internalized perceptions of self and society by white and Negro Southerners, jarring loose to varying degrees the bedrock attitudes and habits of mind instilled in these Southerners with all the force of childhood conditioning." In order to understand the transformation that the movement wrought, one had "to go back and feel the quality and texture of life in the South before the changes came, to re-enter the southern psychological reality of the pre-movement days."[61] For him the best way to explain that reality was through his own childhood memories. African American lawyer and activist Vernon Jordan cited a similar motivation for writing his autobiography. In 1970 the family's black housekeeper, Mrs. Gaines, recalled a memorable bus trip she had taken in the segregated South.

When she boarded the bus, the only other passenger was a white man sitting near the front. When another white man boarded the bus, he came to her seat halfway back and demanded that she move. Jordan remembered his daughter, Vickee, having anxiously asked Mrs. Gaines what she did. Mrs. Gaines told her, "just in a totally matter-of-fact manner," that she had moved.[62] When Vickee insisted that *she* would not have moved in that situation, Mrs. Gaines knowingly told her, "Yes, Vickee. You would have moved." Jordan resolved that he would work "to bridge the gap" between the perspective of adults who knew what the consequences could have been for Mrs. Gaines and that of young people like his daughter, who had grown up during and after the movement and found "unfathomable" the idea that they might have been made to conform in that way.[63] Through autobiography one can enter the reality of the pre-movement days and gain a greater understanding of what the movement accomplished in overcoming the conditioning of black and white southerners.

An examination of racial instruction in homes, schools, and churches will provide access to that pre-movement reality. The first chapter explores what white children learned at home about life in the segregated South. White parents discouraged questioning and discussion of segregation lest their children endanger the system or jeopardize themselves or their family's status by expressing doubts about the system in public. The second chapter reveals that black parents confronted a much more difficult task in determining what to teach their children about segregation. The dilemma they faced was how to raise their children so as to protect them from harm without sacrificing their sense of self-worth. Black parents devised a variety of strategies for approaching this task, some of which encouraged their children to come to terms with segregation.

The third chapter draws on state board of education records and textbooks, along with individual memories, to examine what southerners learned about race and segregation in the region's public schools. In addition to school buildings and supplies serving as visible evidence of inequality, the official curriculum used for both white and black schools was largely silent on the role of African Americans in the nation's past. When black southerners did learn positive messages about black achievement, they did so through the initiative of individual teachers, who sought out materials with which to supplement the official curriculum. The fourth chapter incorporates Sunday school lessons, denominational publications, and individual memories to explore how churches approached issues of race and segregation. Black southerners had more control over what was taught in their churches, which, even more than schools, were sites within black communities where children's self-worth was cultivated. While white schools were largely able to contain the message of equality explicit in the study of American democracy by marginalizing African Americans within the historical narrative, white churches, which taught about the commonality of all people as children of God and sang "Jesus Loves the Little Children," faced a greater challenge in obscuring the implications of that message. The glaring discrepancy in singing about "red and yellow, black and white" in an all-white body of Christians could raise questions that had no easy answers.

The fifth chapter considers how some southerners were able to see through their racial conditioning and begin to imagine alternatives to segregation. These moments of awakening often came in the form of personal interactions within the rituals of segregation, but they could also occur through means such as travel outside the region, attending college, and military service. Some of the most profound awakenings experienced by black southerners involved the realization that segregation was not inevitable, that it was possible to challenge the system. For white southerners the most significant moments of awakening were often based on the realization that maintaining segregation came at a high personal cost. The project concludes with a consideration of the civil rights movement as an educational campaign. From their own experiences and those of others who became critical of segregation in the years before the movement, civil rights leaders gained an appreciation for what it would take to overcome racial conditioning. Black southerners had to be convinced that it was possible to mount a broad-based, public challenge to the system. The movement meanwhile forced white southerners, whose loyalty to segregation was often based on an emotional connection to a system they had not thought very much about, to make a conscious choice about whether to defend segregation or let it go. If white southerners could be convinced that segregation was costing them something—morals, sales, or self-control—they might be persuaded that defending the system called on them to make sacrifices they were no longer willing to make. The accomplishments of the civil rights movement thus depended on an understanding of childhood racial conditioning and the means through which it might be overcome.

CHAPTER 1

"THE SOUTHERN NEVER-NEVER LAND"

Racial Instruction in White Homes

W riting in the late 1950s, after being the target of years of harassment for her stance on civil rights, white Kentuckian Anne Braden did not blame the segregationists in her community or consider them "evil men." Instead, she considered them "trapped." Like many white southerners, they had learned myths about segregation "as they learned their ABC's; they had absorbed it with the air they breathed."[1] Lillian Smith described the process by which white children learned about segregation in similar terms: "We learned far more from acts than words, more from a raised eyebrow, a joke, a shocked voice, a withdrawing movement of the body, a long silence, than from long sentences."[2] White southerners who have written about what they learned about race and segregation at home have focused more on what was unspoken, assumed, or taken for granted than on specific lessons from their parents. This phenomenon can likely be attributed to the very way white parents went about educating their children about the system. Segregation was not to be questioned or even acknowledged in many white households, so intentional instruction would have presented the system as something to be consciously considered. Smith remembered, "Like *sex*, the word *segregation* was not mentioned in the best circles."[3] Parents often relied, instead, on nonverbal cues within the home, along with the signs and scripted performances of segregation in the larger community, to teach their children what was expected of them.

The recollections that follow are primarily those of white southerners who grew up in the segregated South and later criticized the region's racial practices as writers and/or activists. Most were considered to be "southern liberals," part of a small group of white southerners who questioned the South's racial order and often its economic system. Many of these individuals experienced some sort of racial awakening, which most white southerners at the time did not, and were eventually in a position to have their recollections published, which most southerners, again, were not. Although these conditions may suggest that the accounts are not representative and thus reveal little about white southern experience in general, this is not the case. While these authors largely recognized that their awakening experiences were atypical, they stressed that their childhoods were ordinary.

In addition to emphasizing that their experiences were commonplace, the authors were interested in establishing the validity of their liberal credentials; they wanted to prove the extent of their racial transformations by showing just how complicit they had been in the segregated system. Fred Hobson has noted that although such authors were writing as white southerners who had experienced racial awakenings, they were writing about a time before those awakenings occurred.[4] For a substantial portion of their narratives, they are believers in and adherents to the segregated system; that is, they are segregationists. Thus, these writers constitute a unique body of informants who wanted both to show how limiting the system could be and to explain how people with humanitarian impulses—themselves, as proved by their later liberal activism—could become so implicated in the system as to be unable to recognize its detrimental impact on themselves and others. While these sources must be used with some degree of caution, they offer a valuable insider's view of a system that those who maintained a belief in its validity have been more hesitant to reveal.

One of the most influential white writers was Lillian Smith, who described *Killers of the Dream,* her autobiographical work first published in 1949, as a "personal memoir" but also asserted that "in another sense, it is Every Southerner's memoir."[5] More than any other firsthand observer, Smith emphasized that segregation was maintained through silence. Her career reveals a deep concern with issues of race and childhood. For many years Smith owned and operated Laurel Falls Camp for Girls in Clayton, Georgia, where she and her partner, Paula Snelling, encouraged the young female campers to think critically about taboo issues such as segregation.[6] Smith and Snelling also edited a journal under a succession of titles, most notably *South Today,* in which they encouraged critical discussion of the South's racial and economic conditions, and Smith's controversial 1944 novel *Strange Fruit* explored issues of interracial sex and lynching in the segregated South.[7] In light of Smith's instrumental role in articulating the notion that segregation thrived as an institution because it was unquestioned, her analysis warrants further exploration.

Smith stressed the idea that an understanding of segregation was absorbed from the atmosphere rather than consciously taught. Born in 1897, Smith explained how her generation, that which saw the establishment of segregation within their lifetimes, was introduced to the institution: "We were born into it. Signs were put over doors when we were babies. We took them for granted just as we took heat and sandspurs and mosquitoes. . . . People find it hard to question something that has been here since they were born." Although she became aware of the existence of racial violence in her youth through the whispers of adults around her, she recalled that by the time she was in her late teens, around the start of World War I, "things had quieted down. Race relations seemed 'settled.' Segregation had hardened around our lives and feelings." Smith believed black children experienced the same ritualized instruction that she had. "From the time little southern children take their first step," she wrote, "they learn their ritual. . . . Some, if their faces are dark, learn to bend, hat in hand; and others, if their faces are white, learn to hold their heads high. Some step off the sidewalk while others pass by in arrogance."[8] Over time these movements became reflexes, or conditioned responses, that southerners performed without thinking and, in the case of whites, Smith concluded, without feeling. Of this aspect of the system, she had observed earlier in *South Today*, "the trouble is, that we have more reflexes than thoughts concerning the race situation. A reconditioning of reflexes must therefore be brought about."[9] Smith sketched a picture of a society in which individuals performed an orchestrated series of movements that were learned by example and intimation early in childhood and became habits, never to be consciously examined. She also highlighted the conditioning of both black and white southerners.

In a revealing analysis Jay Watson drew on aspects of Smith's language to further explain the choreographed nature of the segregated system. Building on her characterization of segregation as a "twisting turning dance," Watson described this dance as "less a spontaneous personal improvisation than a kind of collective lockstep."[10] Of the ritualized steps that Smith described, Watson wrote, "As these rituals become progressively internalized, white Southerners can practice segregation without the need for any legitimating ideas at all. They simply live their ideology, to their benefit and detriment at once, without thinking about it." Watson noted how the ideology of segregation could control the body, often against its own interests and without its conscious input.[11] Smith had questioned, "What white southerner of my generation ever stops to think consciously where to go or asks himself if it is right for him to go there!"; instead, the "muscles know" where to go, whether it was to the front of the bus or to the bigger school.[12] Darlene O'Dell referred to this phenomenon as "habit memory (memory stored in the movement of the body)."[13] Watson expanded on this theme: "When the muscles know, when belief is quite literally incorporated, abstract or strictly cognitive forms of understanding, such as ethical reflection, are superfluous."[14] Once the movements of the body had been disciplined by the ideology of segregation in childhood, the individual southerner need never make a conscious choice about whether to accept the system or not; he or she endorsed it through motion. Such childhood conditioning was hard to overcome. Smith concluded, "These ceremonials in honor of white supremacy, performed from babyhood, slip from the conscious mind down deep into muscles and glands and become difficult to tear out."[15] For this reason an individual's response to breaching the segregated code could be quite visceral.

Killers of the Dream served as a devastating critique of segregation's impact on white as well as black southerners. Like white southerners in subsequent generations who became critical of the system, Smith did so in part because she began to realize the intellectual and emotional limitations it placed on the lives of whites. She explained, "I began to understand slowly at first but more clearly as the years passed, that the warped, distorted frame we have put around every Negro child from birth is around every white child also. Each is on a different side of the frame but each is pinioned there."[16] Earlier Smith had written, "We need to understand the great injury that the philosophy and practice of segregation inflict upon white children as well as upon colored children. To hate tears up the mind and heart as surely as to be hated. To segregate is as injurious to character growth as to be segregated."[17] The system had crippled both black and white children, in her view, and even after the metaphorical frame was removed and a critical assessment begun, the impact of having lived in a society that encouraged one to deny feelings and ignore doubts lasted a lifetime. White children, in her analysis, "became little crooked wedges that fit into the intricately twisting serrated design of life which THEY WHO MAKE THE RULES had prepared for us in Dixie."[18]

Although she was somewhat vague about who had actually made the rules, Smith clearly had specific villains in mind. Throughout much of her text she referred to what "THEY" did or what "Southern Tradition" wanted people to believe. She wrote rather cryptically, "Southern Tradition taught well: we learned our way by doing. You never considered arguing with teacher, because you could not see her. You only felt the iron grip of her hand and knew you must go where all the other children were going."[19] In Watson's assessment Smith viewed segregation as "an authorless theater," "a stage set on which social actors are moved about like puppets by Southern tradition, mouthing lines they did not write."[20] Smith sought to convey the sense that southerners were being led by an "invisible power" that controlled their movements and that they were incapable of resisting.[21] Segregation thrived precisely because the system obscured what the source of its power actually was. Although reluctant to name a villain, Smith explored elsewhere in *Killers of the Dream* who the killers really were. She had several suspects, including politicians—who told "lies about skin color," thus "forcing decayed pieces of theirs and the region's obscenities into the minds of the young and leaving them there to fester"—and Mr. Rich White, who had made a bargain with Mr. Poor White that he could "boss the nigger" if he let Mr. Rich White "boss the money."[22] Smith's primary villains were elite white males, whom she saw as culpable for the ways in which segregation limited the lives of black men, poor white men, and women of both races.[23]

In her account of how segregation came to be seen as immutable, Smith asserted that even the region's "responsible" elites "did not know how to stop this monster created of poverty, fear, ignorance, guilt, political greed, and crazed by the drug of white supremacy." Unable to find a solution to the region's social problems, these elites "laid down a smoke screen of silence over the South's racial tensions." She explained how this process was accomplished: "It became taboo to talk of these problems; bad form to question; 'irresponsible' to discuss the issues in newspapers or write about them in books. They hoped silence would cure what intelligence and good will felt helpless to combat. If one did not mention these ghosts, maybe they would just go away."[24] Smith was surprisingly conciliatory in this analysis, suggesting that a segment of the elite white population would solve the region's racial problems if only they knew how, though the very practices she condemned had been established to serve the interests of the white community. Separate from the issue of who created the system and why, Smith's analysis conveys the sense that segregation had somehow slipped free from the control of its creators and was now functioning without their active involvement, that it had become self-perpetuating, a "Frankenstein," in historian James W. Silver's terms, that could no longer be stopped.[25]

Other contemporary critics of segregation and later observers of the institution have likewise attributed the system's power and persistence to the way in which it became self-perpetuating as it matured. Carl Rowan described segregation as "its own best defender and perpetuator."[26] John Cell argued, "Force lay behind segregation. . . . Yet most of the time segregation was largely self-enforcing."[27] Of racism in American society more broadly, Andrew Young observed, "The historical roots of American racism are conscious and deliberate, but sheer ignorance perpetuates it without any extra effort."[28] Likewise, psychologist Beverly Daniel Tatum wrote, "Because racism is so ingrained in the fabric of American institutions, it is easily self-perpetuating. All that is required to maintain it is business as usual."[29] Although deliberately established for the benefit of the white community, the segregated system seemed to take on a life of its own as it matured. This feature unfortunately served in the minds of many to divorce responsibility for the system's functioning from those whose interests it served.

Much of Lillian Smith's effort to assign culpability for maintaining segregation to some invisible force or to the South's political and economic leaders was an attempt to acquit the more likely candidates for blame: the parents of white children. By shifting blame from white parents in general, she may have been trying to shift responsibility from her own parents. Smith remembered of her childhood, "The mother who taught me what I know of tenderness and love and compassion taught me also the bleak rituals of keeping Negroes in their 'place.'" Her father taught her about the equality of all people and scolded her for her arrogance toward working-class children at her school but also "trained [her] in the steel-rigid decorums I must demand of every colored male." Yet she dedicated *Killers of the Dream* to them because they had "valiantly tried to keep their nine children in touch with wholeness even though reared in a segregated culture." Smith believed white parents had no choice but to teach their children contradictory messages. Her parents taught their children "ideals they did not practice and did not expect us to practice and which we could not have practiced had we wanted to." Smith held the pressures of the segregated system responsible for white parents' ambiguous racial messages, concluding that white parents lived in "terror" lest their children "be other than orthodox southerners."[30] White families faced real consequences, primarily in terms of social ostracism, if their children did not learn to conform to the prevailing racial order.

Smith had previously explored the implications of white parents' racial instruction in *South Today*. She observed that as white southerners grew up and had experiences that might have served to challenge their childhood conditioning, they were faced with the predicament that to question the received regional wisdom about race constituted questioning their own parents. Smith explained, "Any new feeling, any profoundly different feeling, would seem to our unconscious minds a betrayal of childhood love for our parents—for most of us have never learned to separate this love from the 'right' and 'wrong' which our parents taught us. All are tied up together and to all we react with indiscriminant emotion."[31] White children viewed the lessons they learned about segregation as sacrosanct because they were imbued with the emotional power of childhood love and respect for parents. Margaret Jones Bolsterli, a white southerner of a later generation who wrote her own memoir about growing up in the segregated South, described Smith's view of the region's racial and sexual taboos: "Those who violate the taboos are traitors to everything the white culture values and has taught them to value."[32] Such considerations provided strong inducement for white southerners to continue their support for segregation even after coming into contact with new ideas or experiences that might otherwise have caused them to question it.

Lillian Smith was not alone in her assessment that segregation was maintained through silence. The idea that segregation was unquestioned served as a veritable refrain in white southern autobiographies written by those who came of age in the two generations after Smith. Lindy Boggs, a former U.S. congresswoman from Louisiana, recalled that "segregation of the races was the law of the land, and few people, black or white, publicly questioned it. It was a fait accompli."[33] Mississippi-born preacher Will Campbell wrote, "Race was not an issue when we were growing up. The prevailing system of racial relationships was never discussed. It was, I suppose, considered a permanent arrangement." He explained, "There were schools for white children and schools for black children. It never occurred to anyone, except an occasional black person who kept it to himself, that it would ever be any other way."[34] Another Mississippian, Willie Morris, described associations with African Americans that were a mixture of affection and disdain. Of these emotions he remembered, "My own alternating affections and cruelties were inexplicable to me, but the main thing is that they were largely *assumed* and only rarely questioned. The broader reality was that the Negroes in the town were *there:* they were ours, to do with as we wished."[35] In his account of growing up in Georgia, President Jimmy Carter was adamant that segregation went unquestioned. He referred to "the days of unchallenged segregation" and to "societal customs that . . . were never questioned at the time," recalling, "I don't remember ever questioning the mandatory racial separation, which we accepted like breathing or waking up in Archery every morning."[36] White civil rights activist Joan C. Browning concluded of her own childhood in Georgia, "Segregation simply was an unquestioned way of life."[37]

In a society with stark physical differences in the accommodations for black and white, the notion that segregation was never discussed or even contemplated seems implausible. Doubts about the morality of the system must have arisen; questions surely were raised as parents taught their children to live within the system. If so, then what accounts for these memories? If white children did have doubts, what happened to them as they grew older? Scholarship on child development will help to provide some answers. This scholarship reveals the insight contained in Lillian Smith's assessment of parenting practices that child psychologists now refer to as "race socialization." It also highlights the role silence plays in communicating racial messages to children.

The process of socialization "transmits values, norms, morals, and beliefs from one generation to the next" and "helps the individual become an active, functioning member of their society."[38] Parents serve as "key socializing agents" in that they provide the initial lessons children learn about the world around them.[39] As children come into contact with other socializing agents, such as schools, churches, and peer groups, they may learn messages that either support or contradict those learned from parents. Building on their understanding of socialization, scholars have developed the concept of race socialization, which "involves messages and actions that provide information on personal and group identity, interracial relationships, and social position related to race."[40] Although early scholarship on race socialization viewed it as an activity that occurs primarily, if not exclusively, in black families, later work recognized that white families engage in it as well.[41] Parents' race socialization messages may be verbal or nonverbal and deliberate or unintentional.[42] Thus, a parent might deliver a message verbally that teaches a child something about race that the parent did not intend for the child to learn, or another might convey a deliberate message about race through, in Lillian Smith's words, "a raised eyebrow, a joke, a shocked voice, a withdrawing movement of the body, a long silence," rather than through "long sentences."[43] The extent to which white southern parents taught unintentional lessons or did so through nonverbal means may explain their children's memories of having absorbed messages about segregation from the atmosphere.

Beverly Daniel Tatum stressed the role of silence in white parents' race socialization practices, asserting the existence of a "White culture of silence about racism." Tatum argued, "Because they represent the societal norm, Whites can easily reach adulthood without thinking much about their racial group." In her view parents teach their children what they were taught and thus pass on their own "unexamined prejudices." Although some white families undoubtedly teach deliberate messages about racial superiority, children more often learn racial lessons through "the passive absorption of subtly communicated messages." When children ask questions about racial matters, adults frequently do not know how to answer or feel uncomfortable doing so and may disregard a question or allow themselves to forget that a child has asked it.[44] Children, in the words of psychologists Joseph Ponterotto and Paul Pedersen, "learn quickly what behaviors, attitudes and values are likely to be met with either approval or disapproval from parents. If dominant-group parents believe that the White race is superior or 'better' than other races, then children are very likely, and in short time, to acquire a similar racial attitude."[45] Children learn to accept the prevailing racial arrangements so as to please their parents, and in order to challenge those arrangements, they must be willing to defy those trusted adults. According to Tatum, the messages children learn from their parents about the existing social order "may go unchallenged and unexamined for a long time." She concluded, "Few of us have been taught to think critically about issues of social injustice. We have been taught not to notice or to accept our present situation as a given, 'the way it is.'"[46] Segregation may have been so taken for granted by white southerners that they rarely presented it to their children as something to be consciously considered.

A key component of firsthand critiques of segregation by Lillian Smith and others involved the extent to which the system limited the lives of white southerners as well as black. Martin Luther King Jr. asserted that "the festering sore of segregation debilitates the white man as well as the Negro" and that "the white man's personality is greatly distorted by segregation."[47] Similar assessments appear in scholarship on child development written at the time and more recently. Such observations have been met with resistance from some critics, who stress instead the ways in which white southerners were privileged by the segregated system. Jennifer Jensen Wallach found Smith's "surprising" claim that white southerners were as injured by segregation as black southerners to "run contrary to nearly all valued historical data."[48] Wallach also cited Fred Hobson's assessment that African Americans might have found such statements by whites to be "self-indulgent."[49] At the very least Smith, King, and their contemporaries employed the claim that segregation limited the lives of white as well as black southerners as a rhetorical strategy to convince whites to give segregation up, a possibility that Wallach addressed.[50] At most the claim was an expression of sincere belief about the impact of segregation on all southerners. In his analysis of Smith's work Jay Watson argued that the lessons whites learned about segregation "crippled as well as empowered them."[51] Jason Sokol explained of segregation, "Jim Crow made it possible for white life to be simultaneously comfortable and oppressive."[52] White southerners clearly benefited from segregation in a myriad of ways, both material and emotional. They had nicer accommodations, better schools, and greater access to political power and economic opportunity, among other advantages. There were, however, costs for them as whites for both the privilege they experienced and the silence that helped guarantee its continuation.[53] Scholarship on child development offers valuable perspective on segregation's impact on white children.

Kenneth and Mamie P. Clark are best known for research they conducted on the self-concept of African American children, much of which involved the children's response to a forced-choice test between black and white dolls.[54] Although this research—which suggested that segregation "damaged" black children because they often showed a preference for the white doll—later became the subject of heated scholarly debate, the Clarks' work played a significant role in the 1954 *Brown v. Board of Education* decision declaring school segregation unconstitutional.[55] Much less emphasis has been placed on Kenneth Clark's argument that segregation "damaged" white children.[56] Clark's 1955 work, *Prejudice and Your Child,* can be read in part as an attempt to convince white parents that desegregation was actually in the best interests of not only black children but their own children as well.[57] According to Clark, white parents opposed school desegregation on the basis of both their own racial prejudices and their belief that they were protecting their children by refusing to allow them to attend school with African Americans. He argued of white parents, "If they understood that the opportunity for a child to meet and know other children of different races, religions, and cultures is beneficial and not detrimental; that it contributes to social competence and confidence; that it increases a child's chances for personal and moral stability—then they would demand, in the name of their children, non-segregated public education."[58] Through such statements Clark sought to teach white parents how much segregation was costing their children.

Clark's warnings about the consequences for white children of remaining in segregated settings were often dire. He argued that although there was "no conclusive and systematic evidence that white children are damaged by racial prejudice and segregation to the same extent as Negro children," there was "suggestive evidence that they are insidiously and negatively disturbed by these contradictions in the American democratic creed." In Clark's view "children who are being taught prejudices are being given a distorted perspective of reality and of themselves, and are being taught to gain personal status in unrealistic ways." Such children learned "to establish their own identity as persons and as members of a group through hatred and rejection of others," and they were "encouraged and rewarded if the persons they reject happen to be members of the minority group."[59] In order to convince white parents that segregation should end, Clark had to convince them that it was hurting, not helping, their own children, who were at risk of becoming disturbed, losing touch with reality, and learning to define themselves through their hatred of other human beings.

More recent scholarship on racism's impact on whites—particularly work that focuses on the benefits for whites of cultivating an antiracist perspective—supports many of Clark's conclusions. Scholars have asserted that racism "supports irrationality," "inhibits intellectual growth," and "negates democracy."[60] Additional effects include "ignorance of other people," "moral confusion," and an emphasis on "group conformity."[61] These scholars concluded that racism has a demonstrably negative impact on whites in that it tends to produce individuals who are irrational, confused, intellectually and emotionally stunted, out of touch with reality, and deeply invested in conformity. Ponterotto and Pedersen went so far as to argue, "It is beyond dispute that the negative consequences of racism for all involved far outweigh any fleeting gains for the oppressor."[62] Focusing primarily on the benefits that accrued to white southerners as a result of segregation overlooks these various negative consequences and their potential utility as tools to convince white southerners that segregation was costing them too dearly, particularly through its impact on the very children the system supposedly protected.

Clark suggested that white children could not help but learn to accept segregation in the course of learning to function as normal adults in southern society. He noted that all children in the South "must take part in" segregation and argued that such participation played a key role in their development of racial attitudes. In Clark's view a society's racial prejudices "are acquired as a natural part of the daily life of the child, as he comes to know the existing values, norms, and attitudes which are essential for his acceptance in the outside world." He argued that children who learned the "prevailing racial attitudes . . . must be considered normal within the framework of the society."[63] In order to be properly socialized—that is, "become an active, functioning member of their society"—white children had to learn to accept segregation, a system in which they were required to participate.

White parents, likewise, had limited options about what to teach their children if their goal was to raise them to be normal, functioning adults; nevertheless, they pursued a variety of methods to impart those lessons. Parents with a strong belief in the necessity of segregation likely taught their children to uphold the system on the basis of explicitly racial reasoning. Others may have found modeling behavior to be a more comfortable means of introducing their children to the system. Some parents may not have thought much about what to teach their children and may have merely been communicating their own unexamined beliefs, as taught to them by their own parents. For their part parents who did not support segregation may have found it difficult to prevent their children from learning white society's attitude toward black southerners even when they tried.[64] Whatever their approach, if white parents wanted their children to be considered normal within southern society and to avoid the consequences of violating the racial status quo, they had little choice but to teach them to accept segregation.

The idea that the word *segregation* was unmentionable and memories of having gleaned knowledge about the system from the stratosphere notwithstanding, white parents did sometimes teach their children deliberate, verbal messages about segregation and race. This racial instruction included, among other aspects, lessons on the South's role in the Civil War and on the subsequent tragedy—in the minds of white southerners—of Reconstruction. Those who had lived through these two defining events offered them to their children as justifications for the prevailing racial order. Katharine Du Pre Lumpkin's autobiography provides a stark example of how this instruction took place. Her father, William Lumpkin, was part of the last generation raised before the Civil War, and he grew up expecting his life as a planter and slaveholder to be very much like that of his father. When the war intervened, leading to a decline in the family's fortunes, William Lumpkin became involved in the postwar Lost Cause movement and included his children in these activities.[65] Born in 1897 during a period of political and racial turmoil in the South, Katharine Du Pre Lumpkin joined the Children of the Confederacy as a young girl and remembered having participated in the formation of a child-sized Ku Klux Klan—complete with parent-provided bedsheets—which was dedicated in part to "the planning of pretended punitive expeditions against mythical recalcitrant Negroes."[66]

Lumpkin also learned why whites felt it was necessary that black southerners be segregated; chief among the reasons was the harrowing ordeal that was Reconstruction in the white southern experience. Lumpkin remembered that when her father told stories about Reconstruction, "it was as though his words were wrung from him, for he obviously hated the memories. Yet it seems that he felt he must tell the story, lest we have no concrete images such as haunted him." Lumpkin's father engaged in deliberate instruction of his children to ensure they understood *why* he deemed it crucial that white southerners remain in control and segregated from black southerners. Lumpkin recalled, "We were told how our world during reconstruction was ruled by 'scalawags'—those native white men who by every loyal Southerner were scorned as base renegades; and also ruled by 'carpetbaggers'—unprincipled without exception; Northerners; interlopers; men who were 'nigger-lovers' or pretended to be; rank outsiders who had come in, so it was said, to feast like harpies upon a prostrate country." She also described the lessons she learned about freed slaves: "To have those born in the womb of slavery, those children of dark ignorance and lowest race, as they were spoken of, put in office over white men! The slave ruling over the master! They who but yesterday were masters and rulers could only look on this as something intolerable beyond words. Nor could they ever shake off the feelings which had once overwhelmed them." Lumpkin's elders determined that she, growing up thirty years after Reconstruction and in a family that had experienced it and the war firsthand, "must still feel" the pain of the war's aftermath if she were to understand why segregation was necessary.[67]

Although Lumpkin stressed the intentional nature of her father's lessons, she also admitted that she, as the youngest child in her family, was less well versed in the various justifications for segregation than her older siblings, who were already speaking at Lost Cause events when she was still a child. Lumpkin wrote, "We can be certain that from the time I could sit in my high chair at table or play about the parlor floor while others conversed, my ears were saturated with words and phrases at all times intimately familiar to Southern ears and in those years of harsh excitement carrying a special urgency: 'white supremacy,' 'Negro domination,' 'intermarriage,' 'social equality,' 'impudence,' 'inferiority,' 'uppitiness,' 'good darkey,' 'bad darkey,' 'keep them in their place.'" She recalled that over time she, too, would learn to speak those words, "even before [she] had the understanding to grasp all they stood for." When she participated in a debate at school about the prospect of black equality, "an exceedingly strange query for a Southern schoolroom," Lumpkin, arguing against, drew on her own handwritten copy of a script she had prepared with her family, whom she was essentially parroting.[68] Lumpkin's account brings to light two important and related aspects of racial instruction in white homes. First, she highlighted the fact that white children often learned the rules of segregation before they learned why they were supposed to follow them. Second, she revealed that, as time went on, white children learned fewer and fewer of the reasons for segregation. Lumpkin was less conversant with the justifications for segregation than her older siblings, and they were less conversant than their father.[69] White children whose parents did not themselves have personal memories of the war and its aftermath likely learned even fewer of these justifications. William Lumpkin taught his children about Reconstruction because he wanted it to *haunt* them as it did him, lest they forget the necessity for whites of keeping black southerners "in their place." He wanted them to feel the pain he and the rest of the family had felt. Later generations of white parents seem to have been less motivated by such visceral concerns and were likely just teaching their children what they had been taught without placing undue emphasis on ensuring their children understood why segregation was deemed so crucial.

Mississippi journalist Hodding Carter II, like Lumpkin, was raised to revere the Lost Cause, though in a less systematic manner. Carter was born in Louisiana in 1907, by which time segregation and disfranchisement had become facts of southern life. Although he saw himself as temporally removed from the Civil War, he considered the legacy of the war and Reconstruction to be an "emotional heritage" passed down by his grandparents' generation.[70] He explained that most members of his own generation were "close to some fabulous father or grandfather, some remembering grandmother, to whom, in our childhood and even our young manhood, the war and its aftermath was a personal, bitter, and sacred reality." His maternal grandfather had been a member of the Ku Klux Klan, and his grandmother, who had made her husband's Klan robes, proudly defended his legacy. Carter also made a childhood game of the Klan, though rather than Lumpkin's mythical victims, he remembered actually having chased black children through the woods draped in a white sheet. He believed his grandfather would have bequeathed the family a large estate if the war and Reconstruction had not intervened and was shocked when his mother once suggested that it was her father's lack of skill at the poker table that was really to blame. Despite having been steeped in memories of the Lost Cause, Carter believed such sentiments "were waning even in my childhood."[71]

In deciding how to raise his own sons, the first of whom was born in 1935, Carter came to the conclusion that they "would not be thus conditioned by any past. We would see to it, my wife and I, that their pride in the South and its past would be balanced, as they grew up, with proper emphasis upon the new South and the nation of which it is an irrevocable and generally wholesome part. None of that ancestor-worship business for them, no sir." Despite his stated intention to avoid teaching his children to revere the Lost Cause, Carter remembered lessons learned on a revealing road trip he took with his family from Mississippi to Maine in the summer of 1946. After a series of wistful stops at Civil War sites in Tennessee and Virginia, Carter recalled, "We reached Gettysburg, and that was our undoing. First, we visited the sad, majestic battlefield, and then the ghost-ridden museum, in whose amphitheater one can look down upon an electrically controlled topographical map of Gettysburg, where changing battalions of red and blue lights illustrate the lecturer's account of the bloody campaign." After the lecture was over, "the two older boys were disconsolate." Carter remembered that when his oldest son, Hodding Carter III, "moodily" remarked, "That was a tough one for us to lose," Carter had to rouse himself "from inwardly cursing at Longstreet and wondering where in hell Stuart could have been all that time, to remind him that it all happened for the best, and, anyway, where would we be today if we weren't a united country?"[72] Carter's account reveals that even parents who felt they were making a conscious effort to avoid teaching their children to revere the South's mythical past could still communicate unintended messages. Meanwhile, children were gleaning lessons about regional pride and the Lost Cause from the culture around them, lessons that could serve as a powerful source of group identity.

Over time the Civil War legacy became less immediately relevant, and pride in the South's past could give way to irreverence. Willie Morris, who was a contemporary of Carter's sons, grew up in Mississippi surrounded by reminders of the Lost Cause. His school, which was adjacent to the town's Confederate monument, featured portraits of both George Washington and Jefferson Davis, and his maternal grandparents often took him to visit a Confederate museum in Jackson. He learned stories about his family's trials and triumphs during the war and its aftermath, including those of his maternal great-grandfather—a newspaperman before the war—whose printing presses were reportedly thrown into the town well by Union troops and who later helped "redeem" the state from Republican rule. Despite such reminders, Morris recalled, "that war seemed increasingly remote." His attention was riveted instead on World War II, and when his grandmother and her sisters began reminiscing about the Civil War, "it was like shifting gears, from boyhood's concerns and the war with the Japs to a different world filled with Yankees, poverty, and death." When two soldiers from a nearby military installation to whom his family offered a ride turned out to be from the North, his mother and grandmother accosted them about the Civil War, Reconstruction, and the fate of the family patriarch's printing presses. His grandmother insisted, "You just don't know how awful you treated us, lettin' the niggers run wild, not givin' people enough to eat, stealin' silver, burnin' down houses." Morris then "began to wonder which side they were on after all, and if they bayoneted babies during Reconstruction." When he asked his mother if "Yankees" could be loyal in the ongoing war, she explained, "Oh, we're one country now. . . . We're united. But it wasn't that way always."[73] His mother, like Carter, thus sought to mitigate the impact of her lessons.

Although Willie Morris had absorbed his family's lessons to some degree, he did not venerate the Confederate past as his forebears did. He took great pleasure in tormenting his elderly great aunts, for whom the Civil War was a living memory. Having purchased a device from a mail-order catalog that allowed him to broadcast his voice through the family's radio, he recalled that he would interrupt a program and announce, *"The Yankees are coming!"* which would send his aunts running in fear to tell their sister that the reviled troops were on their way. Despite his grandmother's attempts to calm them with assurances that it was just her grandson having some fun at their expense, Morris reported that they repeatedly fell for the trick.[74] Few white southerners of Katharine Du Pre Lumpkin or Hodding Carter's generation would have mocked the Confederate legacy or their elders' memories in this way. The change suggests erosion in reverence for the Lost Cause over time. Memories that were a "sacred reality" for those who had lived through the war and its aftermath and an "emotional heritage" for their children were passed on with more caution to the third and fourth generations, who heard the stories but could not feel their pain and were not haunted by the same ghosts. Repeated less often and with their power diminished, the stories became less effective as justifications for segregation as the system matured.

Deliberate lessons about segregation also involved provisions on naming, eating, and other deeply symbolic forms of social interaction. Virginian Sarah Patton Boyle's parents were notably intentional in the way they taught such lessons. Boyle recalled that on her twelfth birthday, in the late 1910s, her parents told her she was a "big girl now" and her "relations with Negroes from now on must be formal."[75] Her parents began a rigorous training program in which they detailed how her life would change. Servants began to call her "Miss" instead of simply calling her by name, and her parents told her she could no longer play with black children. After she snubbed a little black boy who had been a favorite playmate of hers, her mother kissed her and said, "Mother saw and heard everything. That was a good girl!" Boyle learned that African Americans were to come to the back porch, and they were to eat in the kitchen. She should be gracious in her dealings with them, but she should avoid undue familiarity, which would embarrass both her and, she was told, her black acquaintances. Boyle recalled, "Over and over I was told that if I didn't adhere to racial conventions Negroes themselves 'would be shocked,' 'would be horrified,' 'would be disgusted,' 'would disapprove,' and—occasionally—even that they 'would be humiliated.'" Above all, she was taught to believe this sort of circumscribed interaction across the color line was beneficial to both parties: "To me our relationship felt wonderful. It brought out the best in me. I assumed it felt wonderful to them and brought out their best, too. It was a traumatic, heart-twisting experience when I learned this wasn't so."[76] Given the nature of her parents' training, it is not difficult to understand why she felt this way. Boyle's racial instruction is remarkable because it was presented in such an explicit, abrupt way, but many white children learned similar lessons.

Anne Braden recalled having been only four or five years old when her mother corrected her after she referred to an African American female as a "colored lady." Her mother explained, "You never call colored people ladies. . . . You say colored woman and white lady—never a colored lady."[77] Embedded in the term *lady* are cultural assumptions about both the class and the race of the woman so designated, and Braden's mother apparently did not feel it was appropriate that a black woman be afforded a term her society reserved for respectable white females. Harry Crews described a similar incident through which he "found out" that his closest childhood playmate, Willalee Bookatee, "was a nigger" because he was black. As Crews was telling his aunt a story about a Mr. Robert Jones, a black man in his community who owned a large farm and was widely respected as a hard worker, she interrupted him to correct his language. "No, son," she said. "Robert Jones is a nigger. You don't say 'mister' when you speak of a nigger. You don't say 'Mr. Jones,' you say 'nigger Jones.'" According to Crews, he "never missed a stroke" and continued telling his story after having dutifully amended his language.[78]

Class could play a significant role in determining what terminology white children learned to use when talking about race. Middle-class families generally prohibited the term "nigger."[79] Lillian Smith learned that "to use the word 'nigger' was unpardonable and no well-bred southerner was quite so rude as to do so." She also learned, however, that no "well-bred southerner" would "call a Negro 'mister' or invite him to sit in the living room or eat with him or sit by him in public places."[80] In other families, like that of Crews, using the word "nigger" was expected practice, and any other term would have been considered pretentious. In his account of growing up in a working-class neighborhood in Birmingham, Paul Hemphill wrote, "It would have been perfectly all right for me to casually use the word 'nigger' around the house—practically everyone I knew did—and I might even have been rewarded with a smile and a pat on the head from my father as an acknowledgement that I was growing up just fine."[81] Fred Hobson explained, "Whether one said 'nigger' or not seems to have been less a matter of morals than of manners— of *class*." When a white southerner "tells us that he or she did not use the word as a child, he or she is telling us, in a sort of code we are all to recognize, not that he was any less guilty of inhumanity toward African Americans but rather that he came from that most cherished of southern institutions, a good white family."[82] Regardless of which term they were encouraged to use, these children were learning that white people were to be addressed with respect and black people were not.

Because fear of unsanctioned interracial sex was one of the key motivations for segregation, rules governing interracial contact between the sexes were among the most likely to be the subject of intentional instruction. Sarah Patton Boyle observed that there were two schools of thought about what to teach white females about black males. The first school made "white girls super-sex-conscious and continually on their guard against doing or saying anything to 'inflame the primitive imagination' when dealing with Negro men." The other school ignored "entirely the simple scientific fact that Negro men are members of the opposite sex" and encouraged white girls "to regard them rather as one does male dumb animals." Boyle's parents chose the latter approach.[83] Margaret Jones Bolsterli's parents chose the former. She was constantly instructed to avoid contact with black men. Bolsterli recalled, "This meant anything from going to taverns or other places where people got drunk to wearing shorts on the farm where I might be seen and therefore spoken to or even looked at suggestively by any of the black men working there. If this should happen, it was implied, my father would be forced to 'do something about it.'"[84] Although often the subject of intentional verbal instruction, lessons on interracial contact between the sexes could also be learned through nonverbal cues. Growing up in North Carolina, Melton McLaurin helped his grandfather, who owned a store adjacent to the black community, by picking up and dropping off black customers, and he occasionally picked up domestic or agricultural workers for jobs at his home. McLaurin had to learn a series of complicated rules about where black passengers should sit in his car. He recalled, "Black men or boys presented no problem; they always sat in front with me. Black women were another matter entirely. I felt ridiculous when forty- and fifty-year-old women automatically climbed into the back seat." As for black girls: "Here the rule was simple. Never, under any circumstances, would I have been alone with them in an automobile."[85]

Young people often found themselves confused by contradictory lessons. The rules prohibiting contact with black girls, for example, were not the only messages McLaurin received about black females. From spending time with his father and grandfather in the company of their friends, he discovered that the taboos he learned were violated in conversation and occasionally in reality by the white men he knew. McLaurin remembered, "Black women were the constant subject of rumor and innuendo, and for what passed as humor. Their sexual exploits and charms, whether they were married or single, occupied a substantial portion of white men's conversation."[86] Teaching a young white boy to avoid contact with black females at all costs and then exposing him to conversations in which it became clear that white men did know something of sexual contact with black women was bound to raise questions in the boy's mind. Willie Morris's father conveyed contradictory messages on another sensitive subject: African American political rights. On several occasions he made statements to the effect that "I don't know why they treat these niggers so bad. They pay taxes just like everybody else. If they pay taxes they oughta get to vote. It's as simple as that. If they don't get to vote they ought not to have to pay any taxes." This man was advocating a sense of fair play in regard to the political rights of African Americans, but in doing so, he used a demeaning term. Morris juxtaposed these statements with an incident in which a man he knew, seemingly his father, called an African American man who had robbed a number of homes in their neighborhood a "nigger" to his face and threatened to "blow [his] head off" if he saw him near his house again.[87] Conflicting messages such as these could not help but raise questions in young people's minds about the lessons on segregation and race they were learning.

The presence of African Americans in and around white homes as domestic and agricultural workers often served, as it did for McLaurin, as another source of racial instruction and subsequent confusion. Although glowing accounts of loving black caretakers from white southern childhoods have become a controversial cliché, white children did learn lessons from black adults about love and acceptance and about the painful humiliations that were inherent to segregation. Because these lessons often did not align with white parents' messages about black southerners, they could serve as a key source of doubts about the system.

Paul Hemphill spent many childhood days following Louvenia, his family's black maid, around the house. He wrote of Louvenia, "She was the first black person I had ever known, and I liked the way she smelled and the way she said 'I S'wanee' to almost everything and the way she would wink and slip me a penny out of the blue . . . wrapping my fingers around the shiny copper, winking again, making me promise not to tell." Hemphill felt what he had heard his family say about black southerners did not apply to her: "I had heard the word 'nigger' plenty of times, from my parents and some of my many aunts and uncles, but this was Louvenia."[88] The woman who cared for him and shared secrets with him could not possibly fall into that category. Margaret Jones Bolsterli remembered a similar relationship with her family's maid, Victoria: "When I was not in school, I was wherever Victoria was, talking and listening. I consider her one of the primary influences on my life. She shaped me as surely as my family did, in many crucial ways undoing their damage." Victoria's most important role in Bolsterli's life was building up her sense of self-worth. Bolsterli recalled, "While the men and boys in the family were agreeing with all white society except my mother that I could not do whatever I wanted to do, because I was a girl, Victoria was agreeing with me that, yes, indeed, I was going to do and be whatever." If Bolsterli found in Victoria a source of friendship and acceptance outside her immediate family, she also learned from her about the implications of segregation for African Americans. Bolsterli observed, "There were other incalculable effects of this black presence, for there were troubles to reconcile." She remembered, "I learned early the shame of betrayals in which I played a part, but for which I was not responsible. When noon came, I would be called to set the table in the dining room for the family; my friend had to wait until we had finished and then eat in the kitchen. This arrangement made me cringe and yet it was beyond my imagination to think of her at the table with us."[89] Bolsterli's relationship with her black "friend" caused her to have qualms about segregation, yet she could not envision challenging her parents' rules.

Male agricultural workers could also provide white children with conflicting information about race. Harry Crews learned lessons from his interactions with Will Bookatee, a tenant on his family's tobacco farm. Crews learned about hard work and punctuality from seeing Bookatee rise before the sun every morning to start working in the fields. In contrast to Crews's stepfather, who often neglected his own work on the farm because he was drunk, Bookatee provided an example of sobriety and constancy. Whereas Crews's stepfather was abusive toward Crews's mother and once sent the family fleeing from the house in the middle of the night when he shot the mantel off the fireplace, Crews never once heard Will Bookatee raise his voice. Bookatee made Crews feel valued as a worker by asking for his help around the farm, in Crews's words, "in a way that made you feel as though you were helping him out of a tight spot he could not get out of by himself."[90] In an environment in which he was taught to disrespect black southerners, Crews found that a black tenant farmer was one of the few people he knew who served as a worthy role model and one of the few adults in his life who instilled in him lessons about his own value.

African Americans who worked in white households occasionally taught their own deliberate, verbal lessons on race. Pat Watters remembered the cook at a friend's house giving him and other white children a lesson in proper pronunciation after one of them called her a "nigger." The cook "very seriously and patiently" explained, "You don't say it that way. It is pronounced Knee-grow. Knee-grow."[91] Watters admitted that even though he always remembered how the cook had told him to say "Negro," most white southerners he knew said "Negra," so he continued to pronounce it that way until he became a reporter working with others who used the correct pronunciation.[92] Lillian Quick Smith, an African American woman who worked for white families while in high school, offered the opposite perspective on a similar encounter. Babysitting a white child one evening, she became very upset when he called her a "nigger." She responded with her own lesson on the meaning of that term: "the word 'nigger,' you know, really refers to an act. Anybody can be a nigger if they commit a niggardly act, and I spelled it for him."[93] The boy admitted that he had heard his parents and other white adults use the term. When his parents returned, Smith confronted them about using the word, thus modeling behavior for their son. Although they apologized, she stopped working for them. One can only speculate about the impact of Smith's lesson on her young charge. Did he change his language in response to her rebuke? Did he, like Watters, continue to use the term even though he knew it was wrong? Or did he dismiss the episode altogether because the discrepancy between Smith's lesson and his parents' actions made him feel confused and uncomfortable?

The contradictory messages about segregation and race taught by parents as well as the presence of black workers in and around white homes may have caused many white children to become confused about the system. When this confusion took the form of a direct question, white parents rarely addressed their children's concerns head on. Parents sometimes chose to provide an "alternative explanation" to their child.[94] John Seigenthaler Sr. recalled having been to the movies a number of times while growing up in Nashville, Tennessee, before he noticed a second balcony filled with black children. He remembered his mother's response when he asked how the children got up there: "'They have their own private entrance,' my mother said, as if 'they' were privileged." Not long after, he was at the theater alone when he spotted the so-called private entrance, which was "down an alley off Church Street and led to three steep flights of narrow stairs."[95] Whatever confusion Seigenthaler may have felt as a result of this incident did not encourage him, however, to develop a critique of the system. Looking back on his own failure to question segregation as a young person, Seigenthaler wrote, "Where was my head? Where was my heart? And where were the heads and hearts of my parents? And my teachers? How could they not have taught me what they certainly knew? Yes, it was the law, but it was wrong. . . . How could we have accepted, without comment or concern, a way of life that was so unjust, so corrupt, and so cruel?"[96] Seigenthaler's frustration at his own inability as a child to develop a critique of segregation is revealing, as is his assertion that the adults around him knew the system was wrong. His reflections do not take into account the pressure to conform and to teach him to conform that his parents were surely under. They may have found it easier to offer alternative explanations to his questions, hoping such answers would forestall further queries.

White parents sometimes responded to their children's questions about segregation with anger. Lillian Smith remembered an incident from her childhood in which a white girl was found to be living with a black family and was subsequently taken in by Smith's parents. Smith enjoyed playing with her new friend until someone discovered the child was in fact "colored." Smith's mother told her the girl would have to return to "Colored Town." After repeated questions from Smith and her sister, her mother admonished them, "You're too young to understand. And don't ask me again, ever again, about this!" Continuing the theme of her parents' regret over their part in enforcing the system, Smith observed, "Mother's voice was sharp but her face was sad and there was no certainty left there."[97] Her mother's possible regret notwithstanding, Smith felt confused, hurt, and guilty, both because she now had to shun her friend and because she had violated the sacred segregated code in the first place. Willie Morris recounted a similar parental response to his interactions with black playmates. He remembered how he used to "go back across the alley to the unpainted houses and play with the colored children. Their houses smelled musty and sharp, and there was always food—gingerbread, cornbread, biscuits, and buttermilk, which we all ate under a big chinaberry tree." This pleasant arrangement went on for some time until his mother decided it should end. Morris recalled, "One afternoon my mother came and got me and yanked me home. 'Don't ever play back here again,' she said. 'But why?' I asked. 'Just you hear me. Just you don't.'"[98] With no room left for discussion, Morris heeded his mother's rebuke.

While such scenes may have done little to diminish white children's reservations about segregation, they probably did discourage them from asking questions or voicing doubts in the future. These episodes reveal that white children struggled to some extent with the lessons they learned from their parents about segregation. Describing her own misgivings about the system as a child, Anne Braden asserted that "many, many white Southern children go through to some extent the same tortures of soul that I did." Although she, too, described her world as one in which "segregation was not discussed; it was accepted," she argued that her personal reservations about the system were representative of white southern experience. Braden wrote, "It is significant to me that very few Southerners, even among those who disagree with me, have in recent years asked me the question so many Northerners ask: where did I get my ideas on segregation? Southerners know."[99] Braden believed most white southerners had doubts about the system even if they felt they could not express them. Kenneth Clark wrote of children's early understanding of injustice, "All children are sensitive to unjust or preferential treatment on the part of adults in authority. Children recognize injustice and—at least when they are young—seem deeply resentful, even if some other child is the immediate victim. It is only later that they become calloused to the subtle injustices of the adult world."[100] The question remains about what happened to white children's doubts about segregation as they grew older.

Some white southerners recognized that segregation gave them privileges and opportunities it denied African Americans, and they dismissed whatever reservations they may have had about the system lest they be forced to give up some of those privileges. This explanation does not, however, cover the range of responses by white children to their doubts about the system. Some children may have simply stopped asking questions that were never answered. When they were very young, white southerners attached little significance to racial differences. They also lacked an understanding of the societal taboos that inhibited adults from discussing racial matters and, thus, initially asked questions that made adults feel uncomfortable or that adults did not know how to answer. These questions were often ignored or shushed, and over time children learned to stop asking them. If at some point in the future an incident or an accumulation of incidents rendered the system of racial privilege visible to them, their doubts may have resurfaced, and they may have experienced anger, discomfort, and/or a desire to end the system. Yet once they realized the costs of criticizing segregation—which were often high for whites in terms of social ostracism and family turmoil—individuals could once again learn not to notice the racism that had briefly been apparent in the society around them.

Other white southerners may have simply been motivated by fear at what would happen to them if they challenged segregation. They had listened closely when promised that cataclysmic results would follow any unauthorized interracial contact, and they were disinclined to learn that lesson again through personal experience. In his work Clark sought to make a distinction between positive and negative prejudices. He cited the human aversion to poisonous food as an example of a positive prejudice and explained, "Such a prejudice reflects the accumulated knowledge of the culture; and it is neither necessary nor reasonable for an individual to try to make a personal verification of what is already known."[101] This is exactly how white southerners felt about segregation. If one's elders had already tried social equality and found the results to be disastrous, as during Reconstruction, individual children need not ingest such "poison" themselves but could rely, instead, on the "accumulated knowledge of the culture" to know which social situations to avoid.

Many white southerners may have felt they were alone in their doubts. Not until her teens did Anne Braden learn that others also questioned segregation. She had bought into "the myth that every other man considers segregation holy and that no one can oppose it and continue to live and work in this environment." Even as a young reporter in Alabama in the late 1940s, Braden was largely unaware of organized opposition to segregation. She explained, "I know now that there were people in the South in those days fighting against segregation; there were probably some in Birmingham, but I did not know them. There were probably organizations, but I did not know them. I—like so many other Southern white people then and now who feel as I felt—believed that I was alone."[102] Social ostracism was one of the most pressing fears among white southerners. In a society that held conformity to be sacred, even a slight deviation from the script could be tragic and irreparable, hence Lillian Smith's statement that parents lived in "terror" that their children would not grow up to be "orthodox" southerners.

An exchange between Smith and a young woman at her Laurel Falls Camp for Girls poignantly highlights this fear. After the campers had performed a play during which complicated issues about segregation were raised, the girl confronted Smith about the lessons she had taught them. She accused Smith of having "done a terrible thing to children" by teaching them to think critically about segregation and admitted, "I almost hate you tonight, for letting us fall in love with beliefs that I see now we can't possibly live." She asked, "Why did you teach us to want to be real persons when you knew there was no place down here for such people?" Smith had "unfitted [them] for the South" when she taught them to criticize segregation.[103] The girl demanded to know how she could ever return to her normal life now that she had learned to think critically about a system she could not change. Any individual effort on her part would ultimately be futile and would only result in alienating her from her family and her community. It was easier just to make the best of life within the system. It would have been easier, in fact, if the subject of segregation had never been raised at all. She angrily told Smith that when she became a mother, she would "teach my children not to *think* about things like this" and asserted, "When I have children, I am not going to give them a single ideal they can't practice. I don't want them torn up like this. I'll tell them Jim Crow is fine, that it's legal, that this is the way things are in the South and the way they are going to stay."[104] Having been socialized by her parents to function as a normal white southerner, the girl realized that Smith's lessons left her unable to live comfortably in her society. In order to dispel her discomfort, she likely chose to forget her doubts about segregation and live as though she had never experienced them. This young woman also gained valuable insight into the race socialization strategy she would use with her own children.

Although their methods ranged from deliberate statements about race to silent modeling of behavior, white parents conveyed a uniform message about segregation: the system was to be accepted without question or comment. Some white parents taught this lesson for the explicit purpose of upholding the South's racial hierarchy, while others did so because they feared the consequences for their children and their families of deviating from the status quo. Still others were unreflective about the messages they communicated to their children and were just passing down the lessons they had learned from their own parents as a kind of familial and regional inheritance. Regardless of the methods or intentions of their parents, young white southerners received little indication in their homes that segregation was a subject open for debate or even contemplation. In deciding how to teach their own children about segregation and race, black parents faced a much more vexing dilemma about how to prepare their children to survive in the segregated South without compromising their sense of self-worth. African American parents devised a variety of strategies for meeting this challenge.

CHAPTER 2

THE AFRICAN AMERICAN DILEMMA
Racial Instruction in Black Homes

Septima Clark wrote of the choices African American parents faced in deciding how to prepare their children for life in the segregated South, "The Negro parent's dilemma is fearsome. There is nothing worse, believe me, and I *know* this, than bringing a child into the world and having to teach him that none of the pleasant things of life are for him, or few of them, at most. How do you teach a tot where to sit, where to walk, where not to play, and where not to go."[1] Martin Luther King Jr. famously articulated the challenge faced by black parents in his "Letter from Birmingham Jail," in which he described the moment as a parent "when you suddenly find your tongue twisted and your speech stammering as you seek to explain to your six-year-old daughter why she can't go to the public amusement park that has just been advertised on television, and see tears welling up in her little eyes when she is told that Funtown is closed to colored children, and see the depressing clouds of inferiority begin to form in her little mental sky."[2] Writing some four decades later about the challenges of raising African American children at the turn of the twenty-first century, journalist Carlton Winfrey wondered how he would be able to "protect" his children from, "yet educate them about, race and racism." He found that the task required "a delicate balancing act" and noted that he was "just the latest in a long line of black parents who have struggled, generation after generation, to strike that balance."[3]

The challenge African American parents faced in the segregated South was how to raise their children so as to safeguard them from being humiliated, assaulted, or killed for violating the segregated code and to do so without destroying their respect for themselves, their parents, or their communities. Based on a consideration of the risks and benefits involved, black parents devised a variety of race socialization strategies for facing this dilemma. Many parents focused on developing the internal resources their children would need to survive the daily assault waged on their sense of self-worth by the ritual humiliation that was a central component of segregation. Others sought to isolate their children from contact with white southerners as long as possible in order to delay their first encounter with racism or instructed them about how to avoid situations in which they would be segregated. Some parents taught their children that although segregation was wrong, they must learn to navigate the system in order to protect themselves and their families. Other parents went one step further: they not only taught their children that segregation was wrong but also educated them about ways to combat it. Finally, some parents refused to discuss segregation with their children at all and greeted their questions with silence or angry admonitions. In practice most African American parents used a combination of these race socialization strategies, selecting between unappealing alternatives to meet each new challenge.[4]

All of the available race socialization strategies had consequences. If children were taught to challenge the system, their lives and the livelihoods of their families would be jeopardized. If they were taught not to challenge it, parents risked having their children come to accept their second-class status while losing respect for themselves and their parents, those who had taught them to acquiesce. If parents allowed their children to remain largely unaware of the rules of segregation either by isolating them from contact with whites—to the extent that class allowed parents to achieve such isolation—or by refusing to answer their questions about segregation, they risked having their children find themselves in dangerous situations through their ignorance of how the system worked. Finally, either teaching children to come to terms with the system or allowing them to remain relatively unconscious of it served to perpetuate segregation. A consideration of the various strategies and their consequences will help to illuminate the "delicate balancing act" faced by African American parents in the segregated South.

In his account of growing up in Alabama, Ralph Abernathy concluded that "what lay at the heart of Jim Crow" was "a desire to inflict pain and humiliation on other people."[5] Because ritual humiliation was a key tenet of segregation, the first line of defense for many African American families was to teach their children racial, family, and individual pride. In doing so, parents sought to give their children the internal resources they would need to withstand the daily assault on their sense of self-worth. Marian Wright Edelman described the task facing black parents from a child's perspective: "They had to affirm and help us children internalize our sanctity as children of God, as valued members of our family, of the Black community, of the American community, and of the entire human community, while simultaneously preparing us to understand, survive in, and challenge the prevailing values of a legally segregated nation."[6] In Edelman's words, these adults worked to "keep the outside messages from Whites that I, a Black child, was inferior from being internalized."[7]

Edelman remembered a number of ways in which her parents sought to teach her and other black children lessons about pride and their value to the community. Whenever the opportunity arose, her father, Arthur Jerome Wright, took her and her siblings to hear and sometimes meet African American educators such as Mary McLeod Bethune, Mordecai Johnson, and Benjamin Mays and artists such as Marian Anderson, after whom Edelman was named. Her parents also placed a high value on reading. Her father's library included various national magazines and the works of Shakespeare but also the poetry of Langston Hughes and Booker T. Washington's *Up from Slavery*.[8] By exposing his children to these prominent African Americans, Wright sought to teach them about both racial pride and the value of hard work toward achieving success. Edelman remembered her childhood as one in which all black adults served as surrogate parents to the community's children. In their capacities as preacher and preacher's wife, Edelman's parents extended the same feelings of worth and security to other children as they did to their own. They built a playground at their church and organized social activities to provide a safe and supportive environment in which local children could play and grow. In turn other adults in the community played the role of parent to Edelman. These adults "provided buffers of love and encouragement that helped combat the negative influences of segregated small-town southern life."[9] Scholarship on race socialization has likewise characterized black parents' role as that of "buffer."[10] Through encouragement and lessons about racial pride, African American parents sought to shield their children from the worst emotional effects of segregation.

The strategy of building up a child's sense of self-worth as a means of protection from the segregated system was not unique to Edelman's experience. Pauli Murray learned the lesson of pride based on family heritage. The stories that her maternal grandfather, Robert Fitzgerald, shared about his service as a black soldier in the Union army during the Civil War served as "an armor of pride" for her family.[11] Her maternal grandmother, Cornelia Fitzgerald, also taught her to take pride in her family's white ancestry. Fitzgerald was born a slave on the plantation of her white father's family. Although she remained a slave until the end of the Civil War, she was raised by her white aunt and instilled with a sense of pride in her past. She then went on to teach that sense of pride to Murray, instructing her, "Hold your head high and don't take a backseat to nobody. You got good blood in you—folks that counted for something—doctors, lawyers, judges, legislators. Aristocrats, that's what they were, going back seven generations right in this state." Murray also learned to derive a sense of worth from her Fitzgerald grandfather's Irish ancestry. Knowledge of these forebears, for Murray, "strengthened the growing shell of pride used to protect the soft underbelly and wobbly legs of a creature learning slowly to navigate in a cruelly segregated world." Although she regretted that much of her African past was "shrouded in shame" and mystery, the competing messages of family pride taught by her grandparents assured her that she was someone special based on both her black and her white heritage. While she drew strength from these messages, she still looked forward to the day when people "no longer needed legends about their ancestors to give them distinctiveness and self-respect."[12] Families used whatever resources were available to them—in this case stories about the family's biracial past—to instill pride in their children.

Murray viewed the lessons taught by her family as a valuable inheritance. The resources they bequeathed were vital to her survival when she left the security of her home and found herself "in a maze of terrifying forces" that she "could neither understand nor cope with." Murray was grateful that her family had taught her to withstand the segregated system from which they ultimately could not protect her.[13] Other African American parents gave their children a similar inheritance based on lessons about individual pride and equality. Benjamin Mays remembered his mother telling him and his siblings, "You are as good as anybody!"[14] Coretta Scott King called this "the black mother's old refrain," given in answer to the "eternal question" of "Why?" asked by black children. King explained, "Every African-American mother says, 'You are just as good as anyone else. It's just the way things are.'"[15] When her own daughter started to cry after learning she could not visit Funtown because "colored" people were excluded, King told her, "Yoki dear, this doesn't mean you are not as good as those people. You know, God made all of us and we are all His children. He made some white, some brown, some black, some red, and some yellow. He must have thought a lot of his colored children because he made so many."[16] King believed it was crucial "for black children to be taught a sense of their own worth that is strong enough to withstand the pressure of a white society which every day tries to show them that they are inferior."[17]

This affirming refrain echoed in the lessons of other black parents. Tennessean Lanetha Branch remembered her mother's lessons: "My mother taught us that you're important; you are somebody, and nobody can tell you who you are. You must decide who you will be. . . . But she also stressed that you're not to think that you're better than anyone else. She was very religious. She would say all of us are God's children. And so therefore, you're not *better* than anyone but you're as good as anyone else."[18] By teaching her children about the value of all people, this mother expressly avoided teaching them to hate whites. Charlayne Hunter-Gault, one of two students who desegregated the University of Georgia in January 1961, discussed the impact of lessons about individual pride on her own life. Explaining why enduring taunts of "Nigger, go home" during the desegregation crisis did not leave her bitter, Hunter-Gault recalled being crowned "queen" of her elementary school in Covington, Georgia, after she raised the most money in a fund-raising drive meant to offset the lack of resources at her segregated school. She described the impact of this event: "The year I won, the notion that I was a queen took up residence in my head and was nurtured by my family and community to such an extent that by the time I got to the University of Georgia, it was inconceivable that I might be the 'nigger' they were talking about."[19] By instilling lessons about individual, family, and racial pride, black parents were able to serve as buffers, absorbing and deflecting the message of inferiority that white society sought to convey.

A counterpart to the strategy of instilling pride in an African American child was that of isolating the child from contact with white southerners so as to delay the inevitable moment when he or she learned that southern society attached notions of difference and inferiority to blackness. If parents could postpone this lesson by shielding their children from contact with the white world until they could be equipped with the necessary internal resources, they frequently chose to do so. A related strategy involved teaching children to avoid situations, such as public transportation, in which they would be segregated. Parents also chose to postpone answering children's questions about segregation or provided alternative explanations to their queries. The overriding goal of these strategies was to defer as long as possible the point at which African American children would become fully aware of the challenges and humiliations they would face as a result of their racial designation.

W. L. Abernathy conveyed a number of messages about black life in the South to his son Ralph. A prosperous farmer who owned five hundred acres of land in Alabama, the elder Abernathy taught his son that African Americans would rise in status through land ownership and education. He also instructed Ralph not to be afraid to confront the injustice he encountered in the world, a message he would remember many years later, at the start of the Montgomery bus boycott. Alongside those messages, however, Abernathy taught his son how to survive life in the South. Ralph learned never to play with white children. If he did wrestle or box with a white boy, his father warned, he would "always have to let him win, otherwise he may become aggravated, and that could lead to trouble." The younger Abernathy recalled, "Such a warning was merely hypothetical to us. We lived on five hundred acres, which gave us plenty of breathing space, and most of the farms around us were owned or run by our uncles and cousins. So we didn't sit around and brood about whether or not to play with whites our age. We'd never met any and had no desire to." Ralph Abernathy also remembered having been "perfectly content" with using separate water fountains and other public facilities because "we were so secure in the honor accorded our family that we didn't consider such practices demeaning or even important."[20] Through his financial success W. L. Abernathy was able to create an almost exclusively black world in which to raise his children.

James Farmer remembered a similar effort on the part of his family to isolate him from contact with the white world. When Farmer was a child, his father, James Leonard Farmer Sr., was a Methodist minister and scholar at Rust College in Holly Springs, Mississippi, and later at Samuel Huston College in Austin, Texas. The younger Farmer remembered having been the "campus pet" at Rust College and wrote, "My memories of life within the campus community are of almost no negatives, only positives—being praised as a paragon, a repository of all virtues and gifts." Farmer was not as isolated once his family moved to Austin, but he still lived in "an all-black world contiguous to a mysterious white one." In his world whites were the "invisible" men.[21] By raising their children in insulated, all-black environments, the Abernathys and the Farmers sought to shield them from the realities of segregated life. The experiences of Abernathy and Farmer reveal one aspect of how class affected black parents' race socialization strategies. These fathers were able to protect their children because they played prominent roles in their communities, as a large landowner and a minister and professor, respectively. Often class was a more important factor than geography in determining a family's ability to protect its children.

When businesswoman and activist Clarie Collins Harvey was growing up in Mississippi—often characterized as the most violent and discriminatory southern state—her family shielded her from contact with whites and from knowledge of her father's activities with the NAACP.[22] Her father was a funeral home director—a position of considerable prominence in a region where people were segregated even in death—and his position and the access to private transportation that went with it allowed him to protect his daughter almost entirely from an awareness of the rules of segregation. Harvey recalled, "The Negro family tried to shelter you from all the prejudices and things that were going on. Growing up as a 'black middle class' I never rode the trolley cars nor buses." Her only experiences with public transportation came on summer trips to cities such as New York, where buses and trolleys were integrated. She recalled first being exposed to segregated transportation on a shopping trip to downtown Atlanta when she was a student at Spelman College: "I just sat down in front or midway on the streetcar, the classmate, or whoever I was going with said, 'Hey! You come back here. You know you are supposed to sit in the back.' I was very nonplussed but I went to the back. She said, 'You come from Mississippi and you pretend like you didn't know that you were supposed to sit back here.' Well I really didn't know." Harvey explained, "My exposure was very limited to the types of things that would make you know the painful tragic truth."[23] Her account reveals that even someone who was raised in the Deep South could be relatively oblivious to segregation because of her family's status and, thus, ability to protect her from experiencing the worst humiliations of the system. Her recollection also complicates the notion that segregation in any one state was uniformly worse than segregation in other states.

Harvey's lack of experience with segregated transportation was not unique. Carolyn McKinstry grew up in Birmingham, yet she recalled learning about the existence of segregated buses not from personal experience but from seeing a story about civil rights activism on television. She explained, "My parents had never really allowed us to ride the bus. There were a lot of things my parents didn't tell us. Rather than saying you can't, they conveniently dropped us off or picked us up." Wanting to witness segregation firsthand, McKinstry obtained special permission from her mother to ride the bus downtown to pay the family's department store bill. On this trip she engaged in a one-woman sit-in near the front of the bus and was surprised to observe the practice whereby black passengers paid their fare at the front, exited the bus, and walked to the side door toward the back to board. McKinstry remembered, "That was one of those things where my parents didn't sit down and say well, this is the way it is." Because her only previous experience on a bus was with the one that took her and other black students to their segregated high school and her parents had never explained the rules of segregated transportation to her, she "didn't have a real sense of what the social background and the history, the historical aspects of why this was the way it was." She recalled that she did not discuss her decision to protest segregation with her parents because she knew they would disapprove of her activism. Only later did she come to understand her parents' choices: "Both of them taught school, they had four boys that they wanted to live to be a male adult. So, a lot of what they did was done with the idea of protecting us."[24] McKinstry's middle-class parents chose to shield their children as much as possible from contact with and even knowledge of the segregated code.

McKinstry's parents appear to have been practicing a strategy of avoidance, directing their children away from situations in which they would be segregated. While they pursued this strategy without fully explaining it to their children, other parents who chose this option were more straightforward. Kentuckian John Wesley Hatch remembered that his father used to catch the train in Louisville very early on Sunday mornings and travel to Henderson County, where he pastored a church. Hatch rose early one Sunday to ride the train with his father, who promised him the "best egg sandwich you could ever imagine" at a local diner once they arrived. When they tried to enter the diner through the front door, a common practice for the father, who ate there often, the owner told them they would have to go around back to be served. Turning away after informing the owner that they were "not that hungry," the father told his son that the owner was "being white" because there was a white customer in the diner that morning. The elder Hatch went on to explain that in the interest of "personal dignity . . . for things that you don't absolutely have to do, you don't go to back doors, you don't segregate yourself." The son recalled of his own reaction, "Although I was starving, I kind of understood it, and we endured until the town came to life, which was hours later. That was the first lesson in Race 101."[25]

In a related approach to those of isolation and avoidance, some parents chose to postpone answering their children's questions about race as long as possible. A particularly traumatic event from Pauli Murray's childhood highlights why a parent might choose this option. When Murray was almost seven years old, she saw the body of a black boy who many in her community believed had been shot to death by a white man. She ran home to tell her aunt Pauline what she had seen, and in the days following the incident, Murray repeatedly asked her aunt why the boy had been shot. Murray recalled of her aunt's response, "'I can't tell you child. There are some things you'll understand better when you get older,' was all she would say."[26] In this instance Pauline Dame probably did not want to burden her niece further by explaining how the boy's skin color may have contributed to his murder. In a more mundane but no less revealing example, John Hope Franklin described his young son's attempt to befriend a neighbor in their new, predominantly white neighborhood in Washington, D.C. When Franklin's son, Whit, who had only recently learned to talk and was anxious to try out his new skill, approached a white man in the adjoining yard, the man ignored him and turned away. Franklin recalled, "Whit ran back into the house and announced that the man out there could not talk. I did not explain to my son what the man's trouble was. I was certain that soon enough my son would discover too many people like our next-door neighbor."[27] In this incident a young black child who had not yet learned to attach meaning to skin color used his child's sense of reasoning to develop an alternative explanation for why the man would not or, in his mind, could not speak to him, an explanation his father did not dispute.

Parents often provided their own alternative explanations for the limits segregation placed on their families. Coretta Scott King remembered that when her daughter asked to play on the swings in what King knew to be a white neighborhood, she "would say something like, 'We have to get home and have lunch, dear,' to try to spare her a little, to give her time to develop her own inner strength before confronting the terrible problem of being black in America." The Kings also stalled for time before finally telling their children why they could not go to Funtown. King recalled, "Martin would say, 'Not this week, children. I have to go on a trip,' or some such thing."[28] In a 1944 letter to Lillian Smith's journal *South Today*, an African American father described the decision he and his wife made to delay explaining the significance attached to skin color to their two sons: "To pour out all the harsh facts of race relations in America to a little Negro child would be devastating to his emotional well being. He could certainly not reason out these matters. The only possible effect is emotional injury." Instead, they let "the experiences come to him gradually." This father explained that when incidents involving race did occur, "we attempt to be sufficiently creative in our interpretation of these experiences so that the child's emotional balance is maintained and his capacity to appreciate people of all races is preserved."[29] This approach can be characterized as "reactive" in that these parents decided to address issues as they arose rather than implement a proactive strategy.[30] In describing their approach, the father explained that when their older son repeatedly asked his mother why he could not go to the theaters in town, she "always managed to give a reason that was not the real one." The father, in response to his other son's increasingly insistent questions, "always managed to escape the answer by evasion." Justifying his strategy, the man asserted, "It is impossible to shelter completely a Negro child from racial prejudice and bigotry in the South, even in his pre-school days. He may, however, sometimes be protected from its full meaning and consequences."[31] This father believed the potential consequences of teaching his sons about the significance attached to race too early outweighed both the risk of creating confusion and mistrust in his children and the threat posed to their physical safety by not knowing the rules of segregation. The decisions such parents had to make were momentous.

Owing to their financial insecurity, many African American families in the South did not have the option of shielding their children from contact with whites, nor could they afford to postpone lessons about potentially dangerous situations. They chose instead to teach their children the intricate rules of the segregated code and to stress that even though segregation was wrong, one had to endure it in order to ensure one's safety and the family's financial survival. This race socialization strategy was captured in the words of Benjamin Mays's mother, not in the assurance she gave her children that they were "as good as anybody" but in her admonition to "be careful and stay out of trouble"—trouble, that is, with white people.[32] Maya Angelou described her grandmother's approach to raising her and her brother, Bailey, in similar terms. She wrote, "Momma intended to teach Bailey and me to use the paths of life that she and her generation and all the Negroes gone before had found, and found to be safe ones."[33] Many black parents, like Angelou's grandmother, found that when it came to their children, they chose the safest paths.[34]

One African American mother described her approach to child psychiatrist Robert Coles thus: "It's like with cars and knives, you have to teach your children to know what's dangerous and how to stay away from it or else they sure won't live long." She explained, "White people are a real danger to us until we learn how to live with them. So if you want your kids to live long, they have to grow up scared of whites; and the way they get scared is through us; and that's why I don't let my kids get fresh about the white man even in their own house. If I do there's liable to be trouble to pay. They'll forget, and they'll say something outside, and that'll be it for them, and us too." Of her children's frustration with the system, she explained that she made them "store it in the bones, way inside, and then no one sees it. . . . The colored man I think he has to hide what he really feels even from himself. Otherwise there would be too much pain—too much." Despite the pain and frustration associated with the system, this mother felt compelled to teach her children that African Americans had to adjust to living among whites; "if they don't seem to learn it," she explained, "like everything else I have to punish them to make sure they do."[35]

Born in Troy, Alabama, in the late 1910s, Henry Hooten remembered that his father "tried to teach his family to do the things that the white man wants you to do and you can get along, and if you don't, otherwise you won't get along." Hooten's father taught him to believe "you don't lose anything" by being respectful to whites, but in being "adamant . . . being boastful, you won't get anything."[36] Hooten never saw his father express anger or dissatisfaction with the system, though he may have felt those emotions. He taught his sons to conceal their true feelings by telling the white man "what he wanted to hear, not what we wanted him to know."[37] Hooten insisted he was willing to work within the confines of the system not because he believed the message of inferiority whites attempted to convey but, rather, out of strategic considerations. One could believe segregation was wrong, but, in Hooten's words, "At the same time, you kept your mouth [shut]."[38] Hooten learned to navigate a system that no one person or family alone could change.

Born in 1940, John Lewis also grew up near Troy, Alabama, and later recalled his parents' lessons about segregation: "My parents told me in the very beginning as a young child when I raised the question about segregation and racial discrimination, they told me not to get in the way, not to get in trouble, not to make any noise." When he repeatedly asked his parents why, they responded, "That's the way it is. Don't get in the way, don't get in trouble."[39] Describing his own anger toward the system, Lewis wrote, "I couldn't accept the way things were, I just couldn't. I loved my parents mightily, but I could not live the way they did, taking the world as it was presented to them and doing the best they could with it." Despite his own decision to fight segregation, Lewis understood his parents' response to the system: "There was no weakness in the way my parents and others of their generation shouldered the burden of their time and made the best of it. Fighting back was hardly an option for them. Fight back against whom? With what?" Lewis explained, "My parents, and millions of other black men and women just like them, bore their load through an age of unbelievable oppression with a grace and a dignity I could only hope to come close to. Theirs was not a time nor a place for turning and facing the system."[40] In such a time and place, black parents made the best of life within segregation's limits and taught their children the lessons they would need to ensure their own survival.

Some of the most important lessons black children learned involved gender. Because the specter of unsanctioned interracial sex loomed so large in white imaginations, boys in particular were subject to special instruction. Growing up in North Carolina in the late 1940s and early 1950s, novelist Cecil Brown remembered a teenage friendship with a white girl. When his mother saw the two playing together and kissing each other's hands, she allowed them to continue, but in the car on the way home, she slapped Brown across the face and told him, "You know you better not get fresh with that girl." Brown recalled that he "didn't know what getting 'fresh' meant," but he "thought it had something to do with [the girl] being white."[41] Brown's mother, like many other parents of black boys in the South, was motivated by fear about what might happen to her son for associating with a white girl or simply for being in the wrong place at the wrong time.

Maya Angelou remembered one night when her brother, Bailey, then eleven, was very late coming home from town. She wrote of her grandmother's fear, "Her apprehension was evident in the hurried movements around the kitchen and in her lonely fearing eyes. The Black woman in the South who raises sons, grandsons and nephews had her heartstrings tied to a hanging noose. Any break from routine may herald for them unbearable news."[42] When Bailey finally did return home, having stayed too late at the movies, he received a whipping for his tardiness and for making his grandmother worry. In both of these instances the physical punishment for the young men's potentially dangerous behavior was identified as a departure from the normal patterns of discipline within their respective families. Brown explained that his mother, who had not raised him and had only recently become a permanent part of his life, "had never had the nerve" to hit him before, and Angelou recalled that her uncle, rather than her grandmother, as was usually the case, had whipped Bailey and that it was the first serious whipping he had ever given either of the children.[43] The way these adults reacted to seemingly innocent departures from the norm by their children indicates the seriousness with which they regarded the danger that boys in particular might face.

If young black men could not be made to conform to the strictures of segregation, both they and their parents faced the prospect that it might not be possible for them to remain in the South. Journalist Les Payne described his upbringing in Alabama and his family's eventual decision to relocate. He explained of his early, sudden refusal to say "Yes, sir" to a white shoe salesman, a refusal that earned him a slap from his mother, "I had no reasons, only questions I dared not ask. Children in black working-class families, even loving, fundamentalist Baptist ones like mine, simply did not talk back to their parents. We were to be seen and to obey in silence."[44] Payne suspected his reluctance to call the man "sir" may have stemmed from the inconsistency he saw in the rules he was learning. Trying to find support for the rule that terms of respect were reserved for elders, he wondered why he was required to say "sir" to an older white man when he had seen his grandmother address a white teenager that way. Payne asserted that he, like all children, "was born free of racial bias" and therefore did not initially recognize the way in which skin color altered the rule about terms of respect. He explained, "In my innocence, I also held the naïve notion that words meant something specific and that their application was immutable."[45]

As he grew older, Payne bent to what he identified as "early parental pressure to get me converted, born again, and socialized into a state of inferiority—to be made a Negro." His parents, he explained, "curbed all signs of rebellion in their offspring, especially in their boys, fearing that it would land them in harm's way." Payne asserted that between the age of six, when he refused to call the white salesman "sir," and the age of twelve, he had been conditioned to accept segregation. He wrote, "I had started out with zero tolerance for the etiquette of Negro behavior. Once it had contorted me like a seizure of the hiccups. Now, at the age of twelve, thanks to socialization within family and community, such petit apartheid drew barely a yawn. My emerging generation was newly primed for our post-slavery role as hewers of wood in a rich, industrialized America." Although his parents strove to teach their children the skills they would need to survive in the segregated South, the family ultimately left Alabama for Connecticut. His mother had explained of her three sons, "I knew I didn't have the kind of boys that could make it down there." Payne wrote of his parents' decision, "Despite careful grooming at home, school, and church, my parents judged us poor candidates for the kowtow."[46] Although Payne himself remembered having been thoroughly conditioned to the system by his preteen years, his parents ultimately decided their family's survival depended on leaving the South.

Although black families in the segregated South faced a special set of challenges in raising sons, they feared for their daughters' safety as well. Sadie G. Mays, the wife of Benjamin Mays, offered a telling account of the lessons her family taught her that also highlights the different strategies that could exist within the same family. Mays remembered that her maternal grandfather took her aside when she was sixteen and told her that although he and her father were both the result of white men having taken advantage of black women, he would see to it that no other such incidents occurred in his family. He told her, "Our mothers were slaves; they could not protect themselves. But you do not have to take insults from anybody. Your Dad and Granddad will spill every drop of blood in their veins to protect you little girls. I am not afraid of anybody; so if you are ever molested by a white man, you let me know."[47] Her father likewise told her and her sisters to tell him if any white man ever bothered them. Her mother, on the other hand, advised her daughters to handle such situations themselves. Mays remembered, "Mother told me to be prepared to protect myself, to carry a hatpin in my bosom, and, if attacked, use it. As I recall, I carried a hatpin with me for a year or more."[48] This mother's advice suggests that she was not only concerned about her daughters' safety but also fearful of the consequences for her husband and her father were they to take action on the girls' behalf.

Carolyn McKinstry recalled that when she was growing up in Birmingham, her father, Samuel Maull, seldom allowed her to go anywhere alone, and she was frequently accompanied by one or more of her four brothers. She understood this rule when it was her two older brothers escorting her around town, but she recalled feeling "terribly embarrassed" when her father sent her younger brothers with her. Maull apparently felt his daughter would be safer with a male member of the family in tow, no matter what his age. The only place she was allowed to go alone on a regular basis was church—where she did clerical work—because it was a "safe place." This exception to her father's rule is ironic given that she was at her church, Sixteenth Street Baptist, when it was bombed in September 1963. McKinstry's maternal grandparents, who lived in Clanton, Alabama, had the same rule as her father: she was not to go anywhere alone. Her grandparents would not even allow her to walk across the street to the beauty shop in their neighbor's home to have her hair done. Accounting for this rule, her grandfather once told her, "Things can happen to little black girls." She recalled, "I later learned that those 'things' meant rape." She believed this was "the greatest fear all black parents had for their girls."[49] Special care had to be taken to teach young black women, many of whom worked in white homes as cooks, maids, or nurses, how to resist and escape the sexual advances of white men. Such lessons formed part of the larger strategy by which black parents sought to protect their children by teaching them how to avoid and, if necessary, navigate potentially dangerous situations.

Other black parents rejected the notion that the system could not be opposed effectively on an individual basis and encouraged their children to challenge the rules of segregation despite the risks involved. Annie Gavin of New Bern, North Carolina, remembered growing up believing whites were superior. She only overcame that idea as she grew older, and once she became a mother, she tested the rules of segregation. When her daughter became thirsty at a department store, Gavin took her to drink from a white water fountain, hoping to provoke a response from the employees. Gavin said, "What's the difference in the water?" Fortunately for her and her child, the white employees did not take any action against them.[50] Unlike Gavin, Alabama native Wilhelmina Jones remembered that her parents had taught her that African Americans should speak out against unequal treatment. Jones, in turn, did not teach her own children about the distinction between black and white and allowed them to disregard the rules of segregation. She recalled an incident in which her children drank out of a white water fountain in a Montgomery department store, and she described a white employee's response: "*Really* I thought she was going to have a heart attack. She said, 'Oh, but they can't drink there!' I said, 'Oh, but they have.'"[51] On other occasions Jones ignored signs indicating separate entrances to public buildings and instead used whatever entrance was most convenient. Although she encouraged her children to do the same, she remembered one instance in which her young daughter refused to make such a test, opting to wait outside while her mother went in. Like Gavin, Jones was fortunate that her choice to challenge the rules of segregation never provoked a violent response from white southerners.

In an effort to explain what aspects of her upbringing had contributed to her activism, Rosa Parks recalled that her paternal grandfather, Sylvester Edwards, always encouraged her to stand up for herself. Owing to his experiences with slavery as a child, he was openly hostile to white southerners and would laugh at them behind their backs. Edwards refused to let Parks and her brother play with the white children who lived nearby, and when rumors surfaced that the Ku Klux Klan was active in the area, Edwards stayed up at night with a shotgun waiting for them. Parks waited with him.[52] His was not the only instruction she received from her family, however, about how she should respond to segregation.

She remembered an incident from when she was about ten years old in which a white boy about her age said he was going to hit her, and she picked up a brick and threatened to hit him back. When she told her grandmother, Rose Edwards, about the encounter, Edwards "scolded [her] very severely about how [she] had to learn that white folks were white folks and that you just didn't talk to white folks or act that way around white people. You didn't retaliate if they did something to you." Parks recalled her grandmother's prediction that if she did not change her behavior, she would be lynched before she was twenty. On another occasion Parks and her cousin were picking berries in a vacant lot near the country club where her aunt worked. A white boy called them "niggers" and told them to stop picking the berries. Parks and her cousin threatened this boy as well, and when they told Parks's aunt what the boy had said and how they had responded, she said, "You all crazy? You keep your mouths shut. If he'd gone and told somebody, they would have had y'all lynched and all we could do was cry a little bit about it."[53] Parks's account again reveals that even within families, there could be a difference of opinion about how to solve the African American parent's dilemma. This lack of consensus fostered divergent and confusing race socialization strategies.

Like Parks's grandmother and aunt, many black adults were simply not willing to risk teaching their children to challenge segregation. Driven by anger at the indignities they had endured, fear for their children's safety, and frustration at their inability to improve the lives their children would have to lead, the most economically vulnerable black southerners often chose the strategy of refusing to discuss segregation or the racial tensions it created with their children at all. Such parents employed silence as a race socialization strategy. A classic example of this approach to childrearing in the segregated South is found in Anne Moody's account of her childhood in Mississippi during the 1940s. Throughout her account of her struggles with both her family and the segregated system, Moody related story after story about her mother's unwillingness to discuss segregation or the racial situation in their community. In response to Moody's questions about why her two light-skinned uncles were not considered white, her mother exploded: "Now, you shut up! Why you gotta know so much all the time?"[54] After repeatedly asking her mother about this issue, Moody concluded, "Every time I tried to talk to Mama about white people she got mad."[55]

As Moody grew older and increasingly frustrated with the tensions in her family and the racial violence in her community, she lashed out at her mother's unwillingness to discuss these matters: "What's wrong with people talking? What's wrong with people? Negroes are being killed, beaten up, run out of town by these white folks and everything. But Negroes can't even talk about it." Her mother's stance on this issue was clear: Moody was not to discuss segregation or the violence that was beginning by 1955 to be used in earnest by white southerners to ensure the system remained intact. As Moody prepared to report to work at the home of a white supremacist only hours after learning of the lynching of Emmett Till, her mother told her to "just do your work like you don't know nothing."[56] Despite her mother's best efforts to protect her by teaching her such lessons, Moody refused to accept segregation.

Richard Wright remembered his mother having used much the same strategy. He described his childhood curiosity about his community: "I soon made myself a nuisance by asking far too many questions of everybody. It was in this manner that I first stumbled upon the relations between blacks and whites." When he asked his mother about an incident he had heard about in which a white man had beaten a black boy, she told him he was "too young to understand."[57] Soon his mother began resorting to physical punishment when he asked questions she perceived to be dangerous. Like Moody, Wright repeatedly asked his mother about a relative, in this case his grandmother, who appeared to be white but was considered black. When his mother refused to answer his questions, he was mystified: "Again, I was being shut out of the secret, the thing, the reality I felt somewhere beneath all the words and silences." When she finally slapped him, he cried. Wright later witnessed the late-night departure of his aunt and her boyfriend, who had come to their house after he had stolen money from a white woman, knocked her unconscious, and set fire to her house to cover the crime. Wright's mother advised him to forget what he had seen and told him he would be killed if anyone ever heard him mention it.[58] His mother, like Moody's, angrily discouraged her child from discussing race and racial violence out of a desire to protect him.

Other black southerners recalled incidents in which their parents discouraged them from asking questions about segregation or challenging its rules. Theresa Lyons remembered shopping trips with her mother to the Kress department store in downtown Durham, North Carolina. When Lyons complained that she was tired and repeatedly asked her mother why they could not sit at the lunch counter and have something to eat, she recalled that her mother "would be fussing, and she would just tell me, 'Shut up.'" Lyons described an incident again involving segregated water fountains that provoked an even angrier response from her mother: "They had two water fountains, and one said 'Colored' and one said 'White,' and I couldn't read, but I knew some letters. I thought 'C' stood for 'cool' and 'W' stood for 'warm.' So I drank out of both of them. I told my mother, I said, 'I drank out of both of those fountains, both of them, and one said 'cool' and [one said] 'warm,' but they were both warm.'" She recalled her mother's response: "I thought she was going to kill me. She grabbed me by the arm. She said, 'Don't you know that's for white? That's for white and colored. You can't drink out of the water fountain for the white people!' She took me out of that store. I thought she was going to kill me."[59] This mother likewise feared for her child's safety and expressed that fear in the form of anger directed at her child.

Even if black parents did not always express their fear with the same vehemence, they made it clear that the topic of segregation was not open for discussion. When asked if her parents ever taught her how to behave in front of white people, Virginia native Alma Mitchell responded, "Yes. They always said, 'Shhh. You're not supposed to talk about that.'"[60] Edith Polk did not remember having any problems with white southerners when she was growing up in Louisiana, and she recalled that white playmates frequently came to her house to play with her and her brothers. When her closest white friend, Alice, reached her preteen years, however, Alice's mother stopped allowing her to play at the Polk home. Polk suspected the reason her friend was no longer allowed to visit was because Alice's mother feared the presence of Polk's brothers, who were no longer little black boys but were becoming young black men. When Polk suggested this possibility to her own mother, she responded, "You think too much."[61] The message was clear: Edith Polk's questions were not going to be answered, and furthermore, she should put the entire matter out of her mind.

Parents who chose this approach may have done so on the basis of class considerations—again, regardless of where they lived within the region—as did those who made the choice to shield their children from contact with white southerners. These families, however, unlike those of Ralph Abernathy, James Farmer, and Clarie Collins Harvey, were not headed by prominent individuals who could provide protection for their children. Anne Moody's mother spent much of Moody's childhood as a single parent working for minimal wages in the homes of white families. Moody herself began working for whites as soon as she was old enough to do so. Richard Wright was raised by his single mother for much of his childhood, and his family moved frequently, often staying with relatives. Theresa Lyons was born to a single mother but was raised primarily by her grandmother, a sharecropper who moved repeatedly from one white landowner's property to another, with nothing left over year after year once her tobacco crop was sold. Alma Mitchell was born into a two-parent, landowning family, but her father's alcoholism caused him to lose his land. Her family, too, was reduced to the status of itinerant sharecroppers, moving from "one bad shanty to another one" throughout her childhood.[62] Mitchell herself began working in the fields at age seven and was forbidden by the white landowners to attend school. Although Edith Polk's father and mother were employed as a carpenter and a laundress, respectively, and thus were in slightly better economic circumstances, Polk still described her family as having been "very poor" when she was growing up.[63]

These families represented the most powerless segment of southern society. Many of them were headed by poor women who, for the most part, raised their children alone. Even when both parents were present in the home, their livelihood was often at the mercy of powerful whites who provided housing and provisions throughout much of the year, made decisions about whether children would work or go to school, and ultimately decided what, if any, profits would be made off the year's crop. Understanding their powerlessness, these parents may have felt they had no choice but to protect their children the only way they knew how: by telling them to accept the system as it was and never openly question it.[64]

Regardless of which strategy or combination of strategies African American parents chose, the task of raising children in the segregated South required compromises. Each of these strategies also involved certain consequences. The approach of building up children's sense of pride and security was problematic if they then went out into the world without understanding that many of the rules of segregation were designed to humiliate them. James Farmer's parents chose to combine the strategies of bolstering his internal resources and shielding him from contact with whites. Farmer recalled that he was raised in "a home with abundant bandages of love" where he was protected by "the armor of my father's position in our proscribed community, sheltering me from the fiercest barbs." Despite the protection ostensibly afforded by this approach, Farmer still questioned his parents' choices: "How well, or how poorly, was I being prepared to accept my own frailties when I learned them, and to relate interpersonally to my fellows, or to face a world that would take my head off?"[65] Farmer recognized that he was perhaps made more vulnerable to the pitfalls of segregation precisely because of the choices his parents had made. He had not learned the rules he would need to survive; he had not learned to anticipate the expectations of whites; yet he had acquired a belief in his own abilities that made him that much more of a target for those intent on squelching any signs of assertiveness in African Americans.

Relying on a family's name or a father's reputation for protection could prove dangerous once a child left the environment in which that name held sway. Consider Ralph Abernathy's experience. As a child, he made frequent trips to the local general store run by Robert Jones, a white man who was a friend of the family. Abernathy entered the store one day to find another white man, a Mr. Fitzhugh, who was drunk and demanded that Abernathy finish the remainder of his Nehi soda. Having been taught by his mother not to drink after anyone, even members of his own family, Abernathy refused, and Fitzhugh took great offence that a black child would refuse to drink after him. Abernathy described Fitzhugh's response: "With a cry of rage he drew back his hand to hit me. At that moment, Mr. Jones, who had been watching to see how far things would go, came halfway across the counter. 'Don't you touch that boy!' he cried. Then he added, 'That's the son of W. L. Abernathy.'" Abernathy recalled that Fitzhugh's reaction was immediate and remarkable: "From a towering bully he was transformed into a bundle of quivering nerves by the sound of a black man's name."[66]

In this situation a sympathetic white observer intervened to save Abernathy from physical harm by invoking the name of Abernathy's father, a prominent figure in the community. Imagine the outcome of a similar encounter if Abernathy had found himself in a store where he did not know the owner and in an area where people were unaware of his father's reputation, or imagine the fate of a young man whose father had the financial resources to shield him from everyday contact with white southerners but whose name did not have quite the same power to save him from harm. When black parents isolated their children from contact with whites and gave them little instruction on how to navigate the segregated system, black children could quickly find themselves in situations in which they had no protection and possibly no understanding even of how they had violated the segregated code.

Farmer revealed an especially compelling example of the limitations of relying on a parent's reputation. He recalled a family outing during which his father accidentally killed a white man's pig with his car. Two white men confronted the elder Farmer and humiliated him in front of his son by dropping the paycheck he had offered as compensation for the pig on the ground in front of him and telling him, "Pick it up, nigger." Farmer recalled the anger and shame he felt when his father complied with their demand, and he remembered thinking, "I'll never do that when I grow up. They'll have to kill me."[67] Following this incident, Farmer and his father could not even bring themselves to look at one another. Although James Leonard Farmer Sr.'s status within the black community enabled him to raise his children in a safe, sheltered environment, his status could not protect him in the larger world, where he was regarded by some as just another "nigger." If he could not protect himself from such indignity at the hands of whites, how could he ultimately shield his children once they came into greater contact with white society?

Consider a different example, this one again involving that minefield of segregated life, the department store water fountain. Recall that Wilhelmina Jones chose not to teach her children about racial distinctions. She encouraged them to disregard signs indicating "white" or "colored," and when her children drank out of a white water fountain in a department store, she laughed off a white employee's anger. Contrast that with a similar situation with a very different outcome. Lil Hooten remembered her younger sister having accidentally used the white water fountain at a Kress department store in Pensacola, Florida, because she had not yet learned to read and her mother had never explained that she was supposed to use the "colored" fountain. Upon witnessing this transgression, a white clerk slapped Hooten's sister, and Hooten's mother angrily explained to the little girl that she was not to drink out of that fountain because it was for white people.[68] Unable to rebuke the stranger who had slapped her young child, Hooten's mother instead directed her anger at the child, whom she had neglected to instruct about the rules of segregation. Parents who did not prepare their children for the restrictions they would face or who encouraged them to challenge the rules could only hope their child would walk away from such an encounter laughing instead of crying.

The potential consequences of teaching black children that segregation was wrong but then encouraging them to make the best of life within its limits were not much more appealing. Once children were made aware of the rules of segregation and of the injustice the system was designed to perpetuate, having their parents then tell them that the system was too big for them to challenge alone and that they must learn to live with it could make life in the segregated South that much more frustrating. Believing segregation was "just the way things were," which many black southerners remembered believing, made day-to-day life easier to bear. From the perspective of black parents maybe it was better, as Edith Polk's mother suggested, if their children tried not to think about segregation at all.

Being taught that segregation was wrong and at the same time that it was futile and possibly deadly to try to challenge it could not only lead to frustration and bitterness but also encourage children to lose respect for the adults who had taught them those lessons. As a young man growing up in a farming community in North Carolina, Cecil Brown had been largely oblivious to segregation. He only truly became aware of how it controlled his life after returning home from his first trip to New York. Brown wrote of arriving at the bus station in Wilmington on his return trip, "Segregation was a fact of life in North Carolina in 1960, but I had never really noticed it before. Now I gazed at the black people, dark and sullen, huddled together in the shabby-looking room on one side of the station and the whites, coolly omniscient of their power over us, spread out comfortably in the green chairs." Driving back to the white woman's farm on which his father was a sharecropper felt to him "like being lowered slowly into hell."[69]

The day after Brown returned, his father, with whom he had always had a troubled relationship, dispatched him to the home of Bertha Long, the white landowner, to borrow some farming equipment. Brown became so incensed by the statue of a black servant that stood in her front yard that he gleefully knocked it over and broke it. Brown had always "detested" the statue, but it had never occurred to him before to destroy it. Long immediately called Brown's father to tell him that his son had broken her "precious antique." Brown protested to his father, "It wasn't an antique and it wasn't precious. It was an Uncle Tom statue." His father admitted, "Hell, I know that, but you should be more careful. You know how these white people are." His father then informed him that, Uncle Tom or no, they were going into town to buy her a new statue. Through this incident Brown lost what little respect he had for his father. He wrote, "How I despised him! He had become the person the whites said the black man was. He was afraid of this old broken-down white woman, and I hated him for it."[70] After having largely accepted segregation throughout his childhood, Brown could no longer do so, and he hated his father for having understood all along that the system was wrong yet encouraging him to go along with it anyway.

The strategy of telling children the truth about segregation and encouraging them to challenge it had perhaps the most straightforward consequences. Parents who chose this option risked economic reprisal at the hands of whites and ultimately the injury or death of their children. The fear that their children would meet such a fate deterred many black parents from teaching them to challenge segregation openly. Encouraging children to disregard the rules of segregation need not, however, always have such dire consequences. Take again the example of Wilhelmina Jones's children at the water fountain. From that encounter her children probably learned that they could challenge the system without retribution. This knowledge likely inspired them to make similar tests of segregation in the future. On the basis of their experiences they may have gone on to teach their own children that segregation was not immutable, that it could be overcome effectively. The challenge of such an approach lay in the element of the unknown: one never knew at which fountain one would be slapped and at which one would have the last laugh. Class considerations and intraregional variations played some role in determining when and where it was safe to disregard the rules, but personal whim—a factor that was impossible to predict—played a significant role as well.

Finally, refusing to answer questions about segregation or forbidding children from discussing it also had potential consequences. As with those who chose to shield their children from contact with whites, and therefore from knowledge of how the system worked, parents who refused to answer their children's questions about segregation or postponed doing so sent them out into the world without the knowledge they would need to ensure their own safety. Children who did not find the answers they sought at home might seek them elsewhere and unknowingly put themselves in danger by broaching the subject with the wrong person. Parents who chose this strategy also risked alienating their children. Years after her autobiography was published, Anne Moody gave an interview in which she contemplated the impact of her mother's unwillingness to discuss segregation or the racial violence in their community. Moody explained, "You kind of lose a sense of closeness to your parents." She believed parents' unwillingness to discuss these matters "creates a barrier, of not just communication, a barrier of feelings, too."[71] In addition to the impact on parent-child relationships, discouraging children from asking questions about segregation ultimately perpetuated the system. Ralph Abernathy remembered that when he was a child, segregation "seemed so old and so ingrained, a part of the landscape, like the slant of a hillside or the hang of a massive oak tree."[72] When parents refused to answer their children's questions about segregation, they reinforced the idea that the system was "a part of the landscape" that was not to be challenged.

African American parents in the segregated South found themselves in the unenviable position of having to develop race socialization strategies through which they could protect their children's lives while at the same time safeguarding their sense of pride in themselves, their families, and the broader African American community. Each strategy and combination of strategies required difficult compromises. Each approach to resolving the African American parent's dilemma promised potentially dire consequences. Whatever their motivations and however difficult their decisions, the cumulative effect of the choices made by many black parents was to encourage young people to view segregation as a fact of southern life. While black parents could choose how to prepare their children for segregation when they were at home, parents could not dictate what their children would learn about segregation and race when they sent them to the region's public schools. Southern schoolchildren, black and white, learned little about the role of African Americans in the nation's past and even less that would have encouraged them to challenge segregation.

CHAPTER 3

SUPPLEMENTARY READING

Racial Instruction in Southern Schools

R egardless of how southern parents chose to educate their children about segregation and race, they sacrificed significant control over what their children learned about these crucial issues once they sent them to school. The school, like the home, served as a key socializing agent in the lives of southern young people. Children learned lessons at school that either reinforced or undermined what they were already learning at home. Anne Braden worried about what her children would learn at their all-white school. She first became critical of segregation through a series of incidents during her college and early professional years, but she intensified her efforts to fight segregation once she became a mother, in the early 1950s. She remembered how her life changed: "I knew that within five years my son would be starting to school—starting to school, unless changes were made, in the segregated schools of the South—and that the whole vicious pattern would be beginning all over again in my life. To strike out against segregation became like a compulsion to me."[1] Braden believed contact with the South's segregated schools would expose her children to lessons about race and segregation that she and her husband, Carl, did not want them to learn. In Braden's view each new generation of children that entered the region's segregated public schools risked learning lessons that perpetuated segregation.

For their part white parents who supported the segregated system were likely very pleased with what their children learned about segregation and race at school, as they encountered little that would have caused them to question the system or view African Americans in a positive light. Schools exposed young people to a narrative of the region's past that minimized the cruelty of slavery, celebrated the heroism of Confederate soldiers, lamented the "tragedy" of Reconstruction, and largely neglected the activities of African Americans both before and after emancipation. Writing in the mid-1950s, Kenneth Clark described the effect of schools on the racial attitudes of children as "more passive than active." Instead of "taking the leadership in educational programs designed to develop more positive racial attitudes," as he believed they should, "the schools tend[ed] to follow the existing community prejudices."[2] White parents such as Anne Braden who sought to keep their children from learning to accept segregation as the natural order of life in the South indeed had much to fear from sending them to school.

While many black parents pursued a strategy at home of building up their children's sense of pride in themselves and in the African American past, they, too, lost control over what their children would learn about segregation and race once they sent them to school.[3] Schools for black southerners were generally poorly funded, overseen by white administrators with varying levels of commitment to quality education for black students, and staffed by highly committed teachers who often struggled to reconcile the official curriculum with the lessons they thought students should learn. Instruction in such schools was largely based on the same textbooks and courses of study used in white schools. One of the most common indignities associated with segregated schools involved having to use secondhand books that had been discarded by white students. Vernon Jordan recalled, "We got the cast-off books the white kids didn't use anymore. In 1951, I was given textbooks that had been used by white students in 1935, the year I was born."[4] Although the textbooks used by black students were outdated, the official curriculum was essentially the same. Because southern schoolchildren would have used textbooks with a range of publication dates throughout the period from 1920 through 1955, it is useful to consider these years as a whole, though changes to the curriculum were under way in some parts of the South by the mid-1950s.

Whether black students learned anything positive at school about the achievements of African Americans depended in large part on the initiative of their teachers in seeking out and in some cases developing materials with which to supplement the official curriculum. Even then, the primary goal of these lessons was not so much to teach black students to challenge segregation as it was "to immunize" them from the "virulence" of segregation's effect on them.[5] Schools, like homes, were sites within black communities where adults focused on building up the internal resources children would need as they came into increasing contact with white society.

Segregated schools were significant not only for the lessons taught there but also for the sense of difference they instilled in children. African American children often first became aware of the significance attached to skin color when they started school. Black and white children in the South played together as relative equals when they were very young, and the first indication that this camaraderie would not last came when black children went to one school and white children went to another. When asked how he first became aware of segregation, Mississippi native Maurice Lucas remembered, "I'm going to tell you how you find out. We had to walk to school and white folk rode the bus. . . . The white folk come by there every day on their little pretty shiny gold bus. Throw rocks off of the bus at us. Didn't take long."[6] Other African Americans likewise recalled walking past a modern brick school for whites on the way to their own one- or two-room school some distance away and being taunted by white children riding buses who not only threw objects ranging from rocks to orange peels but spit at them as well.[7] Rosa Parks explained how she and her friends adapted to white students throwing trash off the bus: "After a while when we would see the white school bus coming, we would just get off the road and walk in the fields a little bit distant from the road. We didn't have any of what they call 'civil rights' back then, so there was no way to protest and nobody to protest to. It was just a matter of survival—like getting off the road—so we could exist from day to day."[8] Their lack of transportation to school, as well as harassment by whites, taught black students early lessons about race.

Once they arrived at school, black children used supplies that had been handed down from white schools. Vermelle Ely, a teacher from Charlotte, North Carolina, recalled that she and her colleagues would go to the city dump at the end of the school year and find first grade reading books, some of which had barely been used, that had been thrown out by the white schools. Ely and her fellow teachers would use these books in their own classrooms the following year.[9] Growing up in Fort Worth, Texas, Ferdie Walker remembered feeling very fortunate to receive a book with fewer than three of the signature lines inside the front cover filled in because it meant that only one or two students had used the book before her.[10] Considering the condition of the books many black southerners remembered using, one would have been lucky to receive a book with any room left to sign one's name. A Georgia State Board of Education member noted that having a record in each textbook indicating which students had used it would "relieve the superintendents of the charge that the books have ever been in the hands of niggers."[11]

In addition to books, equipment such as desks, football uniforms, band instruments, and home economics supplies all came secondhand from white schools. Ely recalled that her school colors—blue and white—were the same as those of the local white high school because the players at her school wore the white players' old uniforms. White Mississippian Willie Morris remembered that in his hometown, the football team at the black high school, known as "Number Two," wore the same colors—red, black, and white—as his school for the same reason.[12] Such memories are no coincidence. Southern state boards of education pursued a deliberate policy of ensuring that black students received textbooks and equipment only after such items had been discarded by white schools. Georgia State

Board of Education minutes from the early 1950s, for example, reveal that orders for textbooks were returned unfilled if they had not been marked as being for "white" or "colored" schools.[13] White officials wanted to ensure that surplus or outdated supplies flowed in only one direction: from white schools to black ones.

Black children were disheartened when they discovered they were using books and supplies discarded by white students. Geraldine Davidson remembered her dismay at the used and torn books she received growing up in Arkansas but recalled that her father told her, "You try to learn what is there in that book. You don't care how many times it had been used."[14] Despite attempts to focus on the content of black children's education rather than on the shabbiness of the environment in which it was often conducted, black students and teachers were troubled by the visible evidence of second-class status. In her autobiography Mary Mebane recalled her excitement at being chosen by her second grade teacher to help pass out textbooks on the first day of class. Her enthusiasm quickly waned, however, when she discovered a tag in one of the books indicating that it had come from a white school. Mebane remembered, "Stunned, I sat down, while the others continued to talk and laugh. I looked in the front of the book, and there were two names and the same words: PROPERTY OF BRAGGTOWN SCHOOL. We were paying book rent for books that the white children at the brick school had used last year." She immediately understood the significance of her discovery: "I looked at the books as the others picked them up. *All of them were secondhand.* They felt dirty to me. I wondered about the girl who had had my book last year. She was smug and laughing at me. I had to use her old book. It wasn't right. I was very quiet for a long time."[15] Anthony Farmer, a teacher in Enfield, North Carolina, remembered feeling physically ill whenever he ordered textbooks for his school because he knew what he was really doing was ordering brand new books for the nearby white school while his school would receive their hand-me-downs.[16]

As black students became aware of the differences between their schools and those for whites, they saw that their schools were old, small, poorly supplied, and lacking in the modern comforts of adequate light, heat, and restroom facilities. As they walked to school each day, they were passed by hostile white students riding shiny yellow buses to clean, well-lit, well-supplied modern brick buildings with indoor plumbing.[17] In other instances black students, particularly high school students in rural areas, rode buses long distances from home each day because there were no adequate educational facilities in their home communities. Such stark disparities in the schools provided for black and white children could not help but communicate how little value the white community placed on education for black students. Kenneth Clark argued that segregated schools were "in themselves concrete monuments to the prevailing racial prejudices in a community."[18] Before the first book was cracked or the first lesson learned, white society sought to teach inferiority to black students.

Because black and white students in the South eventually used the same textbooks, it is instructive to consider how those books approached the subjects of race, segregation, and the role of African Americans in the nation's past. In his 1929 study, *Race Attitudes in Children,* sociologist Bruno Lasker examined how various aspects of children's lives, including schools, contributed to their development of racial attitudes. Of civics textbooks in particular, Lasker wrote, "To the question, what, more precisely, is being taught in the civics class on the subject of race and race relation, the answer is—for most communities—nothing at all." He found that students were more likely to learn about race in history classes, where they learned about slavery, or in geography classes, where they learned about Africa in terms of "aboriginal life at its most primitive." Even in such classes, he considered the "purposeful teaching" of "race and race relation" to be "rare." In cases where such instruction was intentionally undertaken, it was "usually owing to the initiative of a teacher who has strong convictions on the subject—whether adverse to inter-racial contact or friendly toward it."[19]

A number of studies of textbooks used during this period likewise found that the most common way of dealing with the subjects of race, segregation, and the African American past was to disregard them altogether. A 1947 report on a study of over four hundred textbooks used in elementary schools, high schools, and colleges around the country revealed that the books "ignore[d] contributions of Negroes to America's progress." While the study found that "with few exceptions the textbooks and courses of study are free of intentional bias toward any population group," it also concluded that "there are frequent value judgments and implications, unconsciously expressed, which tend to perpetuate antagonisms now current in American life."[20] Clark concurred, writing, "Standard textbooks in American schools almost never deliberately attack or humiliate any of the groups that comprise the American population"; they merely failed to mention the contributions those groups made to the country's development. This approach to the study of the American past ran the risk, according to Clark, that "the average child may well assume that the greatness of America is solely the result of a Northern European or even an Anglo-Saxon heritage."[21] Writing in 1970, after some improvement had been made, a group of scholars nevertheless found that "more often than not, the American Negro has been given the silent treatment" in history textbooks and courses.[22]

Studies specifically of textbooks used in southern schools arrived at similar conclusions about the lack of attention paid to African Americans. In a 1934 study of history textbooks used in sixteen southern states, African American historian Lawrence D. Reddick identified a number of omissions and misrepresentations. He noted the dearth of photographs of African Americans in the otherwise "profusely illustrated" texts and wrote of the coverage of the antebellum period, "There is no photograph or illustration of any sort of individual Negroes as personalities. The most common illustration shows a group of Negroes in a cotton 'patch.'"[23] Reddick found it remarkable that one book included not only a picture of Tuskegee Institute but also one of Booker T. Washington, the one African American most likely to have had his picture appear in the textbooks of the era. Reddick discovered that mentions of Frederick Douglass, Sojourner Truth, and Harriet Tubman were rare and concluded, "From reading the histories, the pupil would get the impression implied by the omissions that the Negroes did nothing, or at the most, very little, toward their own freedom." He noted that during discussions of Reconstruction, the authors "usually depict the Negroes as pawns, passive instruments in the hands of others."[24] Reddick also observed that aside from the occasional reference to Washington and his program of industrial education, "the place and development of the Negro in the national life since the granting of freedom and citizenship are ignored almost completely."[25] On the issue of African American military service, he determined that "there is practically nothing in the South's American history textbooks about the Negro and national defense." Reddick concluded of the texts he studied, "The picture of the Negro is altogether unfavorable: As a slave he was happy and docile. As a freedman he was shiftless, sometimes vicious, and easily led into corruption. As a freeman his activities have not been worthy of note."[26]

Robert B. Eleazer, longtime educational director of the Commission on Interracial Cooperation (CIC), produced a pamphlet in 1935 entitled "School Books and Racial Antagonism," in which he summarized the findings of three studies, including Reddick's, of textbooks used in southern states and then conducted a review of his own.[27] One of the studies he consulted was written by James Overton Butler, a graduate student at George Peabody College for Teachers in Nashville, who looked at fifty-six textbooks on history, civics, and "Problems of American Democracy" that had been adopted by various southern states and were being widely used in schools. Butler summarized his findings: "Generally speaking, the textbooks analyzed fail to give the Negro his rightful place in American life and to engender in the public attitudes which would be useful and even necessary eventually to solve the race problem."[28] Peabody professor U. W. Leavell conducted the third study at the request of the Tennessee State Department of Education in an effort to assess how twenty textbooks then in use were likely to affect racial attitudes in the state. He found the material in the textbooks "entirely too limited to afford the future citizens of Tennessee an adequate basis for judgment and the development of a wholesome attitude in regard to this question."[29] More significant even than this finding is the fact that state officials thought to investigate the books in the first place.

In his own survey of more than fifty textbooks adopted for use in southern states, Eleazer concluded that the findings of the three studies he consulted were "a great deal milder than the facts warrant." In the twenty history books he studied, he, like Reddick, found little mention of African American military service, and he unearthed only four names of individual African Americans: Harriet Tubman, Nat Turner, Denmark Vesey, and Booker T. Washington. Eleazer summed up his findings: "One gets the impression that the Negro has figured in American life only as an ignorant, semi-savage slave and as a dangerous freedman, unprepared for citizenship and consequently a menace to the white man's civilization." He wrote of the civics textbooks he read, "If fourteen children each should study one of the above texts, seven would be left in utter ignorance that there is a racial situation in the South involving civic problems and responsibilities; four would touch the subject so lightly as to receive no definite impression whatever, either good or bad; and three would probably come out with initial prejudices confirmed and deepened." He concluded that "only one of the fourteen would be given any conception of his civic responsibilities in the light of the bi-racial situation, or any preparation for meeting them wisely and fairly." Eleazer's review of thirty-eight American literature textbooks turned up few negative sentiments, an occasional mention of Paul Laurence Dunbar or Phillis Wheatley, and little else.[30] As with history and civics texts, most collections of American literature used in southern classrooms throughout this period overlooked African Americans. These studies reveal that marginalization of African Americans spanned decades and characterized textbooks used both inside and outside the region. Only with the advent of the civil rights movement did officials and publishers begin to devote more attention to the roles played by African Americans in the nation's past.

While these studies reveal much about what was not covered in southern classrooms, samples from textbooks adopted by various southern states provide a glimpse into what was taught. From a textbook adopted for use in Alabama elementary schools, students would have learned that during colonial times "there were many who believed that the condition of the negro was improved by bringing him from the darkness of Africa and putting him into civilized and Christian communities."[31] The author also asserted that Africa was the most convenient "country" from which to obtain the large number of laborers needed in the colonies.[32] An elementary textbook adopted by the state of Kentucky read, "As a rule, no doubt, the slaves were kindly treated when their work was in the household, and even in the fields when they worked with their owner on a small farm. . . . In such cases the relation was personal, and a friendly feeling existed between the white man and his slave." Plantation owners took pains, the author stressed, to avoid separating slave families.[33]

Likely in an attempt to stress national reconciliation while at the same time celebrating Confederate leaders, elementary school textbooks adopted in Alabama and Tennessee profiled "heroes of the Civil War," including Jefferson Davis, Ulysses S. Grant, Stonewall Jackson, Robert E. Lee, Abraham Lincoln, and William Tecumseh Sherman.[34] The author of a high school textbook adopted in North Carolina explained that after the war the "emotional nature" of the former slaves "led them to believe that miraculous prosperity was to be bestowed upon them without their effort."[35] Unfortunately, the author continued, they were "encouraged in these ideas by many low-minded adventurers and rascally, broken-down politicians, who came from the North and posed as the guides and protectors of the colored race, poisoning the minds of the negroes against the only people who could really help them begin their new life of freedom well,—their old masters."[36] Of the white South's response to Reconstruction, the author wrote, "Secret organizations, called the Ku-Klux Klans, made up mostly of young men, took advantage of the black man's superstitious nature to force him back into the humble social position which he held before the war."[37] The author of a textbook adopted for use in Alabama high schools listed the ways in which "radicals" in the South "caused trouble" after the war, including "taking the part of the negro in quarrels with the white man," "attempting to educate the black man," "putting the negro on an equality with the white man," and "conferring manhood suffrage on negroes."[38] Textbooks used in southern classrooms during this period were virtually unanimous that Reconstruction had been a mistake.

When textbooks did mention segregation, they offered novel interpretations of the institution. One book noted the complexity of the "race problem" in the South but heralded as a positive development the fact that "in some sections [African Americans] are segregating in black belts where they are free to develop their own communities."[39] As this was the only mention of segregation in the text, the author left the impression that African Americans had adopted segregation on a completely voluntary basis and that their subsequent ability to pursue separate development would serve to alleviate racial tensions in the South. A textbook used for twelfth grade "Problems of American Democracy" courses in a number of southern states reported that although African Americans were segregated in the South, "the idea works the other way too"—that is, "a white person may not attend a colored school, nor ride in the street car or coach reserved for the negro."[40] In this account the physical movement of white southerners was equally constrained by the institution. The author of another textbook explained that African American leaders such as Booker T. Washington and his successor at Tuskegee, Robert Moton, "desire social segregation for the present,—but with a difference. To the White, Negro segregation means Negro inferiority. To these Negro leaders separate cars and separate schools for their people mean a better chance for the Negro to 'find himself'; but they insist that the 'Jim Crow car' shall be cared for and equipped as well as the car for Whites who pay the same rates."[41] While this description is notable in that it states plainly the sense of inferiority segregation was meant to instill, it nonetheless left students to conclude that both black and white southerners preferred segregation.

The overall story of the region's history inscribed in textbooks used in southern classrooms went something like this: in need of a marketable crop and a ready labor supply by which to establish viable colonies, early settlers bought slaves from passing traders. These "heathen" slaves, who had been captured in the wilds of darkest Africa and, as textbooks were quick to point out, had been sold by other African peoples, were transported to America—often by New Englanders—where they enjoyed the fruits of civilization while contributing to the prosperity of the southern colonies. Their labor was necessary to the growth of the colonies because they were purportedly much easier to control than white indentured servants. Slaves became even more valuable after Eli Whitney, blessed with American ingenuity, invented the cotton gin. Because cotton became the South's primary export as well as a key raw material for the nascent industries of the North—another fact that textbooks hastened to point out—slavery became central to the prosperity of the nation as a whole.

After many years of peace and compromise on the issue of slavery, the story continued, radical agitators in the North began causing trouble; a tragic war was fought over the issue of states' rights, not slavery. Each side, the North and the South, honestly believed in the cause for which it fought, and soldiers on both sides served bravely as heroes. After the war was over, dishonest men from the North stirred up ignorant freedmen, and the South suffered terribly under their rule. Southern men had no choice, so the story went, but to form the Ku Klux Klan to defend the honor of their women and regain control. Once they had re-established their power, southern white men realized what a mistake it had been to give social and political rights to a group of people unable to use them responsibly. Black men were thus removed from the political process so that it would be impossible for such abuses to occur in the future. The story ended with the prediction that if black southerners continued to follow the advice of their great leader Booker T. Washington and seek advancement by pursuing the agricultural and domestic tasks for which they were supposedly best suited, whites and blacks in the South would continue to pursue successful separate development so long as there was no social intermingling. Little in this distorted narrative of the South's past would have caused white students to doubt that segregation and disfranchisement had been the best ways to solve the region's racial problems.

Despite such narratives, which sought to excuse the actions of white southerners while spreading the blame for the nation's racial past, textbooks used in southern classrooms were subject to constant scrutiny and often became the source of considerable controversy. Concern about the content of books used in the South predated the Civil War, and legislatures in various southern states passed resolutions in the late nineteenth and early twentieth centuries discouraging the use of textbooks deemed "unfair" to the South.[42] Starting in the 1890s, various "Lost Cause" organizations, including the United Confederate Veterans (UCV), the Sons of Confederate Veterans (SCV), and the United Daughters of the Confederacy (UDC), undertook campaigns to ensure southern young people learned an "unbiased" history of the Confederacy.[43] In her study of the UDC, Karen Cox explained that the organization "rejected the contention that southerners had been traitors and rebels and instead promoted them as heroes and defenders of a just cause." That just cause, these groups hastened to stress, was states' rights and not slavery. The activities of these groups included compiling lists of approved textbooks, lobbying state boards of education to remove texts they deemed objectionable, and in some cases producing their own state histories that presented a view of the Confederacy with which they agreed. Cox argued that by the end of World War I the UDC and other groups had largely been successful in their attempt to institutionalize the "true" history of the Confederate past, that is, a version of the region's history that was sympathetic to white southerners.[44]

Various state board of education records reveal that efforts by Lost Cause groups and others to promote a so-called unbiased history of the South continued well into the twentieth century. In the early 1920s considerable controversy surrounded David S. Muzzey's textbook, *An American History.* Deemed "Muzzey's history" for the duration of the conflict, this text was opposed in North Carolina and elsewhere by the Rutherford Committee to Disseminate the Truths of the Confederacy—a joint undertaking by the UCV, the SCV, and the UDC—on a number of grounds.[45] Although committee members commended Muzzey for noting that

"New England Rum was used for enslaving the African," they faulted him for not stressing "that the bringing out of slaves was in New England ships and controlled by New England men." Such men, in the committee's view, subsequently "damned the South for using and caring for the slaves the Yankee inhumanely brought from Africa." The committee defended slavery, deeming slaves "the happiest and best cared for peasantry the world ever saw." They described Muzzey's charge that the South fought the Civil War for an "unworthy cause" as "Yankee calumny!" and deemed it "scandalous to teach the children of North Carolina that their heroes of Bethel and Gettysburg and Appomattox were fighting for 'an unworthy cause.'"[46] Letters written by Rutherford Committee members to the North Carolina state superintendent of public instruction recommended a history written, not surprisingly, by Mildred Lewis Rutherford, the one-time historian-general of the UDC.[47]

Later controversies involved charges that textbooks used in southern classrooms were "subversive." One such charge was leveled in Georgia in 1940 at the works of education professor Harold Rugg. David Muzzey's history was evidently still considered controversial almost twenty years later, but when one parent expressed her concern about that book to a Georgia State Board of Education member, he told her not to be so concerned about Muzzey's history but instead to "watch the Rugg books" and "not allow them to get in the schools." State Board of Education members held a public meeting to give concerned citizens an opportunity to voice their criticism of Rugg's works. Despite the fact that almost none of the audience had read the books in question, parents and interested observers held forth for hours on the dangers of allowing subversive literature to influence the minds of Georgia's youth in favor of communism. Virtually the only specific charge made against Rugg was that he "openly advocated racial equality" in one of his books, a charge that Rugg, who traveled to Georgia to attend the meeting, repeatedly denied.[48] This accusation highlights the regional habit of equating calls for racial integration with communist activity. Without ample supporting evidence, however, the board found it difficult to substantiate the claim that Rugg's books were actually subversive.[49]

In light of the watchfulness of organizations such as the UDC and of the public, a condition exacerbated by the increasing anticommunism of the post–World War II period, southern state education officials were particularly sensitive to controversy. They tried to strike a balance between the interests of those who called for more and better treatment of African Americans in textbooks and those who continued to promote what they viewed as an unbiased history of the South. The deliberations of a Virginia textbook commission in the years from 1950 to 1956 reveal the sort of conflicting pressures under which such officials worked. The members of the commission were charged with approving textbooks on Virginia history for use in fourth, seventh, and twelve grade classrooms. They considered part of their task to be determining how much information on potentially controversial issues should be presented at each grade level and frequently decided that omitting certain information was better than leaving a subject open to misinterpretation. Working in the years immediately before and after the *Brown* decision, these commissioners were torn between the desire to develop textbooks that were sympathetic to the South, particularly to Virginia, and the conflicting desire to respond to the political climate by devoting more attention to African Americans.

Many of the commissioners' comments reveal an effort to cast southern history in a positive light. In critiques of the proposed texts, the commissioners asserted, for example, that the harshness of conditions on slave ships and the cruelty of slavery had been "overemphasized."[50] One commissioner, D. A. Cannaday, wondered if the issue of slavery had been tactfully handled in the seventh grade text and noted that the issue would "probably come under close scrutiny."[51] It is unclear with whose scrutiny he was concerned. Cannaday questioned the discussion of states' rights in the high school text and argued that such discussions "should be written from the Virginia point of view, the Southern point of view, for it is to be a *Virginia* history."[52] He also noted that because the text was supposed to be a history written for young Virginians, it should depict the Confederate victories in Virginia in the early years of the Civil War with more "*warmth* and *enthusiasm*."[53] Several of the commissioners expressed concern that the texts did not include enough information on Robert E. Lee.

Another commissioner, Thomas Abernathy, noted an instance in the high school text in which the term *Civil War* had been used and recommended that it be replaced, explaining, "This, if we let it stand, will bring down on our heads the wrath of the UDC and many others. Use War of Secession or War Between the States or War for Southern Independence."[54] Commissioner Cannaday cautioned that causes for the war other than slavery should be stressed and observed of a discussion in an early draft of the seventh grade text, "As here put, entrance into the struggle hardly seems justified."[55] The textbooks' treatment of Reconstruction was roundly criticized, with the commissioners agreeing that if the author of the high school text had consulted the Dunning School's now infamous work on that period, the book would have been more "acceptable" to them. As it stood, the commissioners agreed that the author "does not see the flavor of our traditions."[56] Even after the original author had been removed from the project, the commissioners had to caution his successor that he should replace the term "dishonest men" in his discussion of Reconstruction with the phrase "carpetbagger political opportunists from the north."[57] As for the role of African Americans in Reconstruction, Cannaday wanted the book to focus more on "the newly freed Negro's misunderstanding of freedom" and the carpetbagger's use of the freedman as a "device" for pursuing the "exploitation of the conquered country to his own material and political advantages."[58]

In the wake of the *Brown* decision the commissioners became increasingly concerned with an issue raised by Cannaday: "Is the Negro question well done?"[59] Several commissioners recommended including more information on the achievements of black Virginians, especially Booker T. Washington. Even his accomplishments, however, were presented in a manner designed to be nonthreatening. Cannaday noted that more emphasis might be given to Washington, "especially to his advice to the Negro student—that it was of more importance to learn to earn a dollar than to spend one in attending the opera."[60] The commission instructed the author of the high school text, "If you think you must have a picture of a Negro in the book, by all means use that of Booker T. Washington—a really great educator." They advised him that the picture belonged in the chapter on education.[61] The commissioners dealt repeatedly with issues of terminology. While they frequently referred to "colored people" in their writings and conversations, they decided that in the history texts "colored people should be called Negroes with a capital *N* not colored." The term *mammy* also became a point of contention. A. G. Richardson, an African American adminsitrator with the Department of Education, had advised the commission that the term was offensive, but one of the commissioners argued that *mammy* was "an affectionate term" used during slavery and thus should remain in the text with an explanation.[62] Richardson also questioned the seventh grade text's description of slavery and asserted, "According to this story, most Negroes lived happier and better as slaves under the kindness and consideration of their masters and mistresses, than they do today as free men." He noted that the book still lacked adequate coverage of black Virginians.[63] While Richardson's suggestions were not always taken, the fact that they were at least entertained suggests a level of sensitivity to issues of race on the part of the commissioners.

By 1956 one commissioner in particular, Natalie Blanton, cautioned that the group should not "obsess" over the texts' treatment of African Americans. In her view the commission's attempts to respond to the contemporary political climate had resulted in placing the issue of race at the center of Virginia history rather than on the periphery, where she believed it belonged. She reported having come away from reading the revised version of the high school textbook with the conclusion that Virginia's history was "not glorious, but a long and arduous and losing struggle," "with the Negro problem the most important single conditioning factor," "with very little to offer the nation in philosophy or ideals," and "with only lip service to the freedom of the individual."[64] These objections demonstrate that education officials at this time, even those who were relatively responsive to the concerns of African Americans, were willing to go only so far in their revision of southern history. The committee's deliberations as a whole reveal the competing pressures on officials and educators who sought to correct the "silent treatment" so often given African Americans but were unwilling to change the traditional narrative of the region's history in the process.

White southerners' memories of what they learned about slavery, race, and segregation in school offer insight into the effect of that traditional narrative on students' understanding of the region's past. John Seigenthaler Sr. attended Catholic parochial school, and he vividly recalled what one of the nuns taught him about slavery. She insisted that "the War Between the States . . . had nothing to do with freeing the slaves. The real cause was simple economics—the plantations of the South against the industries of the North." In her view "the nigger slaves . . . were far better off on plantations in the South than white workers were in Northern factory jobs."[65] Larry L. King remembered his high school teachers in Texas conceding that "perhaps slavery *was* slightly awkward in its arrangements when considered in hindsight," but once they were past "the temporary embarrassment of human bondage," they "plunged with ill-concealed relief into what a dark Reconstruction we in the misunderstood South had suffered, what with all those looting Billy Yanks, profiteering Carpetbaggers, and sullen black 'freedmen' blighting land intended for us by God and Jefferson Davis." King was embellishing for dramatic effect here, but judging by the language of some of the textbooks used in the region, students would have learned similar lessons. King remembered being a grown man before he discovered that many of the country's founders had been slaveholders, despite their love of liberty. As for the role of African Americans in the nation's past, King wrote, "Nowhere, in my early association with our educational or other institutions, was it hinted that black people had played sustaining roles in our national history or had made significant contributions to American culture."[66]

History lessons about race extended beyond the classroom. As part of their study of the nation's past, King's American history class was taken to see *Gone with the Wind*. King wrote, "I do not recall that Rhett Butler, Scarlett O'Hara, or Butterfly McQueen did or said anything to alter our racial misunderstandings."[67] The practice of encouraging southern schoolchildren to see the film may have been fairly common. African American novelist Raymond Andrews recalled that both black and white students in his hometown of Madison, Georgia, were dismissed early one Friday afternoon on the condition that they attend the matinee showing of the film at the town's theater.[68] One assumes this was a segregated showing. Andrews reported that when the film was first released in 1939, popular opinion among African Americans in his community held that it was "a 'white folks' picture" that showcased a stereotypical portrayal of the Old South. Andrews's take on the film when he saw it in 1948 was somewhat different: "What I remember most was sitting through the entire picture wondering just why in the world Scarlett was so much more interested in the weakling Ashley than in the more adventurous Rhett? Didn't she know Rhett was Clark Gable?" A fan of action movies, he wished the film version of the Civil War had lasted longer.[69] While Andrews seemed unfazed by the depiction of race in the film, white students who viewed *Gone with the Wind* likely absorbed stereotypes about loyal yet ignorant slaves, a heartbreaking military defeat at the hands of the "Yankees," and white men forced to resort to violence to rescue the South from Reconstruction.

Roy Blount Jr. remembered having been taken to see another racially charged depiction of the South's past, *The Birth of a Nation,* when he was in school in Decatur, Georgia, in the early 1950s. He contacted his mother years later to learn more about the circumstances under which he had viewed the film, first released in 1915, which glorified the Ku Klux Klan. Blount's mother became somewhat defensive and explained, "At that time the race issue was practically nonexistent so far as we knew in the area. [The film] was not sponsored by any one group and you-all were carried to see it from a historical standpoint only. The Ku Klux Klan was nearly dead at that time—rarely heard from. Your father and I saw it, and I remember it being a magnificent movie and we did not at that time consider it as racial."[70] Whether they were conscious of it or not, parents and teachers who sent children to see these cinematic depictions of the South were inculcating them with a version of the region's history that cast African Americans as either loyal, contented slaves or as a menace to white society and simultaneously glorified racial violence.

Instead of learning about southern history through a school fieldtrip to the movies, future civil rights activist Sue Thrasher learned her early lessons in Tennessee through trips to nearby Shiloh National Military Park, where her elementary school held class picnics. Her memories of these outings were of "deviled eggs, macaroni salad, and Confederate flags."[71] Thrasher recalled that she, like her classmates, was dutifully upset that there was only one Confederate monument in the national park. She bought Confederate flags in the gift shop, decorated her room at home with them, and "succumbed to the mythological history of the

South."[72] Thrasher was not alone among white southerners in turning childhood lessons learned at school into regional pride. Jewish author Edward Cohen found inspiration and a sense of belonging by embracing stories about the South's mythical past. He wrote of his childhood in Jackson, Mississippi, "The version of history that I absorbed both in the classroom and out was the same one in which my fellow southerners were steeped. There had been no civil war but a War Between the States, and, almost a century later, I, like my classmates, referred to northerners as 'Yankees.' When we sang 'Dixie,' we stood as if it were the national anthem." He remembered of visiting the Vicksburg battlefield nearby, "I ventured into the imposing Union monuments and felt as if I were standing in enemy territory. In fiction and in fantasy, I rooted hopelessly for the South to win, and I cherished the *Look* magazine article about what would have happened if we had not lost."[73] Although Cohen could not claim Confederate ancestry as most of his classmates could, he still found heroes among the Confederate dead, and he identified a commonality between southern and Jewish people in that both had historically been considered underdogs.[74] Cohen's adoption of the South's heroic past as his own reveals the powerful training white southerners received at school.

Based on their textbooks and their memories, white schoolchildren appear to have learned little that would have caused them to question the prevailing racial order. What they did learn about the South's history and about race relations in the region likely reinforced what many of them had already learned at home: racial segregation was a natural and fixed state of affairs that was rooted in the region's past. Such lessons would have affected not only how white southerners viewed the African Americans in their midst but also how black children, who were being taught from the same texts, viewed themselves.

Andrew Young wrote of his education in New Orleans, "In the textbooks available to us, African-American history was hardly touched upon; when it was, we read in a few sentences of the long painful past that was slavery. The sustained, varied and heroic battles against slavery by black and white abolitionists and those of our ancestors who had escaped to freedom were absent." Instead, he remembered, "The story of the South included in our textbooks was more a collection of myths and legends than actual history. It was closer to *Gone With the Wind*. . . . The books described the War Between the States as a defeat rather than the victory that it was for my people. The achievements of blacks during Reconstruction, which were spectacular in Louisiana, were completely ignored in any book or class." Young believed the accomplishments of African Americans during this era were "sadly, generally unknown even among our teachers."[75] While Young may have doubted his own teachers' historical knowledge, many black teachers in the

South made a concerted effort to supplement the official curriculum with lessons on African American achievement.

When asked whether she had learned anything about black history in school, Marguirite DeLaine laughed, "Surely you jest."[76] On the rare occasions when her teachers did discuss African American history, they taught the lessons on their own rather than relying on the official textbooks. Georgia Sutton, a teacher from North Carolina, noted of black history that teachers had to "sneak that in" if they wanted their students to learn it.[77] Despite his skepticism about the extent of his teachers' knowledge, Young remembered an English teacher who introduced her students to African American literature: "Innovative teachers had to reach out on their own to find black literary material to weave into their classes in the same way black choral directors wove spirituals into their repertoires."[78] The initiative of individual teachers determined what lessons, if any, students learned about the African American past.

Like her white counterparts, Lillian Quick Smith of Wilmington, North Carolina, was issued state-adopted textbooks that included little information on the accomplishments of African Americans and presented an account of slavery that she felt ignored many of the nuances of the institution. She recalled that her teachers brought in supplementary materials to introduce their students to a more accurate depiction of slavery and to familiarize them with the activities of African Americans in various fields. When she became a teacher in the early 1950s, Smith found that it was still necessary to supplement the official curriculum with materials she gathered on her own from the local black library, among them those developed by Carter G. Woodson, founder of the Association for the Study of Negro Life and History. Smith taught her students about prominent African Americans such as Marian Anderson, Mary McLeod Bethune, Countee Cullen, and Frederick Douglass and led her students in singing James Weldon Johnson's "Lift Every Voice and Sing," also known as the "Negro National Anthem." When she became a school counselor, she designed bulletin boards on the success of African Americans in various professions, attempting to impress upon her students that they did have occupational choices.[79]

When Mary Mebane became a teacher, she, too, regarded the state-adopted history textbook as insulting to African Americans. One day she came across a box in the back of her classroom that contained a set of books on black history. When she approached her principal about using the books, she argued that her students did not "know anything about their own culture" and asked to be allowed to temporarily substitute a study of black history for the required course on North Carolina history. After reminding Mebane of her responsibility to adhere to the official course of study, her principal added, "I'm up here. I don't know what you're doing in your room."[80] Mebane took this as a cue that she was free to continue with her plan, and she spent an entire month teaching her students about black history, passing the contraband books out at the beginning of class each day and picking them up at the end.

Owing to the resourcefulness of teachers such as Smith and Mebane, African American students in the South were able to learn about black history despite the intentions of state and local boards of education. Through the efforts of their teachers, students learned about the athletic talents of Joe Louis, the educational philosophies of Booker T. Washington and W.E.B. Du Bois, and the literary talents of black poets and authors ranging from Langston Hughes to Richard Wright. Teachers brought in black newspapers such as the *Chicago Defender,* the *Norfolk Journal and Guide,* and the *Pittsburgh Courier* to show students pictures of prominent black figures. Students sang the Negro National Anthem with the same enthusiasm that white students sang "Dixie." African American dignitaries visited schools and provided students with living examples of black achievement.[81] Many of these activities were undertaken as part of Negro History Week celebrations.

Understanding that a lack of available materials for teaching African American history and literature was a significant challenge facing black teachers in the South, several organizations worked to overcome that obstacle by publishing materials that could be used to supplement the official curriculum. The most influential of these organizations was the Association for the Study of Negro Life and History (ASNLH). The association's founder, Carter G. Woodson, argued in his 1933 work, *The Mis-Education of the Negro,* that because black students were taught the same history, literature, economics, and philosophy as white students, "the Negro's mind has been brought under the control of his oppressor. The problem of holding the Negro down, therefore, is easily solved. When you control a man's thinking you do not have to worry about his actions."[82] Woodson noted the lack of positive attention to Africa and the skewed depictions of both slavery and Reconstruction in American history textbooks used by students ranging from elementary school to college. He asserted that black teachers were not effective at countering these lessons because they, too, had been miseducated. In a particularly harsh assessment of black teachers, he wrote, "Taught from books of the same bias, trained by Caucasians of the same prejudices or by Negroes of enslaved minds, one generation of Negro teachers after another have served for no higher purpose than to do what they are told to do."[83] Black parents came under fire as well for having "learned from their oppressors to say to their children that there were certain spheres into which they should not go because they would have no chance therein for development." Woodson concluded that the existing educational efforts did "not show the Negro how to overcome segregation" but instead taught "him how to accept it as final and just."[84]

In his study of black teachers in the segregated South, *A Class of Their Own*, Adam Fairclough noted of Woodson's work, "Like most polemics, *The Mis-Education of the Negro* was overheated."[85] Despite Woodson's harsh criticisms and his rhetorical excess, he did not see the situation facing black educators as hopeless. He believed the past harm done by the education system might be undone by an initiative that would not only teach black students and teachers a positive view of African and African American history but also incorporate such lessons into the general curriculum alongside those about the Greeks, Shakespeare, and Thomas Jefferson. Woodson thus launched a one-man effort to reeducate the population of the United States about black history. In addition to his own lengthy publication record, Woodson worked under the auspices of the ASNLH to promote research in and preserve documents relevant to black history; to encourage the formation of local black history clubs; to produce textbooks; to publish the *Journal of Negro History*, a scholarly forum, and the *Negro History Bulletin*, a periodical intended for use in primary and secondary education; and to promote Negro History Week.[86]

Starting in 1926, the association designated the second week of February, encompassing the birthdays of both Abraham Lincoln and Frederick Douglass, as Negro History Week.[87] The week was intended to serve multiple purposes: it introduced black history to students who did not normally study it; it drew attention to the subject in hopes that educators and administrators would recognize the need to add it to the official curriculum; and it celebrated in one week work the association hoped was ongoing throughout the year. The *Negro History Bulletin* repeatedly stressed that the study of black history was not to be confined to just one week. Instead, the designated week in February was a time to showcase how the study of African American history and culture had been pursued throughout the year.[88] For Woodson and his colleagues, every year was Negro History Year.

Fairclough argued, "For teachers who feared the personal consequences of activism or disliked introducing politics into the classroom, the Negro history movement provided a safe vehicle for conveying lessons about oppression, resistance, and black identity."[89] Recommended activities for Negro History Week included designing bulletin boards with clippings from black newspapers and magazines, creating artwork depicting African scenes, inviting former slaves to address students, and asking local libraries to display books on black history or to purchase such books if they did not have any in their collections.[90] Suggestions for Negro History Week and the pages of the *Negro History Bulletin* showcased an expanded cast of black characters, including Richard Allen, Anna Julia Cooper, Paul Robeson, Sojourner Truth, and Harriet Tubman, in addition to traditional textbook favorites such as Paul Laurence Dunbar, Booker T. Washington, and Phillis Wheatley. Among the "usual suspects" who graced the pages of the *Negro History Bulletin* was also Crispus Attucks, the black man who became the first casualty of the American Revolution when he was killed during the Boston Massacre and the presence of whose name, by the 1970s, had become the acid test for determining a particular textbook's stance on African Americans.[91] One rare issue of the *Bulletin* included a list of "Advocates of Social Justice," among them W.E.B. Du Bois, A. Philip Randolph, William Monroe Trotter, and Walter White.[92] This issue is notable because the publication generally shied away from highlighting such political figures.

Evidence of the reach of Negro History Week is substantial. The *Negro History Bulletin* printed enthusiastic reports from students and teachers around the country about their Negro History Week programs. The majority of these letters and reports came from schools in the North and Midwest, and most of them, North and South, came from African Americans. There are indications in the *Bulletin*, however, that some white schools celebrated Negro History Week.[93] Evidence of the Negro history movement can also be found in state education records. On at least two occasions during the 1930s and 1940s, committees of African American educators presented lists of books on "Negro Life and History" to members of the South Carolina State Board of Education, asking that they be approved by the state for use in black schools.[94] Perhaps these educators had been inspired by Negro History Week celebrations. Jeanes Fund supervisors, African American teachers who oversaw rural black schools across the South, issued reports on Negro History Week activities that had been carried out in their schools.[95] N. C. Newbold, a white administrator who oversaw education for African Americans in North Carolina during the 1930s, periodically circulated reminders about Negro History Week, along with materials sent to him by the association, encouraging teachers in black schools to observe the event.[96] Woodson's goal of providing materials for the study of black history was successful even to the point of being sanctioned by some white administrators.

Although contemporary observers such as Bruno Lasker and Swedish social scientist Gunnar Myrdal likened the material produced by the ASNLH to propaganda, Woodson and the organization he created played a vital role in the education of black students.[97] Without Woodson, black teachers' individual efforts to supplement the official curriculum with resources that celebrated the role of African Americans in the nation's past would have been much more difficult, and black students would have learned far fewer lessons about individual and racial pride. Daryl Michael Scott explained, "Through Negro History Week, teachers who taught in black schools could be armed with the truth about the black past and effectively counter the harmful myths that circulated in the larger society."[98] Myrdal, despite his criticism, thought the "propagandistic" component of the Negro history movement was justified, and he described the movement as "a counterpoison to the false and belittling treatment of the Negro in newspapers and books written by whites."[99] While the material produced by Woodson and the ASNLH was central to the work of instilling racial pride in African American students, one should note that the version of black history offered by the Negro history movement was primarily contributionist. That is, it focused more on populating the story of the nation's past with African American characters than on fundamentally rewriting the traditional narrative of American history to reflect the role played by African Americans. In that respect the Negro history movement fell short of undermining the official curriculum.

Although some black southerners remembered their teachers incorporating lessons about the importance of voting and seeking greater political rights, black teachers seem to have been more focused on the strategy of instilling self-respect and racial pride in their students.[100] Carolyn McKinstry remembered the feeling of group pride she had learned at school: "You know I guess I've always had that sense of pride because all of the teachers I had in elementary school were wonderful and all of my high school teachers were wonderful. So, where was this inferiority that I kept hearing about? That we couldn't make the grade."[101] Vernon Jordan wrote of his teachers, "For every attempt by the outside community to make me believe that I was inferior, there were multiple efforts by my teachers to make me feel like a star. . . . Working against huge odds, with few resources at their disposal, they taught us as best they could."[102] In the same spirit John Hope Franklin wrote of his high school principal, Ellis W. Woods, "Knowing better than we did the degree to which we suffered from inequalities that made a mockery of the doctrine of separate but equal . . . Principal Woods instilled enough self-confidence in us almost to compensate for them."[103] Many black educators chose to prioritize student achievement rather than emphasize ways to confront segregation and disfranchisement.

This strategy was not without its detractors. Marian Wright Edelman remembered her teachers having pursued the same approach, but her discussion of it had a very different tone. She observed, "While most of our teachers did not stand up for children in the White world where they felt disempowered and on which they depended, many of them tried to compensate by giving each Black child personal attention." While Edelman recognized the pressures under which black teachers worked, she was still frustrated that teachers in her community did not speak out forcefully against segregation. She wrote, "The racial tightrope my public school principal and teachers walked, trying hard not to rock the segregationists' boat or to jeopardize their jobs, was not lost on me or, I'm sure, on other Black children. They were content to timidly request incremental resources to help equalize educational offerings for Black children but unwilling to push hard or publicly for what was just."[104] Such sentiments aside, it should be noted that black teachers in the South made significant progress toward establishing the principle of equality in education, if not yet toward challenging segregation itself, through a campaign in the 1930s and 1940s to equalize the salaries of black and white teachers.[105]

Edelman was not alone in her criticism of black teachers. Andrew Young questioned his teachers' emphasis on cultivating individual and community pride through "respectability."[106] Young described the approach of two memorable teachers: "They seemed to believe the path to freedom was found in manners and diction as much as intelligence and morality." Young came to believe this strategy "was an illusion, that somehow if you really got yourself together nobody could enslave you." He remembered his high school teachers having stressed that "it was important to go along with the etiquette required by segregation" in the interests of both proper deportment and survival, and he recalled, "We were neither trained nor expected to protest against racial injustice, for that was not considered possible, or even desirable." Young ultimately found the "politics of respectability" as practiced by his teachers to be an inadequate means of challenging segregation, even to the point that this strategy promoted adherence to the system's rules, lest one appear to be stepping outside the bounds of propriety. While this approach in black schools may not have served to challenge the system, Young nonetheless remembered finding through such community institutions the "psychological support" to imagine a better future.[107]

Black teachers in the segregated South worked under incredible strain. They lacked the resources available to white teachers, yet they not only taught the official course of study but also obtained materials, frequently at their own expense, through which to teach their students lessons about black history and to correct the misinformation contained in their textbooks. Unlike many black preachers, teachers were dependent on white officials for their jobs, and if they spoke out, they risked losing their livelihood. Talk of school desegregation raised the question of what that prospect would mean for the jobs of African American teachers. Fairclough concluded, "If teachers shied away from discussing, let alone challenging, segregation, that is understandable. Jim Crow was the law of the land, and in

1940 it seemed immovable."[108] Instead of actively challenging segregation through either their own actions or what they taught their students, black teachers worked "to inoculate" their students from the effects of the system by building up their internal resources and the institutional strength of black communities.[109] They also worked to undo the harm that was subsequently done by that system.

Owing to the efforts of their teachers, black southerners learned lessons about racial pride and their own worth that would help to protect them from segregation's virulent impact on their lives. Instruction by these educators did not, however, have as its primary focus encouraging students to confront segregation. Carl Rowan described the mind-set of his principal in McMinnville, Tennessee, as he advised Rowan and his classmates to cede the town's sidewalks to white students: "With the wisdom of a man who has been burned, lecturing children against playing with fire, the principal explained that we could not win."[110] Already working within restrictions set by white authorities, black teachers and administrators knew the risks involved for both themselves and their students if they used the classroom as a venue to question segregation. For their part white students learned lessons at school that reinforced what most of them were already learning at home: segregation was the way things were supposed to be, and the system should be taken for granted and not discussed. The lessons learned about the region's past in southern classrooms did little to encourage students, black or white, to actively question segregation.

In addition to homes and schools, the region's churches were a crucial socializing agent. Like schools, churches were sites within black communities where adults built up the internal resources of young people, though here they had far more control over what was taught. Meanwhile, white southerners—who had largely been able to sidestep the implications of American democracy by leaving African Americans out of the school curriculum—had to reconcile segregation with the message of equality inherent in Christian teachings.

CHAPTER 4

"RED AND YELLOW, BLACK AND WHITE"

Racial Instruction in Southern Churches

Many children growing up in the segregated South would have sung "Jesus Loves the Little Children" at church. The sentiment captured in this simple song had potentially revolutionary consequences for black and white children. The lyrics read:

> Jesus loves the little children,
> All the children of the world;
> Red and yellow, black and white,
> They are precious in His sight;
> Jesus loves the little children of the world.[1]

The notion of the "brotherhood of man," based on a common condition as children of God, contained within it a powerful and seemingly obvious critique of segregation. Through this sentiment black children might learn that they had value equal to that of whites, while white children stood to gain an understanding of segregation as sinful based on the way it denied the value of other members of God's family. Lessons on the value of all people were central to the racial instruction black children received in their churches, and such lessons served to immunize them further from the messages about black inferiority that segregation sought to convey. Meanwhile, other lessons black children learned in their churches inadvertently served to reinforce the system. White children, who were learning the same lesson about the commonality of all people in their own churches, seldom realized the radical implications of that message and were often instilled with the notion that segregation was divinely ordained. Adherence to Christian faith could thus serve to solidify support for the system. Despite efforts by denominational leaders to bring the power of "red and yellow, black and white" to bear on race relations in the South, white prejudice based in part on beliefs about a divinely sanctioned social order could rarely be educated away.[2]

The contours of the southern religious landscape were complex. Divisions within the major Christian denominations both before and after the Civil War meant that a variety of churches competed for the souls and the loyalty of black and white southerners. National organizations of Baptists, Presbyterians, and Methodists split over sectional issues in the years before the Civil War. As a result of these splits, three new regional organizations formed: the Southern Baptist Convention (SBC), the Presbyterian Church in the United States (PCUS), and the Methodist Episcopal Church, South. While the Methodist Episcopal Church, South, reunited with the Methodist Episcopal Church in 1939 and the PCUS reunited with northern-based Presbyterians in 1983, the Southern Baptist Convention endures as an independent, national organization.[3] Contingents of the Episcopal Church also separated briefly during the Civil War but reunited soon after its conclusion.[4] The Catholic Church, for its part, did not experience an institutional split over issues surrounding the war and slavery.[5]

Before the Civil War slaves had often worshipped in white congregations on a segregated basis, though some established independent black churches or worshipped in more informal settings. After the war the newly freed slaves' desire for autonomy in worship and church governance prompted the major religious denominations to develop a variety of arrangements in response to their demands. Both the PCUS and the northern-based Presbyterian Church in the United States of America (PCUSA) organized black synods and presbyteries in the South, thus providing black Presbyterians with local control while retaining the influence of the larger denomination.[6] Black Episcopals likewise remained within the national organizational structure, though with considerable local autonomy.[7] Recognizing African Americans' desire for a greater measure of control over their own religious affairs, the Catholic Church increasingly segregated its parishes in the South, though some black Catholics continued to worship in white congregations on a segregated basis. Catholics also established segregated parochial schools for black children.[8] After experiencing a rapid decline in African American membership during and after the war, the Methodist Episcopal Church, South, seeking to retain some influence over its former members, encouraged the organization of the Colored Methodist Episcopal (CME) Church in 1870.[9] The Methodist Episcopal Church also established schools and churches for African Americans in the South after the war.[10]

In addition to the CME Church, which retained some ties with white Methodists, African Americans established other more or less independent denominations in the South. In 1895 black Baptists formed the National Baptist Convention (NBC), which, though autonomous, participated in some joint endeavors with the white SBC, including efforts to found a seminary to train black ministers.[11] The

NBC itself split into two separate denominations in 1915, after a dispute involving the denominational publishing house.[12] Meanwhile, two older, northern-based independent African American denominations, the African Methodist Episcopal (AME) Church and the African Methodist Episcopal Zion (AMEZ) Church, experienced incredible growth in membership among black southerners in the years following the Civil War.[13]

When considering racial instruction in black churches, attention must be paid to the range of experiences remembered by black southerners. Religion scholars C. Eric Lincoln and Lawrence H. Mamiya concluded that the history of the "black church" in the United States can be characterized as having involved six "dialectics," or sets of tensions, two of which—"other-worldly versus this-worldly" and "resistance versus accommodation"—provide particularly useful ways of thinking about how black churches responded to segregation.[14] An orientation that was "other-worldly" was "concerned only with heaven and eternal life or the world beyond, a pie-in-the-sky attitude that neglect[ed] political and social concerns."[15] By contrast, churches and ministers who were "this-worldly" placed significant emphasis on adapting the teachings of Jesus to the everyday social, economic, and political concerns of their parishioners. As for the tension between resistance and accommodation, Lincoln and Mamiya asserted, "Every black person and every black institution has participated in making compromises between these two poles."[16] Thinking about how black churches responded to segregation as an enterprise that mixed other-worldly with this-worldly thinking and operated on a continuum between resistance and accommodation helps to account for the variety in black southerners' experiences.

Benjamin Mays remembered the sermons preached by his Baptist pastor when he was growing up in South Carolina in the early 1900s as having been other-worldly, describing this type of preaching as an "opiate" for church members. Mays explained that his fellow worshippers, "beaten down at every turn by the white man, as they were," "believed the trials and tribulations of the world would all be over when one got to heaven." He recalled that his preacher never once spoke out against lynching and that on one occasion the preacher interrupted a visiting speaker when he began criticizing whites.[17] John Lewis also remembered the other-worldly approach of his Baptist preacher when he was growing up in rural Alabama in the 1950s: "It always bothered me that he knew, as we all did, how sharecroppers were cheated by our landlords right and left, underpaid and overcharged every year, but not once did he ever speak about this in his sermons." Instead, he preached about "how the soul must be saved by and by for that pie in the sky after you die" and said "hardly a word about *this* life, about *this* world, about some sense of salvation and righteousness right *here,* between the cradle and the grave."[18] Anne Moody observed a similar approach to religion in rural Mississippi in the early 1960s. She wrote of watching older African American congregants sing freedom songs, "They sang them as though they were singing away the chains of slavery. Sometimes I just looked at the expressions on their faces as they sang and cold chills would run down my back." She explained, "Whenever God was mentioned in a song, I could tell by the way they said the word that most of them had given up here on earth. They seemed to be waiting just for God to call them home and end all the suffering."[19] Although these worshippers sang the songs of the civil rights movement, they viewed their faith as a means of being delivered from rather than a means of solving the problems they faced.

Focusing on a heavenly escape from the difficulties of southern life could serve to promote an acceptance of segregation by emphasizing how African Americans would overcome their problems in the afterlife rather than seeking ways of tackling their concrete concerns in this life; such a focus, however, could contain empowering messages as well. Maya Angelou remembered a revival she attended when she was growing up in Arkansas in the 1930s at which the preacher extolled the virtues of charity and the reward to come for those who practiced it but warned of the punishment awaiting those who did not. The congregation, she recalled, "lowed with satisfaction. Even if they were society's pariahs, they were going to be angels in a marble white heaven and sit on the right hand of Jesus, the Son of God. The Lord loved the poor and hated those cast high in the world. Hadn't He Himself said it would be easier for a camel to go through the eye of a needle than for a rich man to enter heaven?" They could rest assured "that they were going to be the only inhabitants of that land of milk and honey, except of course a few whitefolks like John Brown who history books said was crazy anyway. All the Negroes had to do generally, and those at the revival especially, was bear up under this life of toil and cares, because a blessed home awaited them in the far-off bye and bye."[20] Even if they could not end segregation in this life, they could at least take comfort in the idea that once they got to heaven, they might be the only ones there.

John Lewis depicted his other-worldly church as a place where people found community and, ultimately, solace in the midst of the harsh realities of their everyday lives. "For people whose lives were circumscribed by the rhythms and routines of hard, hard work, with relatively little time or opportunity for contact with others beyond their immediate neighbors," he explained, "church was literally a time of congregation, a social event much like going into town." As a child, Lewis saw church as "an exciting place" that was "colorful" and "almost festive." He remembered his Sunday school teachers "drilling" their pupils as they "recited and memorized" Bible verses. Lewis also remembered the release provided by the singing in his church: "These people sang with no self-consciousness and no restraint. Young and old alike, all of whom lived the same hard life, toiling in the fields, struggling with poverty and doing their best to make the best of it, found joy and meaning in the midst of hardship and pain."[21] Although an other-worldly focus encouraged black southerners to transcend the effects of segregation rather than actively oppose the system, it also served, in Benjamin Mays's words, "to enable them to endure and survive the oppressive conditions" under which they lived in the segregated South. While Mays characterized the other-worldly focus as an "opiate," he added, "I am not necessarily condemning the use of religion as an opiate. Sometimes an opiate is good in medicine. Sometimes it may be good in religion. Certainly religious faith has helped me in my struggles." He speculated that African Americans in the segregated South "could perhaps not have survived without this kind of religion."[22]

Because black churches were for the most part not under direct white supervision or control, they actually served as ideal sites for addressing this-worldly concerns. In his memoir, *The Last Radio Baby*, Raymond Andrews remembered his church in rural Georgia as "our *only* possession entirely independent of the white world": "At no other place within, or outside, the community could the entire colored family meet like at church; it was the only place we could rightfully call our own where for a few hours each week we conducted our life in our own way."[23] Alabama native Ira Lee Jones remembered church as the center of her community, a place where people socialized, where they derived inspiration, and where they met to express grievances.[24] Others remembered their churches having been used as meeting places for groups such as union members.[25] Boasting open meeting space free from white control, churches were ideal locations for holding such gatherings even if the church itself was not actively involved. Drawing on the memories of black southerners, one derives the overall impression that the extent to which black churches emphasized this-worldly concerns during the era of segregation depended on the individual institution and the particular personalities involved. Some preachers seem to have opposed segregation and lynching quite openly, while others shied away from discussing such risky topics. Some congregations made regular donations to the NAACP and encouraged the use of their buildings as sites for discussing political activities, while others were more reticent to do so. In addition, the newspapers of a number of African American denominations were fairly outspoken in their opposition to lynching and other aspects of the racial status quo, which likely impacted the political outlook of their local congregations.[26]

Regardless of their stance on political engagement, black churches worked to counter segregation's impact by building up the internal resources of young people through teaching lessons about individual and racial pride and about the value of all people. In this way churches served a function similar to that of black schools, but they did so in an environment in which black adults had far more control over what was taught. Black churches did not have to sneak in lessons about racial pride but instead could make them a regular part of their message. Coretta Scott King observed that even though the preachers at her AMEZ church in Alabama rarely addressed political and economic concerns, "they laid a strong psychological and social foundation for coming generations."[27] Bertha Todd likewise remembered that when she was growing up in North Carolina, her Baptist church seldom involved itself with social issues, but by "implementing and solidifying the values, the church played [its] role."[28] One of the church's key roles was encouraging children. Occasions such as Christmas, Easter, and special Children's Days were opportunities for young people to stage plays and recite Scripture for their congregations and receive lavish praise in return.[29] Mays remembered his church's response when he recited part of the Sermon on the Mount from memory: "The house went wild: old women waved their handkerchiefs, old men stamped their feet, and the people generally applauded long and loud. It was a terrific ovation, let alone a tremendous experience, for a nine-year-old boy." Mays explained that while members of his congregation did not contribute financially to his education, they gave him "something far more valuable. They gave me encouragement, the thing I most needed."[30] Like homes and schools, black churches could serve as a buffer against the harshness of segregated life.

In addition to lessons about individual self-worth, churches taught lessons about racial and denominational pride. In a 1921 address before the annual meeting of the National Baptist Convention, USA, Inc., Reverend P. James Bryant advised African American parents to "inoculate yourself and your children with race respect and race pride. For our race according to records of sacred and profane history has kept step to the music of civilization. . . . We rocked the cradle of science, art and letters. We builded [sic] the Pyramids, etc."[31] In a 1926 report the convention's Sunday School Publishing Board stated its commitment to promoting racial pride: "We offer no apology for bringing to light, and emphasizing the part that Negroes have played in Bible history, and the influence that such noble characters had on civilization and community life during Bible times. Others will not bring out these truths and it is left for us to do so."[32] To foster denominational pride, AME churches honored the February birthday of their founder by celebrating "Richard Allen Youth Week," which allowed young people not only to showcase their own abilities and receive encouragement in return but also to learn lessons about church history.[33] Meanwhile, the *AME Zion Hymnal* featured a song praising that denomination's founders, and its newspaper, the *Star of Zion*, encouraged young people to celebrate the February birthday of Joseph C. Price, founder of the denomination's Livingstone College, in conjunction with Negro History Week.[34] Young people were also encouraged to honor the accomplishments of other notable African Americans during Negro History Week, including Crispus Attucks, Benjamin Banneker, Booker T. Washington, and Phillis Wheatley.[35] Such lessons imbued black youth with a sense of pride in both themselves and their communities.

Other lessons about racial pride were more subtle. The January 1941 "Family Altar" section of the *Star of Zion* featured a story about a boy named Roddy, who, along with his sister, had pledged to donate a dollar to their church to support the "Indian Sunday school out West." After finding a dime on the street, Roddy passed the corner drugstore, where he saw a container of black gumdrops in the window. Roddy was elated: "Black gumdrops!" The author explained, "Whenever anyone passed a dish of gumdrops Roddy always chose a black one." After spending his precious dime on a whole pound of black gumdrops, Roddy felt guilty for not doing his part to raise the donation, and he worked to earn another dime to support his church's missionary efforts.[36] A March 1941 story in the *Star of Zion*'s "Youth's Corner" section chronicled the adventures of another little boy, Bobby, and his neighbor's cat, Shadow, who was "big and black." Each day before he left for school, Bobby would accompany Shadow to and from the fish store. Concerned that Shadow had not appeared for several days, Bobby went to her house and discovered the reason for her absence: she had given birth to kittens, three black ones and three black and white ones. When Shadow's owner offered Bobby one of the kittens to thank him for his kindness toward Shadow, Bobby asked for "the very blackest kitten that looks like Shadow."[37] Taken separately, one might surmise that Roddy just liked licorice or that Bobby wanted the kitten who looked the most like his friend Shadow. Taken together, these stories read as a concerted effort to encourage African American children to develop positive associations with the color black, likely as a means of countering the positive associations with whiteness that were prominent in southern society.

Black churches also taught biblical lessons about the value of all people. In his address to the National Baptist Convention, Reverend Bryant had argued that the racial problems in the nation would not be solved "until all men regardless of race, color or nation will acknowledge in theory and practice the Fatherhood of God, the brotherhood of man, the equality of the human race, and the Golden Rule as the universal law of life and conduct."[38] Denominations passed these lessons on to young people through Scripture. The most significant biblical passage that expressed the notion of equality before God was Galatians 3:28: "There is neither Jew nor Greek, there is neither bond nor free, there is neither male nor female: for ye are all one in Christ Jesus."[39] Also powerful but more open to interpretation was Acts 17:26, which stated that God "hath made of one blood all nations of men for to dwell on all the face of the earth, and hath determined the times before appointed, and the bounds of their habitation." While those who promoted the message of commonality found support for that position in the first half of the verse, those who believed God himself had segregated the races on different continents and in different nations found validation for their position in the second half. For his part Jesus offered unequivocal instructions on interpersonal relations: "Thou shalt love thy neighbour as thyself" and "As ye would that men should do to you, do ye also to them likewise."[40] That is, Christians should practice the "golden rule."

In addition to these messages of commonality, personhood, and love, the New Testament featured a number of stories and parables in which Jesus reached out to those the world valued least or chided those who placed their own wealth above the well-being of others. In perhaps his most radical encounter of this type, Jesus approached a Samaritan woman at a well and asked her to draw water for him. The woman was of a despised ethnicity and a devalued gender; she had been married five times; and she was at that time living with a man to whom she was not married. Despite these aspects of her biography, Jesus did not hesitate to associate with her, to engage in theological debate with her, and to reveal to her his true identity.[41] In the parable of the Good Samaritan, Jesus praised the merciful behavior of the Samaritan, who proved himself a true neighbor by stopping to help a man who had been robbed and beaten; meanwhile, religious leaders had passed by on the other side of the road.[42] Jesus thus encouraged his disciples to value character over their own prejudices and to include all of humanity in their concept of neighbor. Elsewhere, Jesus warned of a coming division between those who would be rewarded for having shown compassion to "the least of these" in the eyes of the world and those who would be punished for not tending to the downtrodden.[43]

Throughout the New Testament, Scripture rebuked those who placed an inordinate value on their own wealth. In one parable God chided a rich man whose barns were so overflowing with his wealth in crops that he planned to tear them down and build bigger ones. Instead of the future of wealth and ease the man had envisioned once his task was complete, God demanded his life that very night. The parable cautioned that such would be the fate for him "that layeth up treasure for himself, and is not rich toward God."[44] In the parable of the rich man and

Lazarus, a poor man to whom the rich man had not shown compassion during his lifetime, both men died and met divergent fates. Angels carried Lazarus to Abraham's side in heaven, while Abraham explained to the rich man as he suffered in hell, "Son, remember that thou in thy lifetime receivedst thy good things, and likewise Lazarus evil things: but now he is comforted, and thou art tormented."[45] As in Angelou's account of the revivalist who assured his listeners that they would be the primary inhabitants of heaven, these passages and parables served as raw materials that preachers and Sunday school teachers could craft into lessons about the value God placed on those who were devalued by the world. The passages also included a subversive message, a promise that the bottom rail would be on top, that "whatsoever a man soweth, that shall he also reap."[46] It would have been left to congregational and denominational leaders to adapt these messages of equality and justice to the concerns of local congregations.

Notions of commonality and "brotherhood" also found expression in hymns and Bible lessons in denominational publications. The hymn that best captured the notion of equality for all was "In Christ There Is No East or West," which was featured in the hymnals of many black and some white denominations.[47] The song begins:

> In Christ there is no East or West,
> In Him no South or North;
> But one great fellowship of love
> Throughout the whole wide earth.

The third stanza makes the message of commonality more explicit:

> Join hands, then, brothers of the faith,
> Whate'er your race may be.
> Who serves my Father as a son
> Is surely kin to me.[48]

The inclusive message of these lyrics was folded into Bible lessons as well, which often featured a mixture of songs, Scripture, and prayer. A daily devotional from the National Baptist Convention's *Star of Hope* incorporated the song into a lesson on "Christianity and the Races." The lesson expanded on the song's message, explaining that "since God saw fit to make all men blood brothers, all the barriers that separate them are artificial." The devotional stressed the need to pursue evangelism despite the divisions of class and race evident in society and counseled, "To lose sight of our resentments and injustices and prejudices and to start real honest-to-goodness sharing with our brothers is Christ's demand for his disciples." The concluding prayer asked, "May we ever keep in mind that thou hast made of one blood all nations. May we see each other human being as a brother. Lift before us thy love. Open our hearts toward all mankind."[49] Such lessons disseminated scriptural mandates about the fatherhood of God, "the brotherhood of man," the equality of all, and the golden rule to African American congregations.

At times the message of commonality was cast in the language of "red and yellow, black and white," as in a lesson on the missionary implications of the New Testament story of Peter and Cornelius that appeared in the *Southwestern Christian Advocate*, a Methodist Episcopal Church publication with a primarily black readership. Falling into a trance while praying on the roof of a house, Peter was convicted of his own prejudice toward Gentiles, and he subsequently welcomed Cornelius, a Gentile, along with his family and friends, into the Christian faith. Through this experience Peter learned that "God is no respecter of persons."[50] The author of the lesson, Reverend D. D. Martin, explained, "God does not, and, in his very nature cannot, think less or more of any one of his children. Race or color can make no difference with the principle of life and relationship." Making an explicit link with missions, he wrote, "Whether it be the yellow or brown of Asia, the white or brown of Europe, the black of Australia or Africa, the red, white, brown, or black, of America, we must not be respector [sic] of persons."[51] Although this lesson invoked the language of "red and yellow, black and white" and one occasionally finds this language used by African Americans, it appears less often in the memories and writings of black southerners than of white ones.[52] Even though the language was less common among African Americans, the concept of equality it encapsulated was central to the lessons black children learned at church.

Many Sunday school lessons reveal only limited information about what was taught regarding racial pride and segregation in southern churches. Such literature, though usually distributed through denominational publishing houses, often drew on uniform lessons used in Sunday schools throughout the country.[53] To complicate matters further, the literature used by black children was not always produced by African American denominations. Some black publishing concerns—the National Baptist Publishing Board, for example, under the leadership of Richard H. Boyd—occasionally obtained literature from white publishers.[54] Northern-based Methodists and Presbyterians appear to have distributed the same literature used in white congregations to their African American congregations in the South.[55] In addition, white congregations from various denominations conducted Sunday school and Vacation Bible School for black children as part of their Home Missions efforts, and in the process they donated used or leftover literature produced by white denominations to black churches.[56] Sunday school and Vacation Bible School literature in general focused more on Bible stories and memory verses than on social concerns, and when such literature did address social issues, it usually did so in the most innocuous way possible.

Although many lessons addressed standard biblical themes, an enterprising black Sunday school teacher could have easily applied these messages to her pupils' daily lives, possibly in a manner very similar to the way in which that same teacher might have taken the initiative to supplement the public school curriculum with lessons about individual self-worth and racial pride. A 1940 Sunday school lesson on the prophet Amos from the uniform series being used in many churches during this period demonstrates the potential applicability of biblical teachings. Entitled "My Responsibility for Social Justice," the lesson detailed how God had sent Amos to rebuke Israel for the "sins of oppression and injustice." The lesson stated, "One who is right with his God will have right dealings with his fellow man. If one loves God, he will love his fellow man. If he loves him he cannot oppress him; he cannot deal with him unjustly. A Christian character is inconsistent with unrighteousness, oppression, and unfair dealings with others."[57] Drawing on the words of Amos, another version of the same lesson from the same week promised hope for Israel: "If she will establish judgment so that it run down as the cleansing waters, and righteousness as a mighty stream, then the Lord may be gracious. In other words, if Israel will repent and seek God, then God will forgive and bless Israel."[58] Likewise, individuals and nations in the present day had the opportunity to repent of their past injustice toward others, and they, too, would be forgiven. Such lessons on injustice would have likely resonated with black Sunday school teachers and their pupils, yet no mention of racial prejudice was ever made in the text, possibly owing to the potentially incendiary nature of the subject in the eyes of whites, many of whom were using the same uniform lessons. An adult version of the lesson on Amos mentioned specific examples of contemporary "social wrongs," such as greed, lawlessness, and war, but made no mention of segregation or racial discrimination.[59] This lesson went only so far in its enumeration of the social wrongs to be righted. The individual teacher would have been left to translate the lesson into one relevant to the South's particular social situation.

Although Sunday school lessons often did not address issues of race, black denominations found other ways to imbue young people with racial pride. Richard H. Boyd of the National Baptist Publishing Board, despite having received assistance at times from the secretary of the white SBC's Sunday School Board, argued that the literature produced by white denominations was unsuitable for black children. He believed white denominational literature reinforced racial stereotypes by depicting angels and other biblical characters as white.[60] The rival National Baptist denomination's Sunday School Publishing Board agreed with Boyd on the need to provide "inspiration to Negro youth by emphasizing the practical thoughts in the lessons by using Negro pictures and illustrations."[61] The *Star of Zion* reprinted an editorial that encouraged African Americans to reject positive associations with whiteness, stating in part, "The pictures in our Bibles and religious literature are all white. . . . We cannot conceive the idea that angels are of any color. Some songs we sing, with such phrases as 'Now wash me, and I shall be whiter than snow,' show that the writer has taken white as an emblem of purity." The author speculated on the impact of these images: "When the Negro accepts such teaching he enslaves himself into the belief that all goodness comes from some white source."[62] Denominations responded to such concerns by incorporating positive images of blackness. In addition to their work in promoting these images, denominational publishing houses themselves served as concrete evidence of black entrepreneurial success, and church members were constantly exhorted to buy and use their church's literature as an expression of racial pride.[63]

African American denominations developed a variety of methods for promoting black pride through visual representation. The *AME Church Review* often featured a photograph of a black "Madonna and Child" on the cover of its fourth-quarter issue in honor of Christmas.[64] This practice was in stark contrast to many white denominational publications, which featured depictions of Jesus and Mary with fair skin and often with blond hair and light eyes.[65] The *Star of Zion* encouraged mothers to enroll their infants in the Cradle Roll Department, for which they would receive a certificate along with a Cradle Roll chart featuring pictures of "colored babies and Mother Zion Church."[66] The paper frequently ran advertisements for black baby dolls, and it printed a letter to Santa from a ten-year-old girl in North Carolina, asking that he please bring her and her sister brown-skinned dolls for Christmas.[67] In addition to the National Baptist Publishing Board, Richard H. Boyd oversaw the National Negro Doll Company, which historian Paul Harvey has credited with having "pioneered" the marketing of black dolls.[68] For its part the Woman's Convention, Auxiliary to the National Baptist Convention, USA, Inc., supported the creation of "Negro Doll Clubs" to promote racial pride among young girls.[69] Yet not all of the depictions offered by African American denominations conveyed a positive message of racial pride. Like white religious literature, black denominational publications made reference to the need to send missionaries to Africa "to save the heathen."[70] Such statements reinforced stereotypes about the "dark continent." The *Star of Zion*, the *Southwestern Christian*

Advocate, and the *Christian Index,* the newspaper of the CME Church, all featured ads for hair-straightening products, and both the *Star of Zion* and the *AME Church Review* published ads for choir robes that featured whites.[71] Ads such as these served to normalize whiteness, which was the very project these publications sought to undermine by featuring visual representations of African Americans.

Judging by some black southerners' memories, African American denominations had their work cut out for them when it came to undermining the image of a white Jesus. Dolores Aaron remembered her Methodist church in New Orleans having borrowed a baby from a white family to play Jesus in the Christmas play. Aaron explained, "We couldn't imagine that baby being black, I guess."[72] Indeed, significant confusion seems to have existed among black children about Jesus's skin color, and adults were reticent to answer their children's questions about this issue. Cecil Brown recalled his aunt having been awarded a picture of Jesus as a token of appreciation from their church for successful fund-raising. The Jesus in the picture "had golden blond hair and serene blue eyes. He was beautiful! But he looked white. Why was he white?" Sitting in church with his uncle, Brown asked him, "Is the Lord a white man?" His uncle responded by telling him, "Shut up!"[73] Future civil rights leader Daisy Bates—having experienced a series of revelations as a child that prompted her to avoid contact with whites—lashed out when her mother tried to encourage her to play an angel in the Christmas play. Bates exclaimed, "I don't want no part of that play about a dead white doll!" When her mother told her that she would not "have that kind of talk" and to "stop that kind of talk this minute!" Bates angrily explained, "All the pictures I ever saw of Jesus were white. . . . If Jesus is like the white people, I don't want any part of Him!"[74] Bates recalled that she spent the night of the Christmas play home alone with her dog and her black doll. Such children were in need of images of Jesus with which they could identify, and black denominations sought to fill that need through their publications.[75]

Efforts by black churches to undermine segregation extended beyond attempts to inculcate racial pride and disseminate positive images of African Americans. Reformers who promoted gradual improvement in race relations in the years before the civil rights movement often focused on education as a means of achieving progress. For some of them education in this context meant pursuing a concerted effort to teach white southerners the "facts" about race and segregation in hopes that their prejudice against black southerners might gradually be educated away. Others conceptualized education as a project that involved elevating African Americans to the point where whites would recognize their progress and grant them equal access to southern society as a right they had *earned.* If African Americans could demonstrate that they were well educated, nicely groomed, and neatly dressed, this line of thinking ran, surely whites would see that their prejudices were unfounded. Then, in response to the social and economic strides made by black southerners, whites would begin to dismantle segregation, the institution having served its purpose as a temporary expedient following the demise of slavery. Many black churches in the South pursued the strategy of attempting to ameliorate race relations by improving their own young people.

Nannie Burroughs, founder and corresponding secretary of the Woman's Convention, Auxiliary to the National Baptist Convention, USA, Inc., embodied this strategy.[76] In annual reports to the Woman's Convention she articulated its goals, which included improving black homes and, through them, black children. In her 1922 report she wrote, "The solution of the Negro problem depends absolutely on the type of homes we make. . . . Negro children must be drilled, rooted and grounded in the ideals of self-respect, self-appreciation, industry, politeness, and self-control. What the race needs is moral and spiritual strength within to meet the organized and evil influences from without."[77] Burroughs viewed the home as a place to instill racial pride and build up internal resources, but she also viewed it as a site to train children how to behave in the larger society in order to challenge racial stereotypes. In 1928 she explained, "The principle of segregation is un-Christian and we must fight it, but if we are going to remove the excuse for segregation, we must remember that the second step in the new home mission program is to bring people up to a high level of living in their homes and in their communities."[78] In order to accomplish this goal, Burroughs preached "The gospel of The Bible, The Bath Tub, and The Broom."[79] She explained this approach in her 1923 report, in this case in regard to combating segregated conditions in the North: "Negro children must be properly fed and sent to school clean and combed. They must devote their time to study and not in attendance at cheap movies and on the streets. The only way to beat segregation is by living up to the standards and ideals of the community." In her view "books studied, bath tubs, combs, brushes, brooms, and yard implements used religiously will do more to keep down or to break down segregation than all the protests and laws that can be made. This phase of the problem is ours to solve."[80] Burroughs thus sought to undermine segregation by training young people.

Others worked to accomplish this goal by providing gender-specific instruction to black youth. In 1919 Reverend J. Harvey Anderson, editor of the *Star of Zion*, argued, "The basic principle of womanhood is virtue and upon the status of its womanhood depends the strength and progress of the race, which cannot rise above the character of its women." In order to ensure such progress, Anderson proposed that mothers form organizations within AMEZ churches to instruct girls "in morals, hygiene, social conduct, self-care, and the rudiments which make for ladyship."[81] In a 1920 editorial entitled "Saving the Boys," Anderson's successor and later AMEZ bishop, W. J. Walls, stressed the need for fathers to keep their sons off the streets and at home—and presumably in church—in order to ensure that they came under positive influences.[82] Those who sought to use racial uplift as a strategy for undermining segregation targeted young people as the most promising candidates for their program, but they also recognized that young people were the demographic most at risk for compromising their efforts. For this reason parents and church leaders alike devoted particular attention to ensuring that children upheld rigorous standards of conduct.

In her influential study of black Baptist women, *Righteous Discontent*, Evelyn Brooks Higginbotham characterized this focus on scrupulous standards of public conduct as the "politics of respectability," writing of these women, "They felt certain that 'respectable' behavior in public would earn their people a measure of esteem from white America, and hence they strove to win the black lower class's psychological allegiance to temperance, industriousness, thrift, refined manners, and Victorian sexual morals." That is, in addition to their work among young people, black churchwomen's missionary efforts had a class component. Through their own impeccable dress and comportment, "their sense of moral superiority over whites," and the values they sought to instill in young people and in working-class African Americans, middle-class black churchwomen sought "to refute the logic behind their social subordination." Higginbotham ultimately argued that the effort by these women to promote an ethos of respectability "reflected and reinforced the hegemonic values of white America, as it simultaneously subverted and transformed the logic of race and gender subordination." The strategy was in her view "a powerful weapon of resistance."[83]

While the strategy can be understood as a form of resistance, it can also be read as an engagement with the logic of segregation on the white South's terms. The strategy endorsed the norms and expectations of the dominant society as the standard to which young people should aspire, yet the power to judge the point at which those standards had been met remained in the hands of whites. Andrew Young remembered being raised in an environment in which his parents and teachers subscribed to the ethos of respectability, and he was critical of this approach. Of the messages he received from his teachers, he wrote, "I sensed no expectation that we would challenge or resist segregation; rather, there was a naive hope that by proving ourselves as good as whites, we would somehow demonstrate that segregation was unnecessary." He saw the promise of respectability go unfulfilled in the lives of his own parents and grandparents, observing, "Their lives were exemplary in every respect. They were educated, responsible, hardworking, taxpaying, church-going Americans. But no matter how hard they worked, or how much they achieved, segregation made no exception for them."[84]

The argument that African Americans had proven themselves worthy of equal rights also invited an effective counterargument. White southerners could simply say that African Americans had not yet advanced to the level where they were ready to exercise those rights. An opponent of the *Brown* decision wrote to Alabama governor Gordon Persons in June 1954 with his assessment of white southern opinion on the decision: "We have lived with colored people all our lives. We respect their many good qualities and we would like to see them continue to improve. But we know from having tried personally to help them that they must help some themselves and *they must have time to grow up as a race.*"[85] Another white Alabamian wrote to Persons in December 1953 after the governor had solicited opinions about what to do if school segregation was struck down. The man wrote, "I have always believed the entire concept of segregation, in our schools and everywhere else, to be unconstitutional. But like so many other injustices, I have realized its necessity. . . . It is an injustice which is necessary if we are ever to raise the standards of intelligence among our Negroes without lowering the moral standards of our own children." He thought better educational opportunities would eventually be made available "for our Negroes" in order to "bring them to a higher plane in our society, collectively and individually, when they earn a right to it."[86] If rights were to be extended only when white southerners conceded that the moral and educational levels of African Americans had reached their own, those rights were likely to be delayed indefinitely.

Ultimately some lessons taught in black churches in the South served to promote an acceptance of segregation, while others served to challenge it. Preachers who promised an escape from the indignities of segregation in the hereafter implicitly acknowledged that little could be done to change conditions in the present. Conversely, young people who read articles in their denominational newspaper criticizing lynching and segregation might be inspired to develop their own critiques of the system. The uniform Sunday school lessons taught in many churches offered little perspective on race relations in the region and depended on the initiative of African American teachers to make them relevant to everyday social concerns. Denominational publishing houses sought to introduce more lessons about racial pride into their literature, but children continued to be surrounded by images that conceptualized Jesus, along with heaven and its host, as white. Black churches sought to impress upon young people the notion that they had value in

God's eyes equal to that of whites; indeed, when they got to heaven, they might find that Jesus was the only "white" person there. Yet many parents and church leaders also placed an emphasis on improving the morals, grammar, grooming habits, and fashion sense of young people as a means of demonstrating to whites that they *deserved* equal rights. In fact, those rights were theirs already by law and by virtue of their birthright as children of God. By encouraging young people to focus on proving to whites that continued segregation was unnecessary in light of the progress African Americans were making, rather than working to expose the faulty assumption of white superiority on which the system was based, some church leaders served to legitimize the very system they sought to undermine.

Although lessons taught at church about the value of all people appear in the memories of both black and white southerners, whites were far more likely to hear that sentiment expressed in the language of "red and yellow, black and white." Growing up in Birmingham, Paul Hemphill remembered church as "a sanctioned diversion, sort of neat," a place where "the ladies who ran the Sunday school classes and Vacation Bible school seemed full of goodness, incapable of ill will," as they taught their students Bible verses and led them in singing "'Red and yellow, black and white' . . . trying to ensure that [they] remained good little boys and girls."[87] He recalled, however, that in 1962 the pastor of his Methodist church, John Rutland—who had been criticized for his liberal views on race since he arrived at the church in the early 1950s—was fired after giving the church's annual "needy family" Christmas offering to a black family.[88] Hemphill recalled of his own response to the firing, "*Red and yellow, black and white / They are precious in his sight.* . . . I never set foot in a church again." Hemphill's understanding of the discrepancy between stated belief and action in his church prompted him to reject the church altogether on the basis of that hypocrisy. When he interviewed Rutland years later, Hemphill gained some insight into the source of his racial views. Rutland remembered his mother having been "an extreme fundamentalist who believed that God had personally dotted every *i* and crossed every *t* in the Bible. . . . If it said they are 'precious in His sight,' it meant *all* of 'em."[89] Although the lyrics themselves did not come from the Bible, the sentiment behind them did, and Rutland's memory of his mother's take on the Scriptures highlights the incongruity inherent in how white Christians in the South—known for being a people of the Book—were able to disregard the letter of the law when it came to matters of race.

The seemingly obvious critique of segregation contained in the message of "red and yellow, black and white" had the potential to prompt churchgoing white southerners to question their adherence to segregation on the basis of their religious beliefs. Had Jesus not said, "Suffer little children to come unto me"?[90]

Had Paul not written, "There is neither Jew nor Greek . . . for ye are all one in Christ Jesus"? The response of Hemphill and Rutland to such sentiments does not appear, however, to have been representative of white southern experience. White southerners were perfectly capable of maintaining a sincere belief in the commonality of all people while worshiping in an all-white body of Christians. By supporting missions to Africa and Asia as well as "Negro work" among black churches at home, white Christians put their belief in God's love for all people into action, but this belief only rarely translated into a critique of segregation.[91] Melton McLaurin remembered of his youth, "As a young child I could sit in church with the other white children of the village and sing, 'Jesus loves the little children . . . Red and yellow, black and white' and never wonder why no black children were in our group." He recalled that it never occurred to him that black children should have been in church with him and speculated, "It also probably never occurred to the adult church members, including the minister."[92]

In his classic study of American race relations, *An American Dilemma,* Gunnar Myrdal argued that a "moral dilemma" characterized the "Negro problem" in the United States. The crux of Myrdal's argument was that the "American Creed" of democracy, justice, and the value of all people, which was based not only on the nation's founding documents but also on many Americans' adherence to Christian principles, conflicted with the treatment afforded African Americans. According to Myrdal, the disparity between white Americans' beliefs and their actions would eventually bring about a resolution of the dilemma.[93] A number of historians have argued that white Christians in the South actually did not recognize a disconnect between their beliefs and their actions. In his study of the eight white clergymen who were the ostensible recipients of Martin Luther King Jr.'s "Letter from Birmingham Jail," Jonathan Bass asserted, "Throughout the first half of the twentieth century, southern white ministers saw Jim Crow as neither an urgent moral dilemma nor an immense social affliction."[94] R. Bentley Anderson found that for Catholics in New Orleans in the years surrounding the *Brown* decision, "segregation, if it was a problem at all, was a social, political, and/or legal problem but not necessarily a moral one."[95] Paul Harvey concluded that, for Southern Baptists, "there was no American dilemma but merely a 'Negro problem' that could be managed successfully by judicious whites."[96]

One reason many white southerners did not view segregation as a moral issue is that they had learned to view the system as divinely sanctioned. Anne Braden remembered having learned as a child that God "had made the white people superior to Negroes."[97] Larry L. King recalled, "Some of the more obvious white-supremacy advocates of my youth were men of the cloth." He met a number of poorly educated itinerant preachers who came to visit his father, who also preached on occasion, at their home in Texas. King remembered, "One of the favored topics of those unlettered priests was the vast amount of Scriptural authority accounting for the black man's lowly state and substandard conduct."[98] They focused particularly on the "curse of Ham" myth. The idea behind the myth was that God had cursed Ham, son of Noah, because he had seen his father naked after a drunken Noah had fallen asleep, and instead of covering him up, Ham had gone to tell his brothers, who, in turn, respectfully backed into the room and covered their father. Noah's three sons were believed to be the means through which the earth was repopulated after the biblical flood, and the myth held that Ham's descendants had been relegated to Africa, destined forever to serve the descendants of the other brothers.[99] King recalled that in the version told by the preachers he knew, "Ham had taken a wife from among a tribe marked by the curse of Cain—some low-rated beast of the field she was, probably little better than a first cousin to the gorilla. From this unnatural union (so ran the prevailing theology) had been produced the most primitive form of the black race." In return God had "forever consigned blacks to be 'hewers of wood and drawers of water,' 'a servant's servant' happiest when waiting tables, playing banjo, or riding in the back of the bus."[100] Melton McLaurin remembered learning that it was the "destiny" of black southerners "to work at menial tasks, supervised, of course, by benevolent whites. All this was according to God's plan and was perfectly obvious to all but dimwitted Yankees and Communists."[101] These authors were embellishing for dramatic effect, but the conclusion they reached was nonetheless telling: white children learned to view segregation as divinely ordained.

Letters written to government officials before and in the wake of the *Brown* decision reveal how white southerners used their understanding of Christianity to justify their belief in segregation. In *A Stone of Hope: Prophetic Religion and the Death of Jim Crow* David L. Chappell argued that southern white religious leaders did not serve as key figures in the segregationist movement and, moreover, that they doubted the "usefulness" of the Bible for defending segregation; however, Paul Harvey has identified the existence of a "folk theology of segregation" among white supporters of the system.[102] This folk, or lay, theology often consisted of ever more creative versions of the curse of Ham myth. After the *Brown* decision a woman wrote to Georgia senator Richard B. Russell opposing those who preached "that God created all men equal." She exclaimed, "No where in the bible will you even find an allusion to such a claim!" According to her reading of Genesis, God had "transformed the youngest son of Noah into a Negro, and made him and wife [*sic*] and children servants."[103] In the actual biblical story Noah cursed Ham's son

Canaan, who many confused with Adam and Eve's son Cain.[104] A woman provided her version of the story to Alabama governor Gordon Persons in August 1954: "I've studied my Bible to find the origin of the Negro and find he originated from Cain whom God turned black the Bible says he was banished from the Garden of Eden he went to land of nod. There he knew his wife. There being no women on earth at that time she had to be an animal. Negro features are that of an ape."[105] While this account may not qualify as theology per se, it does offer a glimpse of how some white southerners used the Bible to defend segregation.

Other white southerners focused on the second half of Acts 17:26 to argue that while God may have "made of one blood all nations of men," he had also set "the bounds of their habitation." That is, white southerners argued that God had put all human beings in their proper place and to undo the divisions he had established was to violate God's will. A woman identifying herself as an "Adult Church School Teacher" wrote to Gordon Persons in March 1954 to argue in favor of segregation on this basis. She made a distinction "between segregation and discrimination," stating, "From Genesis through Revelation the BIBLE TEACHES SEGREGATION and every time God's people ignored this teaching trouble, strife and sin brought chaos." As she saw it, "the Bible teaches there must be NO DISCRIMINATION against any individual because of race, color or creed in regard to rights of salvation, livelihood, justice and mercy. In this sense, God is no respecter of persons, but He would have us give them these things separate and apart, in their own sphere of society." Invoking the Bible story, she argued, "When Christ forgave the woman of Samaria, He did not take her out of Samaria and into Jerusalem. Instead, He left her to witness in her own sphere of society."[106] In this teacher's reading of the Bible, African Americans were to be left in their own segregated world.

White southerners repeatedly invoked a related argument involving nature, especially birds. An Alabama woman explained to Governor Persons, "Nature and God made the *different* trees, plants flowers animals and birds, each stays in its proper place with its own kind. Look, at the blue, red, yellow, black, and white birds, how beautiful they are, shall man be less wise than they."[107] This alternate meaning of "red and yellow, black and white" could be applied to human beings as well. A former pastor from Georgia observed, "Among all the millions of books the Bible is the plainest on segregation. God created five great races to people the Earth; he set them in families—*White* in Europe, *Black* in Africa, *Brown* in India, *Yellow* in China, *Red* in America. They are as distinct today as the colors of the rainbow."[108] This man, along with many of his fellow white southerners, hoped these distinctions would remain in effect and used his reading of the Bible to justify his faith in segregation.

Aside from learning to believe the system was divinely ordained, white southerners remembered learning that the act of violating segregation constituted a
"sin," rendering one "guilty."[109] Christian teachings were thus marshaled in support
of rather than in opposition to segregation. Kenneth Clark cited evidence suggesting that when conducted in a segregated environment, religious instruction, instead of improving racial attitudes, might actually make one "more prejudiced."[110]
For her part Lillian Smith saw commonalities between unquestioned adherence
to religious faith and unquestioned adherence to segregation.[111] Sunday school lessons and memory verses were quite literally lessons learned by rote. Congregants
could have easily sung along to powerful lyrics such as those of "In Christ There Is
No East or West" without paying much attention to their meaning. Adherence to
Christian faith and adherence to segregation were both often based on emotional
connections to a belief system that people felt but likely did not think very much
about, and questioning one's belief in either Christianity or segregation could be
viewed as sacrilegious. Instead of providing a foundation upon which to build
a critique of segregation, the racial instruction white children received in their
churches could actually serve to reinforce their commitment to the system.

Nevertheless, some white southerners, such as Paul Hemphill and his pastor,
did criticize segregation based on lessons they had learned in church. In fact, some
used these lessons to critique segregation at church. Humorist Roy Blount Jr. recalled that while singing "Jesus Loves the Little Children" one Sunday morning at
his church in Georgia, it occurred to him "that all of us were white. I didn't make
a stink about it. Jesus would have, but I was only nine, and I doubt there were any
red or yellow children in Decatur at the time, and the black ones were in a separate world back then, and since I didn't fit into that class very well as it was, who
needed complications? I just wondered, Why did they teach us that song if they
didn't mean it?" Blount admitted that he was known for taking things too literally
and concluded that the source of his confusion lay in the fact that he seldom knew
"*how* literally" things were supposed to be taken.[112] Civil rights activist Dorothy
Dawson Burlage likewise experienced confusion as a result of lessons she learned
at her white church while growing up in Texas. She recalled that in high school
she appeared on the surface to be a typical teenage girl, worried about dresses,
dances, and the like; meanwhile, she explained, "I was inwardly preoccupied with
issues of social justice and the moral teachings of the church. I kept struggling
with the contradictions between the messages I heard about segregation and the
ones I heard in church about love and brotherhood, justice and righteousness."[113]

Those messages resonated as well with Drew Gilpin Faust, who uncovered
much about her childhood views on segregation when an archivist helped her

locate a letter she had written to President Dwight D. Eisenhower when she was nine years old. Faust recalled that she had often told and even "committed to print" a story about how her civil rights activism and her work as a historian derived from her realization—after hearing about the *Brown* decision on the radio—that her Virginia elementary school was "all white" and "that this was not an accident." She had written of her response to this realization, "I quickly penned a letter to President Eisenhower to say how illogical I thought this seemed in the face of the precepts of equality I had already imbibed by second grade."[114] When she consulted her letter, however, she found that it had not been written immediately after the *Brown* decision but instead in February 1957, probably, she surmised, in response to a radio report about some action taken in the course of Virginia's resistance to school desegregation. Although she remembered her critique of segregation having been grounded in her understanding that the system contradicted the American values of equality and democracy, which she had presumably learned at school, her actual letter revealed that her critique was based on the way segregation violated the Christian principles she had learned in her Episcopal church. Her family was not "particularly religious," and "neither race nor the Civil Rights movement was ever mentioned in [her] all-white local church." Such "stunning silence" would encourage her by the 1960s to "abandon organized religion permanently." Despite this silence on racial matters, she had nonetheless "imbibed some sort of egalitarian message from the church." In her letter she had informed Eisenhower that Jesus was born to save "not only white people but black yellow red and brown."[115] Even if local church leaders did not translate their religious beliefs into criticism of segregation, individual white southerners might be inspired by the church's message to oppose the system.

Other white southerners were likewise inspired to translate childhood lessons learned at church into civil rights activism. Sue Thrasher remembered of her Methodist church, "It taught me some of the basic values I brought to the Freedom Movement—like the fatherhood of God and the brotherhood of man."[116] Like other female activists, Thrasher did not extend her critique of the church's stance on race to include a critique of its stance on gender and gender-specific language.[117] Like Faust and Hemphill, Thrasher responded to what she saw as the church's failure to practice Christian beliefs in the realm of race relations by turning away from the church in later years.[118] These white southerners used a critique of segregation grounded in lessons learned at church as the basis for a subsequent critique of the church itself for its stance on segregation. Recognizing that a church did not practice what it preached did not necessarily dictate a rejection of organized religion. Some white southerners saw their activism as an extension of their religious faith. Joan C. Browning, for example, concluded of her childhood church in Georgia, "In sermons and song, Scotland Methodist Church prepared me for the congregational singing and intense emotionalism of Freedom Movement mass meetings."[119] Browning thus highlighted the extent to which the civil rights movement was based in the common, though separate, religious heritage of black and white southerners.

Anne Braden credited the lessons she learned at her Episcopal church in Anniston, Alabama, with both inspiring and sustaining her civil rights activism. Although Braden remembered segregation as having been "unquestioned" when she was a child, she also believed that at some level she had always had doubts about the system. In addition to learning that God "had made the white people superior to Negroes," Braden learned that "the Bible said all men were brothers." Early on she perceived a disconnect between belief and action in her church: "The pictures on the Sunday School walls showed Jesus surrounded by children of all colors, the black and the yellow along with the white—all sitting in a circle together. Long before I could put it into words even in my own mind, I sensed that this did not square with the relations I saw practiced and which I practiced myself in the world around me." The only black children she knew were those of the women who cleaned her house or did her family's laundry, and she wrote of these children: "We did not sit in a circle together. We did not sit anywhere together." She remembered watching one of the girls as she sat waiting for her mother in the kitchen of Anne's home, wearing one of Anne's hand-me-down dresses: "She would sit there looking uncomfortable, my old faded dress binding her at the waist and throat. And some way I knew that this was not what Jesus meant when he said to clothe the naked." She continued, "I recalled that Jesus had also said, 'Therefore all things whatsoever ye would that men should do to you, do ye even so to them.' And I knew that if I were in her place, if I had no clothes, I would not want the old abandoned dresses of a person who would not even invite me to come into her living room to sit down."[120] The golden rule had the potential to make white southerners feel very uncomfortable about segregation.

Visiting her former church in Anniston in the fall of 1954, after she and her husband had come under considerable attack for their stance on civil rights, Braden reflected on the lessons about the commonality of all people she had learned there and on those who had taught them: "The people who taught me these lessons had not mentioned what this concept did to their society's fetish of the color line; perhaps they never analyzed it, and at first neither did I. But I am sure that the seed that was planted in my mind and heart here was the thing that made me able to seek a larger world later—that, in fact, made it imperative that I do so." Braden characterized her affluent church as "the most far-reachingly decent influence" on her "walled-in childhood" and probably the most "radical" influence in her life. For someone who was repeatedly accused of harboring communist sympathies, this was high praise indeed for a segregated southern church. Braden concluded that the same institutions that had given her "so many weaknesses," by teaching her to practice and accept segregation, had also given her "the reserve of strength" she would need to face her adversaries and continue her activism.[121] For white critics of segregation like Braden, childhood lessons learned at church served as intellectual raw materials that could be refashioned to provide motivation and sustenance in later years.

Recognizing the potential for the message of "red and yellow, black and white" to effect change in racial attitudes, concerned individuals within the major Protestant denominations in the South undertook efforts to reeducate white young people by promoting such messages. These individuals thus pursued the other avenue for using education as a means of gradually improving race relations, one focused on educating away prejudice. Women's groups and those involved in home missions took the lead in these efforts.[122] Una Roberts Lawrence, for example, who served as young people's secretary for the SBC's Woman's Missionary Union (WMU) and later as mission study editor for the Home Mission Board (HMB), was instrumental in the SBC's efforts to improve race relations by reeducating young people.[123] Through writing and editing works on subjects such as "Negro Life in the South," Lawrence sought to achieve "better understanding" between black and white southerners. In an effort to promote such understanding, she developed literature that discussed the educational and artistic achievements of African Americans, the history of black Baptists, black entrepreneurial activity, and interracial activity undertaken by black and white Baptist women. Through this literature Lawrence worked to create "an outlook of hope for better living together in the South."[124]

Other organizations within the SBC likewise sought to reeducate young people. Virginia's state WMU was active in developing literature intended to cultivate better understanding. The organization distributed lessons on "World Friendship" that suggested activities such as singing "Jesus Loves the Little Children" and "In Christ There Is No East or West," creating a poster with pictures of "children of many lands" surrounding a picture of Jesus, and, more problematically, building models of African huts out of cardboard. Lesson aims emphasized "the thought that Jesus wants all people of all races to be friends with Him and with one another" and "the thought that our African brothers and sisters, in whatever land they live, need to know and love

Jesus; and that each of us should help to make Him known." Another lesson celebrated the "great and noble" life and work of Booker T. Washington.[125]

At the denomination level the WMU published a magazine for children called *World Comrades*, which took as its motto "To Girdle the World with Friendliness" and often featured an illustration of children of many lands on its cover.[126] A 1946 lesson in this publication, entitled "America, the Rainbow Land," advised, "Jesus himself was a Jew. He taught the people with whom He lived that He loved them enough to die for them. Jesus's love also reaches out to the Japanese Americans, Mexican Americans, Negro Americans and all other people who live on the face of the earth." The lesson then encouraged children to sing "Jesus Loves the Little Children."[127] A lesson for smaller children, so-called Sunbeams, from the same month suggested an activity in which teachers would pin different colored pansies on children as they entered the classroom. Teachers were also advised to assemble "large paper pansies . . . one each of red, yellow, black, brown, and white" and use them to initiate a conversation about difference by asking, "Do they make you think of different members of God's family? What about this lovely black one? Let's put the face of one of our Negro friends there." The lesson explained, "We certainly know about the white one, for that is us. Now we have five lovely pansies in five different colors, but each one is a pansy. It is the same way with God's children. We are all different, but we are all his children."[128] Elsewhere *World Comrades* suggested that young people investigate African American schools in their communities to find out how many students attended, what the conditions were like, and if they had enough seats, library books, and other supplies.[129] Through these activities Baptist young people were encouraged to acknowledge and work to improve unequal conditions in their communities.

In his study of Southern Baptist missions and race, Alan Scot Willis argued that WMU leaders "believed that educating young people about race would lead to better, more Christian race relations in the future." That education stressed three main principles: "the biblical mandates of racial equality and unity, the international dimensions of the race question, and the personal responsibility of each Christian to work for better race relations."[130] In this era one might have expected white denominations to disseminate literature that explicitly supported segregation; instead missionary, women's, and children's literature in particular sought to foster concern and understanding that would help to improve race relations in the South and build support for missions overseas. While the literature produced by white religious denominations in the South was embedded with racial stereotypes and seldom questioned segregation, it was ultimately well-meaning in terms of encouraging young people to sympathize with and improve conditions for African Americans.

Sadie Mai Wilson of the Methodist Episcopal Church, South, explained this approach, "If in our plan of missionary education we can build up appreciation for the contribution of other races, if we can help people to see both sides of the race question, if we can bring about better understanding, we will have opened the way to the development of more Christlike attitudes and practices."[131] In this spirit the Woman's Section of the Board of Missions of the Methodist Episcopal Church, South, published a pamphlet on African American educator Mary McLeod Bethune. The piece stressed Bethune's intelligence, her perseverance, and her greatness as seen in her efforts to promote the education of "her people."[132] The Methodist Church, which was formed when northern and southern Methodists reunited in 1939, distributed a pamphlet written by Robert B. Eleazer entitled "'The Curse of Ham': A Conversation Concerning a Myth That Dies Hard." In this piece Eleazer exposed the many discrepancies between the myth and the actual biblical account, among them that Noah, not God, had done the cursing; Ham's son Canaan, not Ham himself, had been cursed; and no reference to skin color was ever made.[133] If this myth—which was repeatedly invoked by white southerners as proof of biblical support for segregation—could be undermined by distributing literature to young people, greater understanding between black and white southerners might result.

In part because the Methodist Church was a unified national organization after 1939, as opposed to the Presbyterians and Baptists, who maintained separate regional denominations, its literature seems to have been particularly forthright in its discussion of race. Even before reunification, however, publications produced by the Methodist Episcopal Church, South, featured lessons that openly engaged with racial issues. The author of a 1929 lesson entitled "Good Will to People of Other Races" instructed readers, "One of the best methods of understanding the feelings of a person of another race is to place yourself mentally in his or her shoes." The lesson continued, "For anyone to make the lot of a stranger or a member of another race a harder one is to go against all the finer teachings of the Bible. It is also to go against the spirit of the Master, who was forever taking the side of the under fellow."[134] A 1935 lesson entitled "Surprises in Friendship" explained, "It dawned on the early church, as it has been dawning on Christians ever since, that Jesus makes his friends through their own characters, and race has not one thing to do with it." The best option for how to approach the issue of race was "to treat a person of any other race as first of all a person, another human being." The lesson concluded by encouraging readers to seek out opportunities for interacting with "friends from other races" and to support the "Home and Foreign Missionary Enterprise" of the church.[135] Lessons of this type usually had an explicit or implicit link with missionary activity.

Literature published for Sunday school teachers by the southern-based Presbyterian Church in the United States reveals similar efforts to promote "mutual understanding" and encourage support for missions.[136] A 1935 lesson in the *Senior Teacher's Quarterly* suggested a number of review questions on recent lessons, including "Do the white people of your town treat the colored people in a Christian way? Do you?"[137] A 1947 lesson in the *Senior Teacher's Guide*, entitled "The Church Is for All People," counseled teachers to pose questions such as "Is there a recognition in this church (and class) of the equal worth of every person in the sight of God and the full right of every believer to our Christian fellowship?" Teachers were encouraged to work with their students to develop "concrete suggestions as to what your class can do to demonstrate its full acceptance of the fact that with God there is but one race—the human race."[138] A 1944 lesson in the *Primary Leader's Guide* explained the moral behind the pictures of Jesus with children of many lands that appeared in Presbyterian publications and those of other denominations: "Leaders will help the children to realize that Jesus loves all children of all races, and that God wants all children to know and love him as their heavenly father. They will want to help them discover ways in which children of other lands are like themselves, and will seek to develop in the children a feeling of fellowship with other children and a desire to help them know Jesus." One way children could help was through prayer, and the author suggested teachers lead a prayer thanking God for "Jesus who loves all children" and for the picture of Jesus with children of many lands that helped spread that message. The author made the missionary emphasis of the lesson clear, explaining, "As the children learn of the work of missionaries, we hope they may find their part in the work our own denomination is doing for people of other lands, and find definite ways of participating in this work."[139] Many lessons of this type encouraged children to contribute to missionary activities by saving their pennies and dimes and donating them to the church.

Although concerned individuals within these denominations made a sincere effort to improve race relations in the South by teaching young people lessons about God's love for all people, the literature they produced often reinforced existing racial stereotypes or an ingrained sense of superiority. A 1924 lesson for boys in *World Comrades* on the topic "Our Black Neighbors" suggested that teachers decorate a poster "with pictures of negroes, watermelons, banjos, cotton fields and other things associated with the negro race." The lesson also advised, "Plan to have this meeting in the woods. A watermelon feast will be opportune."[140] A lesson for girls from the same month encouraged teachers to make construction paper banjos with "NEGRO" spelled out on them for the girls to take home as souvenirs. The lesson recommended writing, "N-ever treat the Negro ill; E-ver show him your good will; G-ive him love and kindness too; R-ealize that he needs your help; O-ffer him your Savior, too."[141] These girls were being taught that they had an obligation to help African Americans, who presumably could not take care of themselves. A 1928 story in the Presbyterian publication the *Story Hour* featured an illustration of a black woman identified as "Mammy" along with a young black boy in a straw hat bringing her a watermelon; both of them were barefoot. Although the story was set in Jamaica, its imagery would have resonated with white children in the South in a way that reinforced stereotypes common in their society.[142] Meanwhile, both Baptist and Presbyterian publications held up Confederate leaders such as Robert E. Lee and Stonewall Jackson as models for children to emulate.[143] While the use of explicitly stereotyped symbols such as watermelons and banjos was less common after the 1920s, racialized assumptions continued to appear in the Sunday school literature of white denominations.

Depictions of Africa and Africans were especially problematic. A 1935 lesson entitled "Jonah's Lesson in World Friendship" described "an African savage boy" who was subsequently "civilized." When two white boys who heard his story wanted "their dad to go out at once and find a little savage to bring in the home and tame," their mother protested that the two little savages she already had at home were enough. While the author inverted the meaning of *savage* for comedic effect, the image of Africa as the home of uncivilized heathens was reinforced nonetheless.[144] A Methodist Episcopal Church, South, publication encouraged young people to donate money for missions in Africa, especially for the benefit of girls who, the lesson explained, were highly valued because "they make such good servants" and became overworked as they grew older. The lesson asked of the Methodist effort to raise money for missions, "Aren't you glad that this blessed Centenary Movement of ours will be the means of teaching the Africans a better way, so that your poor little black sisters of the Dark Continent will know that the God who made them really cares?"[145] African girls were thus depicted as natural-born servants who should be pitied for their plight in their benighted native land. Another issue of the same publication featured a picture of an African "Medicine Man," and Africans and African Americans were often characterized as religious or superstitious by nature.[146]

Much was also written about the impact of missionaries on Africa. In one story a young boy was inspired to write a letter to "an African friend" after a missionary just back from Africa visited his church. The boy exclaimed to his new "friend," who had presumably embraced the missionary's message of Christianity, "You must be glad that you're not afraid of evil spirits any more."[147] In addition to impacting the religious beliefs of African converts, missionaries were credited with having changed Africans' appearance by introducing them to "civilized" clothing. An author in *World Comrades* explained how to build an African village to illustrate a missionary lesson. She encouraged teachers to build huts out of oatmeal boxes covered with clay and advised them on how to depict the village's inhabitants before and after their contact with Christian missionaries: "A little African boy wears only a loin cloth, a girl may wear a grass skirt or a cloth wrapped around her body. After the children go to the mission school they learn to dress very much like American children."[148] A Presbyterian publication made the same point through visual representation, depicting an African village with a divide between residents who had come under missionary influence and wore westernized clothing and residents, mostly women and children, who were in various states of undress.[149]

Depictions of Africans in illustrations of Jesus with children were also problematic. Pictures of Jesus with children generally fell into two categories: those that illustrated the message of "suffer little children to come unto me," which featured more or less light-skinned versions of Jesus and children, and those that depicted Jesus with children of many lands.[150] Perhaps the most well-known rendering of the latter type is Harold Copping's "The Hope of the World," which features a light-skinned Jesus with a diverse mix of children, including a white girl whom Jesus holds near to him and a naked African boy with his back to the viewer who sits the furthest away from Jesus.[151] The boy is not only depicted as uncivilized or unconverted, as represented by his lack of clothing, but he is also physically separated from both Jesus and the other children, perhaps because of his nakedness, perhaps because of his unbelief. Another notable illustration, which appeared in Presbyterian Sunday school literature, featured a group of Africans gathered around a picture of a white Jesus that had been posted on a tree.[152] Such depictions of a white savior were exactly what troubled African American leaders about white Sunday school literature. Meanwhile, pictures for lessons with titles such as "Working for a Healthy Neighborhood" and "Friends Who Help Me" featured all white children and adults, serving to further normalize whiteness for the audience of primarily white southern children.[153]

Stories built around the concept of "red and yellow, black and white" could inadvertently reinforce whiteness as well and made for interesting interpretations of the message of commonality. A particularly telling lesson featured a story about an artist who was commissioned to paint a picture of a group of children gathered around Jesus that would serve as the template for a stained-glass window in a church. Having gone to bed after finishing his painting, the artist dreamed that Jesus came and painted the faces of the children, previously all white, in five different colors. In the dream Jesus questioned why the artist had only used one color for the children's faces when he had so many different colors available and asked him, "Who told you [the children] were all white in my kingdom?" The artist replied, "Why, no one ever told me. . . . I just didn't think." When the artist woke up and realized he had been dreaming, he began fixing the painting, "making a little yellow child with slanting eyes, brown and black faces with smiling lips."[154] Even this otherwise admirable attempt to promote positive racial attitudes in children could not escape the racial stereotypes that pervaded southern culture. Meanwhile, a version of this story that appeared in a Presbyterian publication had the artist returning to his studio after waking up from his dream to find "all the little faces were *white*, just like yours!" The author thereby revealed her assumption about the race of the story's audience and, thus, that of the membership of local Presbyterian congregations in the South.[155]

Stories involving dreams that imagined the way the world could be were quite common in Sunday school literature. In a story entitled "The Boy Who Didn't Know His Own Family," the main character, Jack, dreamed he went to heaven. He was pleased once he arrived to see there were no poor, dirty, or foreign children there and exclaimed, "How nice it is to be among a lot of boys and girls of my own kind." Upon learning that some of his new playmates were actually from such places as Africa, India, and Japan, he was confused until a helpful angel told him that all people looked the same in God's eyes, which, given the context of the story, presumably meant they all looked white like him.[156] In another story in the same genre a black boy named Paul was ecstatic to be welcomed as a playmate by a white boy and invited into the boy's home until he realized he was in the "City of the Colorblind." In what turned out to be a dream, the white family only welcomed Paul because they could not distinguish his skin color.[157] In another story a white girl named Sarah was amused when she found out a local black church was looking for patterns to make angel costumes for its Christmas play. Meanwhile, her brother, Sam, was surprised to learn that the local mission was looking for props for Chinese shepherds to use in its play. Sam exclaimed, "Chinese shepherds and black angels! Sis, the Christmas programs in this vicinity are certainly going to be colorful this year." When Sarah fell asleep studying history one night, she dreamed of a singing heavenly host, including people who "looked like our American Negroes and, yes, some wore shining white robes and had the appearance of angels."[158] Surprised to learn that African Americans could become angels or play them in this life, she still imagined them clothed in white. Although such stories attempted to teach lessons about commonality and acceptance, they could neither escape racial stereotypes nor avoid maintaining whiteness as a cultural norm.

White Protestant denominations in the South often approached questions of race relations in terms of obligation and responsibility.[159] White Christians saw themselves as helping to lift African Americans up from a lower condition than they themselves occupied, and this missionary activity reinforced a sense of white superiority. Bruno Lasker observed of religious literature, "Even some seemingly innocuous books, just because they endeavor to arouse zeal for missionary work, emphasize the gifts which the American has to offer the non-American, or the white to the colored peoples of the world, and thereby make for self-satisfaction and a sense of national or racial superiority." He deemed this attitude one of "benevolent paternalism."[160] That attitude was perfectly encapsulated in a 1949 Sunday school lesson for senior-level students that featured a picture of young white women raising money to build a segregated swimming pool for black children. Driven by a desire to promote "Christian understanding," the women welcomed the opportunity to interact with African Americans, who reportedly came by to thank them "for the wonderful way we are helping them."[161] Although these young women understood themselves as doing something good for black children, they were motivated by a sense of obligation to help those who were less well-off than they, and their project explicitly reinforced segregation. Denominational leaders were not unaware of the potential liabilities of the literature they produced. Methodist writer Sadie Mai Wilson observed, "To speak of these other children as 'poor little black children'—or 'little heathen Chinese'—to tell of the strange customs or queer idols which are quite outside the range of the little child's experience and understanding, is perhaps to create in the mind of the white child the impression that he is different and superior, and that those other boys and girls are inferiors to have pennies doled out to them."[162] Even when white religious denominations meant well, the literature they produced often reinforced the South's racial status quo.

Despite the limitations of this literature, some white southerners remembered the positive impact it had on their racial views. Paul Hemphill interviewed a man named Bob Corley who had attended the same church he had and learned the same lessons about the value of all people. Corley said he had not turned against the church as Hemphill had because his "whole thinking shifted" after he read some literature on "race and brotherhood" published by the national Methodist Church, literature that he remembered having angered adults in the local congregation.[163] Ed King, a white minister who played a key role in civil rights demonstrations in Mississippi, likewise remembered the impact of literature distributed to his local Methodist church by the national denomination, writing, "The white southern church was responsible for my first questioning of the morality of segregation." He also recalled efforts by more conservative church members in his community to have Methodist Sunday school literature banned.[164]

Evidence of the reach of such literature can also be found in contemporary letters from those who opposed its use. Many Southern Baptists sent letters to denominational officials criticizing the distribution of materials that they felt promoted integration. In 1958 a man from Alabama wrote to the SBC's Christian Life Commission, headquartered in Nashville, declaring, "I would like to make my Personal Protest, to the literature that is being published by you, on the question of Integration. We Southern People, like to think of Nashville, as still being in the South, but some of the articles that you are sending out, sound as if they were written by [a] questionable character from Brooklyn." He believed the dissemination of this literature was making the racial climate in the South worse and argued, "Your NAACP propaganda type literature, is only aiding the Communist program, NOT the Christian Program, in the South, at least."[165] Two church leaders from Louisiana wrote to James L. Sullivan, executive secretary of the Sunday School Board, to oppose a reference to Gunnar Myrdal in a Baptist quarterly because, they claimed, "known Communists" had contributed to *An American Dilemma*.[166] In both instances the letter writers intimated that their financial support for the denomination would be withdrawn should these materials continue to be produced. Other correspondents returned literature they deemed objectionable or requested that their names be removed from denominational mailing lists.[167] One of the central objections to this literature was its assumption that there was only one Christian response to the racial situation in the South. A Baptist official from Alabama wrote to A. C. Miller, executive secretary of the Christian Life Commission, in 1957 to oppose the distribution of a recent report by the commission to pastors in his state: "The burden of the report as a whole is an appeal that we assume a Christian attitude on this question. . . . Many have become quite resentful of any inferences that they are not Christian if they oppose integration."[168] Denominational literature that supported a "Christian" solution to the race question was disseminated widely enough to generate substantial opposition from church leaders and members who thought their denomination should either support segregation or remain neutral, if not silent, on the issue of race.

Ultimately, the attempt by white religious denominations to improve southern race relations was ineffective for a number of reasons. These efforts—like those undertaken by secular organizations such as the Commission on Interracial Co-operation—were not intended to dismantle segregation; they merely sought to promote better understanding between black and white southerners. Although Alan Scot Willis generally lauded the SBC's educational efforts, he conceded that "before 1954 some progressive Baptists hoped to create racial harmony without attacking segregation directly."[169] Instead, they emphasized gradual improvement within the confines of the segregated system. Moreover, the strategy assumed that white southerners recognized or could be fairly easily convinced that a moral di-lemma existed because of the disparity between their beliefs and actions, and this was often not the case. The strategy of making patient appeals on the basis of reli-gious principles was not effective in undermining the lifetime of racial condition-ing white southerners experienced, especially because some of that conditioning took place within the church itself. As a 1949 report from the PCUS concluded of the denomination's educational efforts, "Like a vaccination that doesn't vaccinate, plainly much of our education hasn't 'taken.'"[170] Although the literature distrib-uted in some white southern churches contained surprisingly strong statements about the need to extend more consideration to African Americans, it did not significantly undermine white southerners' adherence to segregation. Instead, the literature motivated white southerners to embrace a missionary stance toward African Americans that ultimately served to reinforce their sense of superiority.

Lillian Smith made a compelling point about the role religion played in the segregated South through her description of a play put on by her Laurel Falls campers, the same play that had prompted one of the girls to accuse Smith of having "done a terrible thing to children" by teaching them to think critically about segregation.[171] In the play, modeled after Antoine de Saint-Exupéry's *The Little Prince*, a character named "Every Child" embarked on a journey out into the world, collecting traveling companions as she went, among them "Conscience," "Southern Tradition," and "Religion." When Every Child encountered a situation in which she had to decide whether to play with a black child, Conscience de-ferred to Southern Tradition, and Southern Tradition quickly blocked the white child's path. When someone suggested that Conscience listen to what Religion had to say on the matter, Conscience replied, "I never listen to Religion where segregation is involved. No one does, down here."[172] The campers' assessment of religion's capacity to counter the dictates of southern tradition is telling, though the overall effect of religious belief and practice on the segregated system was more complex than these young southerners suggested.

Religion had the power to instill in black children a vision of their own worth in God's eyes. Black churches served as autonomous institutions through which

African Americans found means of surviving segregation with their faith and their dignity intact, and churches sometimes served as sites where black southerners organized to demand their rights. This role would become much more apparent in later years, during the civil rights movement. Even as some churches began to facilitate activism, however, others continued to emphasize an otherworldly escape from the problems of this life, a focus that acknowledged the limits on such activism in the years before the mass movement. Black religious leaders also promoted a strategy of attempting to ameliorate segregated conditions by improving the morals and personal habits of black children and thus lent legitimacy to the very system they were working to undermine. For white southerners Christianity offered intellectual raw materials that might have served as the basis for a critique of segregation; the potential inherent in the golden rule and "red and yellow, black and white" went largely unrealized, however, in part because white southerners were also learning to view segregation as divinely ordained. Growing up in an environment in which religious principles were marshaled to support segregation, white southerners were unlikely to question either set of beliefs or recognize a discrepancy between the two. For most white southerners the choice between "Jesus Christ and Jim Crow" was not one they felt they had to make.[173]

Even if religious convictions did not serve as a widespread source of doubts about segregation, some white southerners did begin to feel their commitment to the system wane in response to their faith and to experiences such as travel, military service, and higher education. At the same time African Americans began to see past their racial conditioning and envision a world without segregation. In the decades before the civil rights movement, individual black and white southerners around the region slowly began to build a critique of the segregated system.

CHAPTER 5

TO MAKE THE TOLERABLE INTOLERABLE

Black and White Racial Awakenings

Writing in response to Richard Wright's 1940 novel, *Native Son*, Mississippi author David L. Cohn concluded, "Mr. Wright obviously does not have the long view of history" because he demanded both political rights and social equality for African Americans and was not willing to wait for them, as Cohn and other like-minded racial moderates had been advising black southerners to do for some time. Cohn stressed, "Justice or no justice, the whites of America simply will not grant to Negroes at this time those things that Mr. Wright demands."[1] The proponent of an elite-led gradualism that he believed would result in the eventual amelioration of race relations within the segregated system, Cohn thought an untimely appeal for immediate change in the social and political status of African Americans in the South would have dire consequences. Thus, he warned Wright and those who might be influenced by his work, "hatred and the preaching of hatred, and incitement to violence can only make a tolerable relationship intolerable."[2]

Cohn's reaction to Wright is revealing in that the act of making the tolerable intolerable is precisely the task that civil rights leaders faced in subsequent decades. Their goal was to convince black and white southerners that the segregated conditions they had lived with for more than a half-century were so unbearable that they must come to an immediate end. White moderates such as Cohn failed to recognize that tensions, like those subsequently created through nonviolent direct action, were necessary to effect meaningful social change through the creation of either disorder for the community or internal conflict for the individual. A number of black and white southerners remembered encounters in the decades before the civil rights movement through which they, as their successors would during the 1950s and 1960s, came to view life in the segregated South as intolerable. These realizations, or awakenings, resulted from a variety of experiences, such as travel outside the region, military service, college education, exposure to social or literary criticism, and personal encounters within the rituals of segregation. Through these experiences black and white southerners began to engage in a critique of the system they had learned to accept as a fact of southern life.

Historians have often identified such awakenings in the work of either black or white southerners. Leon Litwack deemed the moments when black children first realized life would be different for them "racial baptisms."[3] John Cell noted, "The moment of discovery, when the black personality first comes to full recognition of the realities of life under white supremacy, is a constant topic of Afro-American autobiography."[4] Fred Hobson drew on the autobiographies of elite white southerners to inform his analysis of "the white southern racial conversion narrative."[5] Recognition of the importance of such moments, whether one calls them awakenings, baptisms, or conversions, is central to the study of southern autobiography from this period; one must also recognize, however, that both black and white southerners remember experiencing such moments. While the content of these realizations differed based on race, their effect was the same: they made southerners question segregation in a way they never had before.

An emphasis on the commonality of black and white experiences reveals the limits of the "racial conversion narrative" concept. Hobson's focus on conversion narratives assumes a confession by whites of their racial guilt and a resulting repentance of past racial sins, but white southerners learned about segregation in such a way that they developed a deep emotional attachment to a system they had not thought very much about. To have experienced guilt over segregation, they would have had to have been thinking consciously about their complicity in the system. The very narratives Hobson explored reveal that many white southerners' participation in segregation was based on "unthinking" compliance.[6] Even when white southerners did feel guilty about their treatment of individual African Americans, that guilt competed with guilt over violating the segregated code as taught by trusted parents and teachers. In addition, racial guilt does not seem to have been the primary factor in the "conversions" remembered by some notable whites. A number of the most influential critiques of segregation by white southerners began not when they were convicted over guilt at their treatment of African Americans but, rather, when they came to the conclusion that segregation was costing them something as whites.[7]

Autobiographies about segregation are more accurately stories of awakening— of how black and white southerners came to *see through* their racial conditioning—than they are stories of conversion. Kristina DuRocher used the more apt term "racial awakening narratives" to describe these accounts.[8] Literary scholar Lynn Bloom wrote of such narratives, "All of these autobiographies deal with the pervasive experience of racial segregation and its searing effects on blacks and whites alike. This does not mean that segregation is exclusively southern, but that it is inclusively southern. No child, black or white, can escape it; no autobiographer can ignore it."[9] When conceptualized as stories of racial awakening, black and white southern autobiographies have much in common.

As southerners sought to attach meaning to their racial encounters, they developed powerful metaphors for both the experience of segregated life and the process by which they began to understand and overcome the system's power over them. Both autobiographers and oral history informants drew on such metaphors to explain segregation. Based on her childhood in Virginia, African American Elnora Hayslette said of the system, "When you've been brought up in this kind of thing, you sort of have a shell. You just get to feeling as though this is the way it is."[10] Margaret Jones Bolsterli wrote of her relationship with her family's African American maid, "We were in transparent spheres like bubbles that passed into one another and then out again; but we could not get out of our individual bubbles, no matter how, in certain situations, they might combine."[11] South Carolina native and U.S. district judge J. Waties Waring said of the system, "White supremacy is a way of life. You grow up in it and the moss gets in your eyes. You learn to rationalize away the evil and filth and you see magnolias instead."[12] James Farmer likened segregation to a "closed door" that he had bumped his head on as a child. His earliest encounter with this closed door "left a wound that never ceased reopening."[13]

From these metaphors one understands segregation as an institution that isolated individuals by keeping them closed off from members of the other racial group even when they encountered them every day and even when they encountered them in their own homes. African Americans were behind a "closed door" or living within a "shell." Black and white southerners could see each other from their separate "bubbles," but they only rarely occupied the same social space; they could never totally leave their own sphere to enter that of the other group. For their part whites had "moss" in their eyes and thus could not see how segregation impacted them and the African Americans in their midst. Darlene Clark Hine invoked a similar image in her discussion of Katharine Du Pre Lumpkin's autobiography when she described the "cataracts of racism" that kept white southerners from becoming fully aware of the implications of segregation.[14] Through the use of metaphors black and white southerners sought to capture the experience of growing up in the segregated South and to show how their racial conditioning clouded their view of what was possible where segregation was concerned.

If most white southerners had moss in their eyes and many black southerners were living within a shell, in which it seemed as though conditions would always be as they had seemingly always been, how did individual southerners come to question segregation? Although some of them described racial awakenings as instantaneous transformations, most realizations occurred much more gradually. Like Farmer, Lillian Smith used the notion of a closed door to explain segregation. She recalled learning about segregation "the way all of my southern people learn it: by closing door after door until one's mind and heart and conscience are blocked off from each other and from reality." Although she remembered a specific incident involving a childhood friendship with a girl who was thought to be white but later discovered to be "colored," an incident that "pushed these doors open, a little," she explained the overall process of becoming critical of segregation thus: "Somewhere along that iron corridor we travel from babyhood to maturity, doors swinging inward began to swing outward, showing glimpses of the world beyond."[15]

Sarah Patton Boyle used an even more compelling metaphor to describe the series of incidents through which she became critical of segregation: "It was as though water purifier had been put into a contaminated reservoir but left in sealed bottles. These incidents were little centers—bottles—of genuine truth and experience which remained sealed off by my indoctrination and training, unable to permeate and purify my over-all conception of the Negro people and their situation in the South." Eventually, she wrote, a "tidal wave swept into my private reservoir, banging my sealed bottles together until they broke, releasing my captive insight into the general stream of my thought."[16] Both Boyle and Smith described a process by which knowledge about segregation and its impact on African Americans and on themselves as whites came to them gradually over a long period of time. Small incidents resonated with them. They encountered situations in which the imperative of upholding segregation conflicted with the tenets of democracy and Christianity as taught to them in the segregated South. Slowly, these white southerners developed a critique of the system.

African Americans made similar use of powerful metaphors to describe how they came to new understandings about race and segregation. The most commonly remembered childhood moments for African Americans involved their initial recognition of the significance white society attached to skin color. Farmer wrote of such moments, "Every black child in the South has an early experience of racism that shafts his soul. For the lucky, it is sudden, like a bolt of lightning, striking one to his knees. For others, a gradual dying, a sliver of meanness worming its way to the heart."[17] The two scenarios Farmer identified were more often than not part of the same process. The narrative structure of autobiographies and often of oral histories encourages people to identify *the* moment when all became clear to them. Not merely a literary convention, this feature is likely key to how individuals make sense of the incidents in their own minds: they access an existing narrative or metaphor in their culture and use it to structure their life experience. Even within the narratives themselves, however, the authors identified not just one moment when they learned something new about race and segregation but several through which they came to an ever deeper understanding of the institution.[18]

Farmer first became aware of difference based on race when he was three years old and his mother explained that he could not buy a Coke at a downtown drugstore because he was "colored." This was the incident in which he described himself as having bumped his head on the closed door of segregation. The hurt from this episode was the wound that never healed. Farmer related each new encounter with racism back to this incident and built his own critique of segregation around its lessons. He went so far as to link his later activism to this childhood event. Reflecting on his imprisonment in Mississippi during the Freedom Rides, Farmer questioned, "Would the man have been in a cell in Parchman in 1961, if the child had not been denied his soft drink in Holly Springs thirty-eight years before?"[19] Such moments had power in that they could form the basis of a life-changing critique of segregation, even if that critique developed only slowly over time.

Daisy Bates remembered a childhood incident with a similar life-altering impact that occurred when her mother, who was not feeling well, sent her to the store alone one day to buy meat for dinner. After standing by patiently as the butcher waited on several white adults in line in front of her and then several who entered after she did, Bates lost her patience when he continued to ignore her order and waited on a newly arrived white girl about her age. After the other girl left, the butcher wrapped up some inferior cuts of meat, thrust the package at her, and told her, "Niggers have to wait 'til I wait on the white people."[20] She went home crying to her mother, who deeply regretted having sent her to town and told her they would discuss it when her father came home. Bates recalled her life before this event: "As I grew up in this town, I knew I was a Negro, but I did not really understand what that meant until I was seven years old [when this incident occurred]. My parents, as do most Negro parents, protected me as long as possible from the inevitable insult and humiliation that is, in the South, a part of being 'colored.'" The encounter with the butcher forced her parents, who had chosen the race socialization strategies of shielding their daughter from whites while simultaneously building up her internal resources, to formulate a response to her confusion. It is notable that her father, to whom the task of explaining the confrontation at the store fell, did not try to postpone the discussion further but instead explained the situation to her as best he could in light of her age. Her parents first retired to their bedroom to discuss how to proceed; then her father took her aside and struggled to explain to her, in her words, "that a Negro had no rights that a white man respected."[21]

Her new awareness of the obstacles she would face because of her skin color rendered her previous life as a "proud and happy child" unbearable for her. Not long after this episode, Bates found out that the couple who raised her were not her birth parents but, rather, friends of her father with whom he had left her after her mother was murdered by a group of whites. The men had apparently expressed sexual interest in her mother, who had been a beautiful young woman, and when she refused their advances, they killed her. Suffering from too many shocks in too short a time, Bates began to avoid whites. When she saw a white playmate at a store who offered her a penny so they could buy candy, Bates slapped the girl and told her she did not need her money. Bates immediately wondered if her actions would bring retaliation to her or her adoptive father. She later regretted having treated her friend that way, but when she started to approach the girl, she "suddenly remembered that she was white" and turned away. Bates also refused to play an angel in a Christmas play because she wanted "no part of that play about a dead white doll!" Later, when her adoptive father was dying, he spoke to her about her hatred of whites. He cautioned her that all of the energy she was expending being angry with them would be better spent working to change conditions for African Americans in the South.[22] Bates remembered following her father's advice by finding a more constructive outlet for her anger in civil rights activism, discovering along the way white southerners who were supportive of her efforts.

Awakenings to the significance attached to race are a staple of African American autobiography, but they also appear in oral histories of African Americans. Arkansas native Le Ester Jones recalled two childhood incidents through which it became clear to her that she was considered different from whites. Jones grew up in a sharecropping community that included seventeen families, some of whom were white. She and a white girl had in the past chosen rows next to each other during cotton-picking season. One day, when Jones suggested they choose rows together, her friend told her simply, "I can't."[23] When Jones asked her mother why her friend had reacted this way, her mother told her it was because she was black. Jones asserted that she had not known anything about racism before this incident. On another occasion Jones threatened to hit a white boy who lived nearby because he had kicked her. His family overheard her threat and warned her not to strike him. When she returned home and indignantly informed her mother that this white family had not stepped in to stop the boy from hurting her, her mother explained that they let him kick her because she was black. Through these experiences Jones began to learn there were "double standards" for black and white. She explained that black children learned this lesson early because "the [grown-ups] see to you learning it, the grown up white people." Jones's mother was not in a position to challenge the dictates of these whites even though they shared a common economic status as sharecroppers.[24]

A growing awareness of the significance attached to race was not the only type of realization experienced by black southerners. As they began to interact more with the larger society, they sometimes had encounters that caused them to think something was not quite right about segregation. Pauli Murray, for example, took incredible pride in her maternal grandfather, Robert Fitzgerald. His parents derived from a variety of backgrounds, including Swedish, French, Irish, and African. Murray's ancestry "seemed very natural" to her despite the fact that Durham, North Carolina, the town where she grew up, "rigidly enforced the separation of the races and had signs WHITE and COLORED everywhere to remind [residents] stringently of this injunction." She wrote of the signs, "Before I was old enough to understand the full meaning of segregation I knew there was something woefully wrong about those signs, since there could not possibly be anything wrong with my Fitzgerald great-grandparents!"[25] Murray could see from the hues in her own family that the idea of separating people in this way was preposterous because European and African backgrounds were so often found within the same individual. She could see that the segregation signs did not make sense.

Mary Mebane, who, like Murray, grew up in Durham, North Carolina, came to a similar conclusion about segregation. She was very covetous one day when her brother brought home a beautiful cup that a white woman had given him. Mebane noticed that when her father explained to her mother why the woman had given their son the cup—she did not want it back after he had used it—neither of her parents seemed pleased with the gift. From their reaction Mebane deduced that "it was something wrong. But I didn't know what. It was a beautiful cup . . . but there was something wrong."[26] The family was accustomed to drinking out of repurposed mayonnaise and peanut butter jars, which made the acquisition of a real cup seem that much more special to Mebane and her parents' displeasure that much more puzzling. Their lack of enthusiasm about the gift and their silence as they contemplated the reason why it was given convinced Mebane that something had happened that she did not understand and that something was seriously wrong with the situation.

South Carolina native Benjamin Adams remembered playing and eating with white friends as a child. When his friend Anne reached the age of thirteen, her mother told his mother that he would have to stop playing with her and start calling her "Miss Anne."[27] Because this white family had not previously made a distinction on the basis of race, Adams was confused and began to learn for the first time that equal respect was not accorded to blacks and whites. On another occasion Adams and his siblings reached an agreement with their parents that they could go to school during cotton-picking time—something black children in rural areas were often not permitted to do—if they worked in the fields both early in the mornings before school and in the evenings when they came home. The white man who owned the land they worked saw Adams in his school clothes one morning and had him call his father away from the breakfast table to talk to him. When his father returned to the house, he told Adams to take off his school clothes because he was not going to be able to go to school after all until cotton-picking season was over. Adams recognized that his father did not have final say over the decisions made in his own home. He said it "stuck in my mind that my daddy couldn't be a man!" because he had to defer to a white man even when his own children were involved. Adams recalled of this incident, "I just knew something was wrong."[28] His father's powerlessness went against his understanding of his father as the ultimate authority figure in his life. Such encounters formed the basis of Adams's critique of segregation, and he vowed that in his own life he would never be in a position to defer to whites where his children were concerned.

A black child's critique of segregation could begin with a statement as simple as that of Mebane and Adams: something was wrong here. Once black southerners became aware of how they were going to be treated differently because of their skin color, they often began to build a critique of segregation around the simple fact that this treatment violated their sense of fair play. Adams could not understand why he had to call his friend "Miss Anne" when they had previously interacted as equals. Daisy Bates could justify the butcher waiting on white adults before her because they were older than she, but when he waited on a white girl her age who had entered the store after she did, she knew she was being treated unfairly. James Farmer had seen a white boy drink a Coke at the same drugstore where his mother had insisted he could not drink one. Indeed, something was wrong here. Such situations inevitably created questions in children's minds, questions that often went unanswered.

Being aware of the existence of segregation and of the way one's racial designation could deny one access to those things white society held dear was not necessarily the same as having experienced the hurt and humiliation intrinsic to segregation on a personal level. Activist and later television host Xernona Clayton recalled attending segregated schools when she was growing up in Oklahoma in the 1940s but explained, "At that time we did not think a great deal about it."[29]

She later attended Tennessee State University, a segregated college in Nashville. When Clayton was in her twenties, she traveled to Louisville, Kentucky, with her husband to visit her ailing father-in-law. When he died unexpectedly, she went to a downtown department store to buy a black hat to wear to his funeral. The clerks ignored her until one woman finally responded when Clayton indicated a hat that interested her: "You know you can't try this hat on. What are you trying to do? Make trouble?"[30] Only after the woman had thrown the hat down and walked away did Clayton realize why she had not been waited on. When Clayton complained to someone in the office that she was merely trying to buy a hat for the funeral of her father-in-law—a prominent man in the community whose picture had been on the front page of the newspaper that morning—she was taken to a higher floor, where the more expensive hats were kept; allowed to try on as many hats as she liked; and given a hat of her choice at no charge.[31]

Clayton speculated about why the incident had caught her so off guard: "Maybe I was insulated while growing up because of my family and friends, both in Oklahoma and Nashville. Maybe I shouldn't have thought that if you worked hard and got a good education, you would never have to face something like my experience in buying a hat." Instead, she remembered, "I had a college degree, money in my pocket, not a lot but adequate funds to afford any hat in that store. I was neatly groomed, but when I walked into that store to buy a hat, I was treated like 'just another nigger.' It hurts to this day."[32] Like many other African American parents, Clayton's had shielded her from contact with the indignities of segregation when she was a child in Oklahoma, and Clayton remembered her childhood as a happy one. Her parents taught her that if she worked hard and got an education, she would be successful. When she went to college in Nashville, she was again largely isolated from whites and surrounded by a supportive black community. Earlier in her twenties, she had worked for the National Urban League in Chicago, going out on job interviews to determine if employers would hire African American workers. Even this experience had not prepared her for an encounter in which she felt personally humiliated because of her race. The emotional power of this incident made conditions she had lived with her entire life much more difficult to bear; what once had been tolerable in her life now seemed intolerable.

An appreciation for how demoralizing segregation could be often came only when African Americans had traveled or lived outside the South for some time and then returned. Emogene Wilson grew up in a well-to-do black family in Memphis, Tennessee. She recalled that she had only become angry about segregation, especially on public buses, after living for a time in Washington, D.C., where she rode buses on a nonsegregated basis. Of her first time sitting at the front of a bus, she remembered, "It was the most traumatic thing that had ever happened to me. I sat on the front of the bus and everybody was sitting like nothing's wrong . . . . Nobody could feel what I was feeling. I had never sat that far up on the bus. I didn't know what it felt like."[33] She vowed never to sit at the back of a bus again, and, when she returned to Memphis, she refused to move when pressured to do so by whites. She explained the change in her attitude toward segregation: "You took things for granted then. It was a way of life. When you've been drinking purple water and you figured that was all the water, and everybody else was drinking purple water, you just drank the purple water. Until you find out there's some green water that you can drink and then you want some of that green water."[34] Wilson's critique of segregation was based on an awareness of alternatives. She only gained that awareness through experiencing unsegregated conditions elsewhere. Black southerners who had not traveled outside their home communities—a high number, given the cost and the obstacles posed by segregated or nonexistent accommodations—often lacked an awareness of alternatives on which to base a critique.[35]

Marian Wright Edelman's autobiography offers a powerful testament to the way in which an awareness of alternatives made segregated life unbearable. Edelman was born in Bennettsville, South Carolina, in 1940. Her parents, like those of Daisy Bates, combined the strategies of shielding their children from whites and building up their sense of self-worth. Edelman attended Spelman College in Atlanta starting in the late 1950s, and there she heard the inspirational words of chapel speakers such as Benjamin Mays and Howard Thurman and learned about civil rights activism from Howard Zinn. Recognizing her talent and ambition, Zinn and philanthropist Charles Merrill Jr. arranged for her to travel to Europe alone when she was nineteen years old. There she experienced life without segregation for the first time, after which she "could never return home to a segregated South and a constraining Spelman College in the same way." She explained, "After wandering the world, sharing the struggles for liberation of Hungarian, African, and Iranian students, sensing the longing for freedom of my Soviet student guides and counterparts who secretly shared their fears and frustrations, discerning the common thread of God in my fellow human beings, the genie of freedom could not be put back into the bottle of racial and gender segregation in America." Edelman had not only experienced freedom from racial and gender discrimination but also learned that other young people and people of color around the world were mobilizing to fight for their own freedom. Returning to the United States determined to work toward achieving an integrated life, she found a "powerful outlet" in Martin Luther King Jr. and the civil rights movement.[36]

Many African Americans had the opportunity to travel outside the region for the first time while serving in the military, especially in World War II. The chance to visit new places and observe different social conditions was not the only new experience afforded by military service. Some black service members interacted with whites on terms approaching equality and through their experience became aware of the existence of sympathetic whites. Andrew Wade, an African American man who in 1954 asked Anne and Carl Braden to purchase a house in a white Louisville neighborhood and then resell it to him, explained to Anne that his service in the navy in World War II helped inspire him to challenge segregation once he returned home.[37] Years later, in an oral history interview, Wade recalled, "I would see a house that I liked, then it occurred to me that this was in a forbidden area. And I said, 'This doesn't make any sense.' I served in the services and . . . felt highly . . . right in trying to buy what I wanted to buy with my own money. . . . And I saw that there's a, a wall built that I'm not supposed to penetrate right in . . . my own country. Then I'm gonna penetrate the wall and get what I want."[38] What Wade wanted was a quality home where he and his wife, Charlotte, could raise their growing family.

Anne Braden based her memoir of the Louisville incident around the concept of walls that separated black and white southerners. In *The Wall Between* she sought to explain both how Wade had been courageous enough to challenge residential segregation and why she and her husband had been willing to help. Of Wade's experience in the navy, she wrote, "For the first time in his life he came to know friendly white faces. White faces that looked you straight in the eye when they talked. White voices that called you man instead of 'boy.' White hands that clasped yours in a grip of friendship. White men who stood by your side as equals instead of standing before you as sentinels on the wall."[39] In short Andrew Wade experienced life without segregation for the first time, and he came home knowing life could be lived on a different basis. Braden theorized, "Somewhere the walls had crumbled in his mind." Segregation would never again have the same emotional power over him, even if he was still physically in its grasp. With the new knowledge that it was possible to find white allies in the struggle to end discrimination, he "began to look for gates in the wall in Louisville."[40] Like Edelman, Wade returned home determined to seek outlets through which to challenge segregation.[41]

Carl Rowan had a similar experience in the navy, where he was among the first African American officers trained for service in World War II. He wrote of his interactions with whites during training, "The white sailors and I found that the things we had in common far outweighed our differences. We all hated early morning calisthenics, Friday afternoon drills, and Saturday inspections."[42] In addition to the experience of simply living with whites on an unsegregated basis, Rowan was profoundly affected by the relationships he developed with whites. One of his bunkmates at the Naval Reserve Midshipman School at Fort Schuyler in the Bronx was a white man from Pascagoula, Mississippi. On the verge of flunking out and being sent home, the man explained to Rowan how their association had affected him. According to Rowan's rendering of the conversation, the man said, "A little while back, down yonder in Pascagoula, if somebody had told me I'd be sitting beside a Nigra tonight I'da called him a damn liar. If they'da told me I'd be sitting beside one and not minding it—I mean *liking* it, *appreciating* it—I'da knocked somebody's teeth out. But here I am, and before I go I just wanna tell you that, and wish you luck." Rowan wrote of this encounter, "As my bunkmate left, so did some of my bitterest feelings about my native South."[43] When black and white southerners trained and served together, they interacted in ways that had the potential to undermine racial lessons that had been learned on both sides.

Rowan wrote of the process by which he had learned to accept segregation as a fact of southern life, "It is only after you break away that you see the weblike nature of the conditioning process, the way it becomes day-to-day living, making segregation its own best defender and perpetuator." Rowan believed that if it had not been for his experiences in World War II, he might never have come to understand that segregation was not immutable; he might have lived out his life as other men he had known did, without ever examining why their society was organized as it was and without ever gaining an awareness of alternatives. Rowan described one incident in particular in which the new awareness he had gained in the military helped end the system's power over him. He stopped in his hometown of McMinnville, Tennessee, one night en route to a training mission in Miami. As he walked through a park in his uniform, he was mocked by a group of white men, one of whom joked to another, a sailor, that he should stand up and let the "nigger admiral" have his seat. As a result of their taunts, Rowan began to think about how there was no place in the park for him to sit down, even in uniform, as African Americans were forbidden to use the benches except when accompanying a white child as a servant. Rowan wrote, "I had walked through the park thousands of times with the subconscious realization that I was forbidden to sit down there . . . and I had accepted this without conscious questioning until a war came along." Now he could see that any white person—even the dirty, drunken sailor who issued him a mock salute—could sit down, while he, an officer in the United States Navy in a clean uniform, was forbidden to do so. Rowan had a physical response to this intellectual awakening: "It seemed as if my head were being inflated, because my jaws bulged with helpless anger. But I walked on, and when the sensation wore away, I was free of the web. The reconditioning process was under way."[44] Having overcome the system's mental hold over him, Rowan was free to imagine alternatives to segregation and began working to attain them.

The idea for *South of Freedom,* the book in which he wrote about this incident, derived from an unlikely friendship between Rowan and a white sailor from Brownsville, Texas, named Noah Brannon. Brannon and Rowan's friendship developed over time spent at the piano enjoying a shared love of music. As he became more comfortable in Rowan's presence, Brannon began to ask questions and make comments based on lessons he had learned about racial differences at home in Texas. He began by asking Rowan why he did not have the offensive odor that all blacks were supposed to have. Brannon confessed that he had never realized African Americans had last names, as he had always called black adults "Aunt" or "Uncle" followed by their first name. He expressed surprise when informed that African Americans in McMinnville could not buy a drink in a drugstore unless the clerk had paper cups available. Instead of responding to these questions with anger or laughter, Rowan recognized the sincerity that motivated them, patiently explained away the myths, and tried to clue Brannon in to the reality of what it meant to be a black man in the South. When word came that Rowan had been ordered to a new station, Brannon, knowing that Rowan planned to be a writer after the war, encouraged him, "Why don't you just sit down and tell all the little things it means to be a Negro in the South. . . . It all was right there before my eyes, but I'd never have known it. You probably can't get a drink of water in a Brownsville drugstore either." Rowan complied, and *South of Freedom* was the result of that request.[45]

Based on his own experiences, Noah Brannon believed white southerners were not fully aware of the differences in accommodations for blacks and whites. He thought that if whites were made aware of the disparity, they would feel differently about the system. He explained to Rowan, "If you're a Southern white person, you see these things and you don't. You're taught not to care. It's something that exists because it exists. . . . There must be many people in the South with big hearts but so little knowledge of this thing."[46] For white southerners to fully understand the impact of segregation on African Americans—and on themselves as whites—they often had to go through the same sort of awakening Brannon did as a result of his friendship with Rowan. One should note, however, that it was likely the emotional impact of this friendship—rather than merely learning more about segregated conditions—that sparked the change in Brannon.

Like African Americans, whites in the South who became critical of segregation underwent a period of gradual transformation before they were able to articulate that critique, and they, too, became aware of alternatives to segregated life through experiences such as travel, education, and military service. Edward Cohen, a Jewish writer from Mississippi, remembered of his childhood, "I didn't question the norm that blacks and whites never shared public facilities. The now-startling image, seen in documentaries, of 'white' and 'colored' drinking fountains was as everyday as a traffic light." When he was ten years old, he took a trip to New York with his parents and was shocked by what he saw. He explained, "There, black people acted like white people. They wore suits and ties, they spoke with educated accents, they used the rest room at the hotel, they sat at the next restaurant table. It was disorienting, as if I'd stepped into a racial *Twilight Zone*." When he returned to the South and matters returned to normal, he felt that "the familiar seemed oddly off-kilter." The experience, however, did not permanently transform his view of segregation. "Once home," Cohen confessed, "I quickly became reaccustomed to the old social order and comfortably categorized what I'd seen up north as an aberration."[47] Cohen's approach of dismissing troubling evidence that went against all the other lessons he had learned about segregation was likely common. The pressure to conform to the prevailing social norms, a pressure that for Cohen was probably amplified by his own status as part of a religious minority, may have been too great for one trip to undermine a lifetime of conditioning about proper racial protocol. Whites in the South who became critical of segregation typically remembered a series of small events that created increasing doubts in their minds.

Margaret Jones Bolsterli remembered a "spark" that made her realize her doubts about segregation might be justified. These doubts derived in large part from the disconnect she felt between the lessons she had been taught about the proper place for African Americans and the warm relationship she shared with her family's maid, Victoria. One day during Bolsterli's sophomore year in high school, her English teacher "ventured the hypothesis that blacks might be as competent as whites if they had a chance to prove it." Bolsterli believed it to be true as well, but she had never before heard an adult express this view. All of the other white authority figures in her life—parents, preachers, teachers, politicians, policemen, judges, and local professionals—"believed in the system" and "predicted the end of the world with the end of segregation." Yet here was a white teacher openly conceding the possibility that African Americans were intellectually equal to whites. Bolsterli wrote of this incident, "The spark had caught; that teacher touched a nerve that had never been touched before, and I wanted to be like her, the first liberal I had ever laid eyes on."[48] From this point on Bolsterli began to formulate a critique of segregation with the knowledge that she was not alone in questioning the received wisdom. Not all white southerners were fortunate enough to have had such knowledge.

An even more powerful moment of transition for Bolsterli came when she left her home in the Arkansas Delta in 1952 to attend Washington University in St. Louis, Missouri. Here she encountered a "shocking" sight that further indicted everything she had been taught to believe about the need for racial separation: she saw African Americans playing golf on a public course. "That glimpse of normality marked the end of the first phase of my life," she wrote of the incident; "for the simple sight of those black men playing golf, a sight that probably would not even have been noticed by somebody from the North, was, in my mind, like turning a corner and running into a burning bush." She recalled that "the sight called into question everything I had been led to believe up to that moment and constituted the first step in a long and painful journey toward revising my vision of the world."[49] Seeing African Americans interacting freely in a capacity reserved in the South exclusively for whites prompted Bolsterli to recognize that the warnings she had received about the end of the world accompanying the end of segregation had been unfounded.

Virginia Durr recalled a similar but more personal encounter that occurred when she left Alabama in the early 1920s to attend Wellesley College in Massachusetts. Like Bolsterli, Durr had learned the lessons of being a privileged white daughter of the South. When she entered the dining hall on the first night of her sophomore year, she was shocked to find a black student sitting at her assigned table. Durr described her reaction: "I nearly fell over dead. I couldn't believe it . . . . I promptly got up, marched out of the room, went upstairs, and waited for the head of the house to come."[50] The head of the house was a no-nonsense woman from New England who informed Durr that she would have to adhere to the rules of the college or else go home. Durr tried in vain to explain that she was "from Alabama" and that her father "would have a fit" if she ate with a black person. She was forced to decide between telling her father, who would almost certainly have made her come home, or staying at Wellesley, where she was dating a Harvard man and generally having the time of her life. Even though she "had been taught that if [she] ate at the table of a Negro girl [she] would be committing a terrible sin against society," she decided to risk damnation rather than forgo the good times at Wellesley. After a month of eating with her, Durr found the girl to be intelligent and polite, and she discovered that they were both southerners who shared an affinity for southern cooking. Hardly a moment of searching internal transformation, this episode did alert Durr to the fact that her northern friends and the college administrators did not share her racial views. Durr concluded that while this incident "may not have been crucial at the time," it nevertheless was "the origin of a doubt."[51] For the first time her faith in the sanctity of segregation wavered.

As it did with African Americans, military service could have a profound impact on the racial views of white southerners. Reverend Will Campbell served in a military unit that was stationed in the South Pacific for several months during World War II. Unlike Andrew Wade, Carl Rowan, and the whites who trained and served with them, Campbell experienced the war on a completely segregated basis, a more common experience among World War II soldiers, as the military had not yet been formally or widely desegregated. Black soldiers had different camps and bases, and he had virtually no contact with them.[52] What Campbell deemed his "conversion" experience was instead brought on by a letter he received from his brother, who was also in the military. Joe Campbell had been injured in a car accident while home in Mississippi on furlough, and during his convalescence he had read Howard Fast's novel about the Reconstruction-era South, *Freedom Road*, which had been issued by the Council on Books in Wartime, an independent agency working with the military to issue inexpensive, easy-to-carry books for service members.[53] Joe Campbell wrote his brother a letter full of "did you knows?" asking if he knew about the many accomplishments of African Americans and the numerous hardships they had endured since the end of slavery. He predicted of the book, "It'll turn your head around." Will Campbell felt compelled by his brother's urgency to read the book, which was also available where he was stationed.[54]

Campbell called the story "the most powerful and compelling words I had read in my nineteen years." He identified with the lower-class whites in the book and explained that the African Americans "were those we grew up thinking we had to oppose. I had never questioned why we were so taught before, that it was because for us to do otherwise would constitute a threat to those who ruled us before the Civil War and who had in just one decade after the war succeeded in ruling us again." As a result of reading the book, he wrote, "I knew that my life would never be the same. I knew that the tragedy of the South would occupy the remainder of my days. It was a conversion experience comparable to none I had ever had, and I knew it would have to find expression."[55] Although Campbell did not experience life without segregation in the military, he was exposed through his service to new ideas about race, and he returned home determined to work toward challenging the system.[56]

In the years following World War II, the military undertook a more concerted effort to experiment with integration, culminating in Harry Truman's executive order desegregating the military in 1948. Larry L. King was the beneficiary of such experimentation when he was assigned to the army's Signal Corps Photo Center in Astoria, Long Island, in 1947. Here the army systematically integrated black and white troops in an effort to assess how best to implement desegregation branch wide. Growing up in Texas, King had been steeped in racial stereotypes, and he originally attempted to join the navy "because it was said to admit fewer blacks." While in the army, however, his views slowly began to change as he encountered African Americans as equals and superiors in the command structure and as he came into occasional social contact with interracial couples in New York City. King described his growing awareness and its impact on his relationships back home: "Though my racial experiences in the Army and in the East had been less complete than I then presumed, exposure to black people at least had taught me that they had minds, dreams, and hurts like the rest of us, and in no way deserved their automatic exclusion." He wrote that learning about "the million mindless 'little' humiliations" endured by African Americans "stirred my tardy rage and soon caused me to be looked on as a little crazy and unreliable."[57] Once King returned to Texas, he found that his new outlook on race and segregation affected his relationships with his father, his friends from high school, and his new classmates at Texas Tech, many of whom had served in the military without having made the same transformation he had. The experience of nonsegregated living made it much more difficult for King to return to the life he had once lived. Conditions he had previously thought nothing of now bothered him to the point that he had trouble interacting with his family and his peers.

Experiences such as those King had in the army and in the eclectic social environment of New York City had the potential to show white southerners that the lessons they had learned about the disastrous consequences of interracial interaction were wrong. More often than not, the rigors of segregation were such that white southerners had to travel outside the region in order to experience such life-altering encounters. When they returned to the South, they found it difficult to resume their formerly comfortable lives, and they could locate neither an outlet for their new energies nor anyone with whom to discuss their insights.

Whites experienced awakenings about race and segregation not only by realizing the myths they had learned about the consequences of interracial contact were false but also by gaining an appreciation for the emotional consequences of segregation both for African Americans and for themselves as whites. James Farmer remembered a road trip he and another black student at Wiley College in Texas took in the late 1930s with a white University of Texas sociology graduate student, Cy Record. Embarking on a trip that took them to Richmond, Virginia, to attend the National Negro Congress and the Southern Negro Youth Conference, the three students shared a commitment to racial justice.[58] For the first time in his life, however, Record discovered how it felt to be discriminated against. When the students entered a restaurant along the way and attempted to eat lunch, they were told they could either eat in the kitchen or go to the home of a black woman nearby who sometimes cooked meals for black travelers. Record indignantly informed the proprietor that he was "not eating in anybody's kitchen." The interracial group resorted to buying groceries and making sandwiches in their car. They also opted to sleep in the car, as there were few hotels where they could stay. Sleeping by the side of the road during the night, they were confronted by a white police officer who, believing Record's story that he was "a Negro," proceeded to speculate on what a "good-lookin' wench" his mother must have been to have had a baby by a white man. Farmer concluded of the education in race relations that Record received on this trip, "Sociology textbooks had not prepared him for this."[59]

Farmer recalled that once they had returned to his professor's house in Texas, "Cy Record was virtually in tears. The trip for him had . . . been at once a revelation and a crucifixion." Record explained of his reaction, "I'm not blind and I'm not insensitive. How could I possibly have grown up and lived in the South all these years without seeing, without knowing, the hell that we put you through every day of your lives? How do you live with it? How do you take it? How do you stand it? Why don't you commit suicide?"[60] There was a difference between knowing segregation was wrong and grasping its full emotional impact on African Americans. Even his commitment to social justice and his graduate studies had not prepared Record for the experience of traveling through the South being refused access to services he had taken for granted his entire life.

While realizing the emotional impact of segregation on African Americans could be jarring, the realization that often had the most profound impact on whites was that of understanding segregation's emotional hold on them. Such a realization could be as simple as coming to understand the strength of one's own racism. Novelist Tim McLaurin, who grew up in North Carolina, remembered a startling episode that occurred when a young black woman, Mabel Williams, who was the sister of his childhood friend L.J., made lunch for them one day. McLaurin wrote of this incident, "I had lifted my sandwich and taken my first bite when I noticed the print of her fingers mashed in the soft bread. No dirt, just a ghost left where her slender fingers had closed the halves. I stared at the bread, chewed what was in my mouth, and felt it grow larger and larger. She had touched my food. Plain and simple."[61] Although he had seen Williams wash her hands before she made lunch and she had made whole meals for him many times in the past, he was overcome by revulsion at the physical evidence that she had touched his food with her bare hands. He excused himself from the table and spit out the food, declining her offer to make him another sandwich if he was still hungry. McLaurin concluded that this incident "proved my own heart was infected with the concept that other human beings might be inferior to me for the matter of their skin colors."[62] He remembered feeling ashamed at his actions because of his affection for the Williams family.

Melton McLaurin, also from North Carolina, recalled a similar incident of physical revulsion involving contact with a black friend. McLaurin and an interracial group of boys were playing basketball one day with a ball that needed to be reinflated frequently. Part of the process of inflating the ball involved wetting the needle with saliva, and one of the black boys, Bobo, wet the needle with which one of the other boys struggled to inflate the ball.[63] Impatient with their efforts, McLaurin grabbed the needle and put it in his mouth to rewet it; upon doing so, he quickly realized the needle had just been in Bobo's mouth. McLaurin wrote rather dramatically of his response, "I was jolted by one of the most shattering emotional experiences of my young life. . . . Bolts of prejudice, waves of prejudice that I could literally feel sent my head reeling and buckled my knees."[64] After he struggled successfully to maintain his composure in front of Bobo, he went around a building, hidden from the view of the other players, and repeatedly rinsed out his mouth, trying to remove all traces of Bobo's spit from his body.

Like Tim McLaurin, Melton McLaurin was surprised by the strength of his reaction. In his study of race and the senses, Mark M. Smith wrote of this incident, "McLaurin's reaction to Bobo's spit revealed the tension facing liberal southerners, people who wanted to use their intellect to explore the inconsistencies of the system of segregation but whose own history, upbringing, and racial privilege rendered them hostage to raw feeling and the compass of the gut."[65] McLaurin recalled that this encounter showed him "the emotional power that racial prejudice and segregation held over whites as well as blacks." For the first time he felt that adherence to the rules of segregation affected him as a white person in ways with which he was not comfortable. While the power of this incident and the confusion it created over his proper relationship to African Americans did not make complete sense to him at the time, McLaurin remembered, "the understanding that segregation was so powerful a force, that it could provoke such violent emotional responses within me, for the first time raised questions in my mind about the institution, serious questions that adults didn't want asked and, as I would later discover, that they never answered."[66] Segregation did not matter much in the lives of whites so long as it merely conferred on them a life of relative privilege that they took for granted, but once white southerners came to understand that segregation controlled and limited their lives as surely as it did those of black southerners, they were much more likely to question the wisdom of the system.

Strong physical reactions rooted in childhood lessons about the perils of interracial contact could occur even in white southerners who had already made a conscious decision to oppose segregation. Like a number of other white southerners, Dorothy Dawson Burlage recalled that she first began to have doubts about segregation when she saw the effect of discrimination on the African Americans who worked in her home. The strength and dignity of these individuals belied all that she had been taught about the proper place for blacks, and she was disturbed by the social barriers that separated them from her. In 1956, after a year at Mary Baldwin College, a private women's college in Virginia, where she had been criticized for writing a paper opposing school segregation, Burlage transferred to the more hospitable climate of the University of Texas at Austin. There she became involved with the YWCA and a group called the Christian Faith and Life Community, both of which were active in the cause of social justice. Driving to a lecture sponsored by "the Community" one evening, Burlage offered a ride to a white student, who in turn offered one to two black students, one of whom was a black male, who sat in the front seat next to Burlage. Such close proximity under these circumstances violated any number of rules in the segregated code, including the most important one about prohibiting contact between black men and white women, particularly in an enclosed space like an automobile. Burlage's response was powerful and immediate: "In a split second, I felt my world turn upside down. For the first time in my life, I experienced being in a situation of apparent social intimacy with a black man—not just in a meeting or a class, but in my mother's car, breaking my mother's rules and violating nineteen years of her training." She recalled feeling "physically sick with fear that I had crossed the color line and worried about possible retribution for breaking this southern tradition."[67] Despite the fact that she was already opposed to segregation, she could not control her response to the situation, nor could she undo the impact of years of racial conditioning.

Burlage learned a valuable lesson about segregation through this interracial encounter. "The very intensity of my reaction taught me how deep had been my socialization into the racist system and how irrational it was to have such a reaction," she explained.[68] She was determined that other white children not be raised learning the lessons about race and segregation that she had, and she reaffirmed her commitment to ending segregation. Gaining this insight—that segregation controlled and limited the lives of white as well as black southerners—was one of the most powerful means by which whites became critical of the system. This was the foundation upon which Lillian Smith had based her critique. She observed that "what cruelly shapes and cripples the personality of one is as cruelly shaping and crippling the personality of the other."[69] Once whites became aware not only of what segregation was doing to African Americans but also of what it was doing to themselves *as whites,* they found much greater cause to criticize the system.

Anne Braden experienced a realization of this kind and went so far as to suggest that the emotional impact of segregation might be greater on whites than on African Americans. She credited early lessons about the "brotherhood of man" that she had learned in the Episcopal Church with forming the foundation of her critique of segregation. Her observation of her housekeeper's daughter—a young black girl who wore Braden's ill-fitting hand-me-down dresses and had to stay hidden in the kitchen when she came to work with her mother—convinced Braden that black southerners might not be as comfortable "in their place" as her parents had suggested they were. Although Braden had begun to doubt that African Americans "were happy with things as they are," she recalled, "the thing that it took me much longer to articulate was the other side of the coin: the fact that I was not happy with things as they were either."[70] Her effort to reconcile the contradictions between what she had learned about segregation and what she saw of its impact on the people she knew led her to a conclusion: "*Racial bars build a wall not only around the Negro people but around the white people as well, cramping their spirits and causing them to grow in distorted shapes.*"[71] Braden was not describing "the wall between" black and white southerners, as the title of her memoir suggested; instead, she envisioned a set of walls, one that worked to keep blacks out of white society and one that worked to keep whites in.[72] To continue with this metaphor, freedom for all depended on blacks working their way through their wall while whites simultaneously worked their way through theirs. Only when both black and white southerners overcame their racial conditioning could segregation be successfully challenged.

A series of encounters helped Braden further transcend her own conditioning. She remembered a conversation with an older white man about the idea of a federal anti-lynching law. She revered this man as a leader in his church and community, a man to whom anyone could go for help, but she also admitted that he believed in segregation. She did not realize the intensity of his belief until he exploded during their conversation with the statement: "We have to have a good lynching every once in a while to keep the nigger in his place." The segregated system had taught this loving man whom she respected to advocate murder. Braden wrote, "I thought to myself then and have often wondered since, *What could segregation ever do to the Negro as terrible as the thing it had done to this white man?*"

She remembered having been "horrified" by the system's impact. In the epilogue to a later edition of *The Wall Between,* Braden identified this man as her father, Gambrell McCarty.[73]

Aside from building a critique of segregation based on what she saw it doing to those around her, Braden made considerable progress toward overcoming her racial conditioning by having dinner with a young African American actress while visiting a friend in New York City. Although Braden was initially apprehensive about eating with a black person, she was interested in becoming an actress at the time, so she quickly became involved in an engaging conversation with the woman. Upon realizing she had "completely forgotten that there was a difference in our color" during the course of the conversation, Braden had a sense that "all the cramping walls of a lifetime seemed to come tumbling down in that moment."[74] Not only had she not suffered any ill effects as a result of this integrated meal, but she had also gained the valuable experience of interacting on terms of equality with an African American who excelled at a field in which she was interested.

Braden recalled a final encounter that impressed upon her the importance of taking action to end segregation. While working in Birmingham as a newspaper reporter covering the happenings at the city courthouse, Braden joined a colleague for coffee one morning, after calling around to check if anything important had happened overnight. When her colleague asked her if there was any news, she replied, "Everything quiet. Nothing but a colored murder."[75] The African American waitress who was at their table pouring coffee immediately tensed up at her words, and Braden squelched the urge to apologize and explain that while she cared about the murder, the paper would not consider the story newsworthy. As a result of this incident, Braden began to recognize her own complicity in the system and came to the conclusion that unless she worked to end segregation, she would continue to be complicit. The only way she could free herself from segregation's effects was by challenging the system.

Braden described the process by which she came to understand segregation's impact on both black and white southerners as "like a picture slowly coming clear in the developing fluid" as "the truth appeared before my eyes."[76] In the decades that preceded the civil rights movement, a number of black and white southerners were affected by the presence of such "developing fluid," which gradually made clear to them the ways in which segregation controlled and limited their lives and the lives of other southerners. Whether through military service, travel away from home for the first time to go to college, a courageous lesson taught by a teacher in a southern classroom, or a subtle moment of transition with a friend, each snapshot of experience helped the individual see the overall picture of segregation in the South more clearly. Each moment of discovery contributed to the individual southerner's critique of the system. Each experience made life in the segregated South a little less bearable.

For African Americans their earliest awareness of segregation involved an understanding that life would be different for them because they were black in a world controlled by whites. Slowly they began to realize "something was wrong here," even if they could not yet say what it was about the interactions between black and white southerners that bothered them. Still, they could live for many years in the system without feeling the full impact of the indignities segregated life had to offer. Once they had experienced those emotional effects and become aware of the existence of alternatives, their lives became increasingly intolerable, and they began seeking ways to challenge segregation. Braden wrote of her friend, "The thing that Andrew Wade had that most of the Negroes of his father's and grandfather's generations did not have was the knowledge that the wall was not gateless—that it was possible to find a way through."[77] Perhaps the most significant awakening that individual African Americans experienced was the realization that there were gates in the wall; there were attainable alternatives to segregation. Life in the South had not always been lived on a segregated basis, and it need not be lived on that basis in the future. Segregation was a condition to be remedied, a problem to be fixed, instead of a fact of life that must be borne. The civil rights movement would provide an outlet for those who had come to find life in the segregated South unbearable; for others it would provide the developing fluid through which they, too, would come to view southern life as such.

For white southerners the realizations of these years were different but no less powerful. Discovering all of the ways segregation made life different and more difficult for African Americans was startling to some whites. Coming to a full understanding of the emotional impact of the segregated system on African Americans was even more so. Whites struggled at times to reconcile the lessons about democracy and the commonality of all people they had been taught in their homes, schools, and churches with those about the sanctity of segregation they had learned in the very same institutions. Travel and the contact with new ideas and new people that accompanied it taught some white southerners that the sky did not fall and the world did not end when blacks and whites interacted on terms of equality. The most profound awakening for white southerners occurred when they realized the impact segregation had on their own lives. They could not deviate from the racial lessons they had learned even if they wanted to. White society would not allow it, and neither would their own emotions. A small number of white southerners in the years preceding the civil rights movement slowly came to understand what much of the white South would realize in the coming years: segregation was costing them something. These white southerners began to recognize that maintaining segregation called on them to make sacrifices they were no longer willing to make. Civil rights activists would work to teach white southerners this lesson even as they sought to teach African Americans that there were alternatives to segregation and viable means of attaining them.

CONCLUSION

I n order to accomplish their goal of ending legalized segregation and disfranchisement, civil rights activists had to target and overcome the childhood conditioning of both black and white southerners. In their homes white southerners had learned that segregation was not to be discussed and questions about the system were rarely answered. In school they learned about American democracy but not how that democracy conflicted with the tenets of segregation. In their churches white southerners learned to save their dimes and say their prayers for their black "brothers" in Africa but were rarely called upon to extend their compassion to African Americans down the street. For their part African American parents and teachers built community institutions that served as sources of strength and stability. Within those institutions black children learned that they had value as children of God, but many of them also learned that the injustice of segregation was a fact of southern life. In order to undermine these lessons, civil rights leaders had to understand both the nature of white southerners' attachment to segregation and the reticence of black southerners to confront the system head-on and then craft appeals to each group.

The movement targeted not only black and white southerners but also the federal government and spectators across the country and around the world. By staging local protests and making canny use of the media, civil rights leaders sought to educate each audience. Movement leaders had to convince black southerners of the efficacy of nonviolent direct action and then train and mobilize them. Demonstrations and the violence they often provoked served to dramatize the injustice of segregation for a national and international viewing audience. The movement worked to leverage the resulting national outcry and international embarrassment, along with fears of social disorder and constitutional concerns about defying federal power, to compel the federal government to intervene. Finally, civil rights leaders sought to use local and regional protests to teach white southerners how much segregation was costing or could be made to cost them and to convince them that dismantling segregation and disfranchisement would benefit not only black southerners but themselves as well.

Civil rights leaders explicitly conceptualized the movement as an educational campaign. John Lewis explained of the use of nonviolent direct action during the 1960 Nashville sit-ins, "Among so many other things, this was about education, pricking consciences, teaching one race about another and, if need be, about itself."[1] Martin Luther King Jr. wrote of nonviolent direct action, "It educates its myriad participants, socially and morally."[2] Thus, when the Southern Christian Leadership Conference (SCLC) initiated a successful boycott of downtown Birmingham businesses in 1963, the organization, in King's terms, "educated them forcefully to the dignity of the Negro as a consumer."[3] King's SCLC colleague Andrew Young also described the educational component of the Birmingham campaign: "From the very beginning we spent considerable time organizing— even orchestrating—the image of our demonstrations. We intended them to tell a story, what [fellow SCLC activist] Jim Bevel called 'socio-dramas'; they were conscious efforts to dramatize the conditions and realities of segregation."[4] The movement thus engaged in intentional instruction of both its actors and its audience.

As an educational campaign, the civil rights movement succeeded where earlier efforts had achieved limited results. In the decades prior to the movement, moderate and liberal voices in the South had sought to bring about gradual improvement in race relations primarily within the confines of the segregated system through education and through communication across the color line. In addition to the educational efforts of this type pursued by white religious denominations, a variety of secular interracial organizations, including the Commission on Interracial Cooperation (CIC), the Southern Conference for Human Welfare (SCHW), the Southern Regional Council (SRC), and the Southern Conference Educational Fund (SCEF), pursued to some extent this measured strategy.[5] White liberals were the driving force behind these organizations, which worked to promote better understanding between racial groups and focused on a slew of related issues, such as preventing lynching, abolishing the poll tax, and improving educational opportunities for African Americans, but were reluctant to target segregation itself.[6] David Chappell portrayed the work of such organizations as an effort to "educate away" racial prejudice and characterized this educational approach as a "tactic of trying to awaken a 'silent South' by mere repetition of dissenting ideas."[7]

Arkansas journalist Harry Ashmore described "the thesis of Southern white liberals" as the belief that "an evolutionary process would in due time bring the Negro justice and equality, while anything that smacked of revolution would only bring disaster."[8] The specter of such a disaster—the often promised race war that would accompany any drastic attempt to challenge segregation—operated to keep liberal and moderate whites from supporting measures that might result in violence or social disorder, thus David Cohn's warning that encouraging opposition to segregation would only make a tolerable situation intolerable. Whatever the drawbacks of a covert gradualism, that strategy was better, in the minds of white liberals, than the perils that might follow an open confrontation with the system. The goal of these reformers was to ameliorate racial conditions without provoking the type of elements that later came to be associated with massive resistance. Anne Braden described the thinking of such "liberal forces" in Louisville, particularly those associated with the city's main newspaper, the *Courier-Journal*: "They believed that the best way was to proceed gradually, inch by inch, altering the segregated pattern of Louisville life so slowly and imperceptibly that the die-hard segregationist would hardly realize things were changing—boiling the frog without his realizing he was being boiled."[9] If only they could figure out a way to initiate change without tipping off the opposition, their thinking went, they might be able to accomplish meaningful social reform.

White liberals argued for improved race relations in the South on the basis of two distinct appeals. The first approach was enshrined in Gunnar Myrdal's 1944 tome, *An American Dilemma,* in which he called for *"an educational offensive against racial intolerance."*[10] Myrdal believed white Americans faced a "moral dilemma" because their treatment of African Americans conflicted with the "American Creed" of democracy, justice, and personhood. Myrdal thought considerable headway would be made in improving race relations if white Americans only "knew the facts."[11] David M. Kennedy described Myrdal's objectives: "He aimed not only to make his white American readers see the enormity of their racial system but also to prompt them to change it, and he assumed that by accomplishing the first objective he would automatically realize the second."[12] Key to Myrdal's argument was his conclusion that "in their fight for equality," African Americans "have their allies in the white man's own conscience."[13] Kennedy explained, "Myrdal adopted a strategy with roots in American political culture that reached back to Abraham Lincoln and beyond: it consisted in the simple belief that a factual appeal to the better angels of their nature would induce Americans to do the right thing."[14] Although Myrdal asserted in one of the appendices to his massive study that "facts by themselves do not improve anything" and only had value to the extent that they made white southerners reexamine their justifications for racial discrimination, Kennedy succinctly captured the primary takeaway from Myrdal's study: a rational appeal to the conscience of white Americans would convince them that segregation and disfranchisement were wrong and should be eliminated.[15] Although Myrdal called for a more comprehensive educational program than had yet been attempted, his work nonetheless validated the liberals' approach.

The second appeal made by white liberals was to self-interest. Myrdal identified this strategy and occasionally engaged in it himself, suggesting that dire domestic and international consequences awaited the nation if conditions for African Americans were not improved. Thus, he warned, "*America is free to choose whether the Negro shall remain her liability or become her opportunity.*"[16] A secondary line of reasoning for Myrdal—appeals to individual, regional, and national self-interest—served for many white liberals as the primary selling point in favor of improved race relations. In his classic study of southern liberals, Morton Sosna traced the tradition of appealing to white self-interest back to the nineteenth century: "From George Washington Cable to Lillian Smith, Southern liberals not only sought to upgrade the status of the region's blacks but also attempted to liberate their fellow whites from what they saw as self-defeating prejudices." Sosna also found the idea that "race chauvinism harmed whites more than blacks" to be "a persistent theme of Southern liberalism."[17] Liberals often argued explicitly on "a cost-accounting basis"; that is, they maintained that the cost to the region in terms of economic growth, educational attainment, reputation, and other tangible and intangible factors was too high for racial discrimination to continue.[18] In holding African Americans down, their argument went, the South compromised its own development; therefore, the racial climate in the region must be improved for the South's own good.

White liberals ultimately believed patient appeals—whether to the better angels of the white South's nature or to self-interest—would bring about social change on the South's own terms. A belief in the prospect of what legal scholar Michael Klarman called "indigenous racial change" rested either on the assumption that material conditions in the South in terms of industrialization, urbanization, and rising education levels were rendering the institution of segregation obsolete or on confidence that the educational campaign of southern liberals would eventually work.[19] Both contemporary observers and historians have viewed the aftermath of World War II as a time when the potential for homegrown change was particularly high. In his study of the era John Egerton identified a "moment of opportunity" after the war "when the South might have moved boldly and decisively to heal itself, to fix its own social wagon voluntarily" and to do so "not simply because it was right, but also because it was in our own best interest."[20] While Egerton looked back on what might have been, Myrdal wrote in the midst of World War II about the prospects for social change once the war against fascism had been won. He believed "the world conflict and America's exposed position as the defender of the democratic faith" were "accelerating an ideological process which was well under way."[21] He thought "the racial beliefs which defended caste" were "being torn away" and saw this trend as "probably irreversible and cumulative."[22] Myrdal's conclusion that the war would hasten the seemingly inevitable resolution of the American "dilemma" in the direction of the American Creed further reinforced white liberals' program of gradual, voluntary change.

Despite such optimism, the argument that segregation would have eventually died out or been educated away without the interposition of an active, black-led civil rights movement is unrealistic. When "indigenous racial change" came to the region, it was the result of open confrontation with the segregated system rather than a by-product of economic modernization or world war and was led by African Americans rather than white liberals.[23] Egerton conceded white liberals' inability to capitalize on the moment of opportunity: "Realistically, they never had the numbers, the discipline, the unity, or the fervor to pull it off."[24] Sosna came to a similar conclusion: "The South's liberals possessed neither the power nor desire to force social change. If Southern blacks had followed only the Southern liberals' prescriptions for a gradual adjustment, it is doubtful whether the region's racial practices would have altered dramatically."[25] The educational campaign of white liberals "failed to awaken a Silent South"; that is, it failed to unearth and mobilize a numerically significant proportion of southern whites who would support voluntary social change.[26]

The chronology of the late 1940s and early 1950s argues against the inevitability of such change. Egerton stressed the importance of the Cold War context in curtailing the moment of opportunity, asserting that by the late 1940s "communism was getting the blame for almost every deviation from the political or social status quo. From then on, social reform of any kind was a hard sell. The time for quietly making little changes was past—if there ever really had been such a time."[27] The Bradens found this to be true in 1954, when, despite having participated in various leftist organizations in the 1940s with relative impunity, they bought a house in a white neighborhood for Andrew Wade and were accused of participating in a communist conspiracy and charged with sedition. Egerton likewise observed that while the questioning of segregation by an individual crusading journalist might "have been tolerated in the Roosevelt-Truman years . . . it was becoming unacceptable to most Southern whites by the political season of 1950, and downright dangerous by the time Dwight Eisenhower was elected two years later."[28] By the early 1950s it was becoming not easier but ever more difficult to work toward gradually dismantling segregation.

The *Brown* decision and the black activism and white resistance that developed in response to it rendered the strategy of gradualism irrelevant and put white liberals largely out of business, except for those who were willing to play a supporting role in the black-led movement. Egerton wrote of these gradualists, "Until the end of World War II, the term 'liberal segregationist' was not an oxymoron in the South, but after the war it gradually became uncommon for anyone to be accorded the luxury of such a contradiction. By 1955, when the middle rock had eroded to a razor's edge, people had to choose to be one or the other, a liberal or a segregationist."[29] The story of white southern liberals after 1955 is actually a story not of less silence but more. Sarah Patton Boyle recalled, for example, that up until the time of the *Brown* decision, she had spoken privately to many white southerners who indicated their willingness to accept desegregation. She observed of the aftermath of *Brown*, however, that "within six weeks after the decision, it was as though a door had been slammed shut. I had every reason to be optimistic until then, but the politicians took over, and the church failed, and the papers failed. It became hard to keep my faith in the South."[30] Martin Luther King Jr., who had expressed some hope in the late 1950s of receiving support from crucial segments of the white community, most notably the churches, later repeatedly decried "the appalling silence of the good people."[31]

As the aura of inevitability surrounding segregation began to disperse in the mid-1950s, white southerners who were critical of the system yet remained silent now did so in more direct response to an awareness of the consequences of speaking out. Sosna observed of conditions in the late 1950s, "Operating in a hostile climate, white Southern liberals, if they spoke out at all, undertook the unenviable task of opposing Southern school boards, sheriffs, politicians, White Citizens Councils, and resurrected Ku Klux Klans in their own bailiwicks and at unfavorable odds. Theirs would be a lonelier, more dangerous struggle than the one Southern liberals had faced when Jim Crow had appeared impregnable."[32] To return to the notion of a series of safeguards for the segregated system, the first two levels—which discouraged conscious examination and discussion of the system, respectively—had ceased to operate as effectively once events such as the *Brown* decision, the Emmett Till lynching, and the Montgomery bus boycott put the issue of segregation's future on the national agenda. With the culture of silence that had served to maintain segregation since the 1920s compromised, the system's additional safeguards—fear of consequences and actual consequences, the most extreme form of which being physical violence or even death—would now operate openly to defend the system.

Egerton correctly diagnosed the fundamental problem with the educational campaign of white liberals: "The progressives couldn't overcome emotion with logic."[33] Myrdal's confidence that a rigorous educational initiative would bring about the eventual resolution of the American dilemma had rested on his underlying assumption that "people want to be rational" and on his belief in the ongoing "decay of the caste theory." Moreover, he argued both that "the basic racial inferiority doctrine is being undermined by research and education" and that "the younger generations of Southern whites are less indoctrinated against the Negro than their parents were."[34] His second conclusion made his first less significant. Even if historical justifications for segregation were being undermined through scientific research and intellectual argument, such "decay" did not matter if white southern children were learning fewer of those justifications as time went on. The argument that segregation could be educated away did not take into account the fact that, owing to their childhood racial conditioning and the silence surrounding the system, white southerners had developed an unexamined emotional attachment to segregation that did not respond to patient, rational appeals. White children learned to obey the rules of segregation before they understood why they were supposed to follow them. By 1920 the justifications they did learn about segregation were more often lessons learned by rote than they were explicit, considered grounds for upholding the system. When children attempted to find out why they had to follow the rules, parents silenced their questions, and children eventually learned to stop asking them. As white southerners grew older, questioning segregation—aside from being foolhardy—could seem to constitute a betrayal of the trusted parents and teachers who had taught them to accept the system. Imbued with all of the emotion of childhood and rarely consciously considered, white southerners' attachment to segregation was not easily dislodged. This aspect of the system was the source of much of its strength and resilience even as the original justifications for the institution lost intellectual respectability, material conditions in the region changed, and critiques of segregation mounted.[35]

Other observers have noted the nature of white southerners' attachment to segregation and the difficulty of overcoming it. Mark Smith argued that the very purpose of segregation was "to make a previously contingent, complex world simple to the point of unthinking when it came to race." Locating the source of racial prejudice in the gut-dictated realm of the senses rather than specifically in the nature of childhood conditioning, Smith characterized white performance of segregation as "unthinking, automated choreography," in which one could *feel* race rather than seeing it or thinking about it.[36] Drawing on her own experiences with segregation, Anne Braden observed that "race prejudice being an emotional thing cannot be removed by intellectual arguments alone." She believed only "some real emotional experience, such as a deep friendship across the race bars . . . can shake the emotional patterns of a lifetime."[37] Jason Sokol argued that white stereotypes of black southerners "proved rarely susceptible to logic, reason, or even events." He explained, "Once white southerners, like any other humans, latched on to a belief and internalized it, that belief died only under extraordinary circumstances."[38] There could be no real moment of opportunity until a more effective method had been devised to combat the effects of white southerners' racial conditioning.

The civil rights movement would provide the "extraordinary circumstances" through which white southerners would come to examine their own commitment to segregation and make a conscious choice about whether the system was worth the cost it would take to maintain it. The significance of those whites who became critical of segregation before the *Brown* decision was not their numbers, as most observers now agree that such dissenters were relatively few.[39] Their significance, instead, was what they taught civil rights leaders about the basis upon which white southerners might be convinced to relinquish segregation. David Chappell argued that these leaders had gained from pre-*Brown* white liberals, "the complex and supple strategic insight that some white southerners had an interest in abandoning the system that claimed to help *all* white southerners."[40] Among those southern whites who became critical of segregation in the years before *Brown,* many did so not primarily out of concern for black southerners but, rather, because they realized the adverse impact the system had on them *as whites.* Virginia Durr explained of her support for ending segregation, "I have never acted from benevolence but from a burning desire to change the South so I could be at home in it."[41] Lillian Smith described her activism in similar terms, writing, "You know, I am rather selfish in my attitude toward race relations. I want to make life easier for all colored people; but I want to make it easier for us white people to live with our own consciences, and easier for our children to continue to grow as human beings."[42] A younger generation of whites echoed these sentiments. Student Nonviolent Coordinating Committee (SNCC) activist Bob Zellner recalled that he was not acting on a "missionary impulse" when he joined the movement: "I was fighting for my own rights as well"; "I got involved to free myself."[43] Likewise, fellow SNCC activist Constance Curry described the significance of her realization that "segregation took away *my* personal freedom as surely as if I were bound by invisible chains."[44] Drawing on such sentiments, civil rights activists learned to target white southerners by teaching them how much segregation was costing—or could be made to cost—them.

Activists appealed to white southerners in terms of individual, regional, and national self-interest. Martin Luther King Jr. pointed to the "crushing price" that lower-income whites paid in terms of "insecurity, hunger, ignorance, and hopelessness" in return for "empty pride" in the "racial myth" that was white supremacy. Segregation, in his view, had "placed the whole region socially, educationally, and economically behind the rest of the nation." He warned of the racial climate in the country, "How we deal with this crucial situation will determine our moral health as individuals, our cultural health as a region, our political health as a nation, and our prestige as a leader of the free world." If the problem of segregation was not solved, however, "America will be on the road to its self-destruction."[45] Looking back, Andrew Young explained, "Segregation was choking off the economic lifeblood of the South," and it took demonstrations, lawsuits, and the spectacle of violence "to persuade white Southerners to do what was really in their own interest." Young observed that in Birmingham, as in South Africa decades later, economic pressure had in the end persuaded white elites that the "price" of racial separation "was too steep."[46] Zellner recalled that as the 1960s wore on, he and others engaged in local organizing efforts did not try to "appeal to peoples' consciousness [sic], their Christianity, their love or anything like that, because everybody who could be appealed to on that basis" was "already in." Instead, they told whites that it was "to their material benefit" to relinquish their prejudices and make common economic cause with African Americans for the good of both groups.[47]

King ultimately hoped "the simple logic and justice in their own interests" would lead whites "to the only acceptable solution—to accept equality and maintain it on the best level for both races."[48] His invocation of logic highlights the rational nature of the appeal to self-interest and thus reveals a degree of continuity with appeals made by white liberals. Young argued, "The nonviolent approach is not emotional"; instead, it was a "rational process."[49] King disagreed. Young remembered King chiding him for being "too rational," telling him, "You would reason your way out of segregation, but it takes more than just reason to get this country straight." Instead of patient, logical appeals, King explained, "You need confrontation to bring the horror and violence of racism to the surface where it can be exposed to the light of truth and be healed."[50] Adam Fairclough argued of King, "Philosophically and in practice, he explicitly rejected the notion that blacks—or any other oppressed group—could overcome their subjection through ethical appeals and rational argument: they also needed an effective means of pressure."[51] Likewise, Chappell characterized King's leadership as having been guided by an understanding that "coercion" and "non-violent *force*" would be necessary to achieve social justice for African Americans.[52] John Lewis understood nonviolent direct action in much the same way, citing the need for activists to dramatize the injustice of segregation, that is, to "raise up the rug and pull out the dirt and force people to look at it, to *see* it."[53] Meaningful social change required the one thing white liberals feared most: confrontation. Although King and other activists frequently made moral appeals and welcomed those whites who supported the movement on that basis, they understood—in a way white liberals did not—that pressure made a much more reliable ally than did the consciences of white southerners.[54]

In addition to economic pressure and the "pressure of public opinion" from outside the region, nonviolent direct action created pressure within individual white southerners.[55] The movement gave whites the opportunity—for some the first opportunity they may have ever had—to *think* about their commitment to segregation and make a choice about whether the benefits they derived from the system were worth the cost of keeping it in place. Jason Sokol wrote, "African-Americans forced those whites to respond to their presence, confront their demands, choose sides, and recognize uncomfortable truths." He cautioned, however, that the change brought about by civil rights activism could be "in the direction of greater tolerance or increased resistance."[56] Like the Clarks' dolls test, the civil rights movement served as a forced-choice test in which white southerners had to make a conscious decision about whether to fight for segregation or let it go.

For many white southerners this decision involved choosing between conflicting priorities. They chose between public education, religious principles, sales figures, and respect for law and social order on the one hand and segregation on the other. Sokol explained of the response to the closing of Little Rock high schools during the 1958–59 academic year in the aftermath of the city's desegregation crisis, "The issue was not whether white southerners wanted segregation, much less whether they supported black demands. But when the very survival of public education was at stake, whites in Little Rock chose their public schools over the dogmas of their heritage."[57] Mark Newman wrote of Southern Baptists, "Regardless of their views toward Jim Crow, Southern Baptists shared primary commitments to scripture and evangelism, and, since at least the end of the nineteenth century, to law and order and to public education. Conflict between their primary commitments and the maintenance of segregation in the civil rights era made moderate segregationists amenable to change."[58] Elizabeth Jacoway explored the response of southern business leaders to the civil rights movement and the social and economic disruption it produced and concluded of these leaders, "They confronted the alternatives available to them, examined their values and priorities, and chose, ultimately, to place economic growth before white supremacy."[59] Chappell argued that civil rights leaders staged demonstrations in a deliberate attempt to "force a practical or financial crisis that would impel white citizens to reconsider their priorities: was segregation worth fighting for, especially if fighting meant a costly war of attrition against telegenic protestors?"[60] Once the issue was framed in this way, white southerners increasingly decided that maintaining segregation was not worth the cost.

This conflict in priorities and values was similar to that highlighted by Gunnar Myrdal in 1944, but the choices made by white southerners in the 1950s and 1960s did not represent the inevitable resolution of Myrdal's dilemma. In practice few white southerners had been conscious of the disconnect between their beliefs and their actions before civil rights activists brought it to their attention. Myrdal admitted as much, explaining of "valuation conflicts," people "want to keep them off their minds, and they are trained to overlook them. Conventions, stereotypes, and convenient blind spots in knowledge about social reality do succeed in preserving a relative peace in people's conscience." He conceded that "most people, most of the time, live a routine life from day to day and do not worry too much. If it could be measured, the amount of both simple and opportune ignorance and unconcernedness about social affairs would undoubtedly be greater than the amount of knowledge and concern."[61] In other words, most Americans did not think about race enough to be conflicted about it. The American Creed may have been objectively in conflict with the racism in American society, but most white Americans did not experience that conflict as a moral dilemma. King characterized the conflict in values as a paradox, a contradiction.[62] The civil rights movement served to turn that contradiction into a dilemma, a conscious choice between two clashing sets of values.

Along with their concern about how maintaining segregation threatened priorities such as public education, social order, and the economic bottom line, white southerners became increasingly concerned about the exposure of regional sins before a national and international spotlight. While King spoke often of conscience and occasionally of guilt, he spoke repeatedly of shame as a factor motivating white southerners to change their racial beliefs and practices. He viewed nonviolent tactics such as boycotts and demonstrations as "a means to awaken a sense of shame within the oppressor."[63] Speaking in Montgomery in December 1956, King predicted that nonviolent direct action would "soon cause the oppressor to become ashamed of his own methods. He will be forced to stand before the world and his God splattered with the blood and reeking with the stench of his Negro brother."[64] The civil rights movement succeeded in redefining segregation as a sin and declaring the white South guilty. Yet *shame*—a self-interested fear of the exposure of sins—served as a far more effective tool for prompting white southerners to change than did guilt, an internal sense of contrition at sins committed and an accompanying sense of regret for those harmed in the process.[65]

Even Lillian Smith, who wrote more often of guilt than did any other critic of segregation, understood that self-interest, whether it took the form of avoiding shame, maintaining order, safeguarding profits, or protecting children, was a better way of inducing white southerners to change their racial views and practices than was a benevolent appeal on behalf of African Americans. Writing as early as the 1940s, Smith explained regarding children, "When the imaginations of white people are stirred, when they become aroused to the great injury being done to their own children, they will have a more profound motivation for changing our segregated way of life than simply that of sporadically doing a 'good deed' for the Negro."[66] Sokol likewise found self-interest to be a motivating factor during civil rights demonstrations, concluding, "Of those white southerners who came to accept integration, more were repulsed by segregationist violence than attracted to civil rights demands."[67] The social disorder and violence provoked by the movement put on full display for local whites and the national television audience the extremes to which a defense of segregation could drive white southerners. To put an end to this regional shame, a growing number of civic and business leaders, along with individual white citizens, became willing to let segregation go. In the words of Numan Bartley, these leaders "finally opted for moderation, a moderation based on the ethics of cost-accounting rather than human justice."[68] Because it was based on an assessment of the costs involved, the change in racial attitudes and practices made by white southerners could be quick, but it only went so far. King admitted as much, writing of nonviolence, "Southern segregationists in many places yielded to it because they realized that the alternatives could be intolerable."[69] In the end the educational campaign of civil rights activists succeeded in convincing enough white southerners that the cost of maintaining the system was too high.

The appeal to self-interest was based on the argument that segregation, a system designed to privilege whites, instead harmed them so much that it must come to an immediate end. Some observers have been skeptical of claims that segregation harmed whites or limited their lives in some way, as many of these claims, especially those made by pre-*Brown* white liberals, focused on the emotional or spiritual cost of participating in the oppression of African Americans. Sokol, who was sympathetic to whites' claims that they had been "liberated" by the demise of segregation, conceded that such statements "possessed an ethereal quality."[70] Fred Hobson was more critical and questioned how black southerners would have responded to such claims, writing, "When one was fighting for the right to use a water fountain or public restroom, redeeming the soul of the white southerner might have seemed a high-minded extravagance."[71] Saving the soul of America, however, was precisely what many African Americans claimed to have been doing, and King's SCLC took this idea as its motto.[72] Chappell wrote of King, "He believed that white southerners held back their region by holding down their black neighbors. He believed that the violence, dishonesty, and miseducation of white people which were necessary to maintain white supremacy, hurt white people in material as well as spiritual ways."[73] For King the appeal to white self-interest seems to have been sincere.

King was not alone among African American leaders, however, in arguing that segregation harmed white southerners as well as black. Speaking in Birmingham in the aftermath of King's 1963 Good Friday arrest, Andrew Young attempted to calm the crowd gathered at Sixteenth Street Baptist Church by explaining the virtues of nonviolence, a tactic he hoped would "put an end to the system which is hurting us both—black and white."[74] Sokol highlighted a host of African American dignitaries—including King, Ralph Abernathy, James Baldwin, and James Weldon Johnson—who espoused some version of the advice activist Fannie Lou Hamer gave a group of black children preparing to integrate a school in Mississippi: "They ain't gonna be savin' *you*. You gonna be savin' *them*."[75] John Lewis remembered SNCC sage Bob Moses having told a group of white Freedom Summer volunteers assembled for training in Oxford, Ohio, "Don't come to Mississippi this summer to save the Mississippi Negro. . . . Only come if you understand, really understand, that his freedom and yours are one."[76] Civil rights leaders could not afford to dismiss the notion of saving white southerners from segregation as superfluous. Apart from the likelihood that some of these leaders sincerely believed they were freeing white as well as black southerners from the system, they found that such an appeal could serve as a valuable rhetorical strategy to convince whites to give segregation up not for the good of African Americans but for their own good.

While civil rights activists were confronting white southerners' racial conditioning, the movement worked to mobilize black southerners as well. The first step toward overcoming the racial conditioning of black southerners was ending the control of segregation over their minds, if not yet over their bodies. Pauli Murray wrote of her unsuccessful attempt to gain admission to the University of North Carolina at Chapel Hill in the late 1930s, "For me, the real victory of that encounter with the Jim Crow system of the South was the liberation of my mind from years of enslavement."[77] Anne Braden described Andrew Wade's experiences in World War II in similar terms: "Somewhere the walls had crumbled in his mind, as they had in the minds of so many others; the body was still shut in, but the spirit for the first time had the room to grow."[78] Andrew Young remembered an African American woman at an SCLC workshop who told a story about how her son questioned her willingness to accept segregation after she opposed his participation in civil rights activism. As she sought answers to her son's tough questions, she explained, "Finally, the cobwebs commenced a-movin' from my brain." Young recalled, "Everyone in the hall knew what she meant."[79] Drawing on such experiences, movement leaders learned that they had to remove the barriers to activism in black southerners' minds before they could mobilize their bodies for protest.

King and his colleagues found the mobilization of potential protestors to be one of the primary challenges facing the movement. Young described "accumulated mental shackles" that must be thrown off, while King invoked "manacles of self-abnegation" that must be removed.[80] Overcoming these obstacles required what Young termed "a tremendous leap in consciousness."[81] King stressed the difficulty of reaching black southerners, citing the propensity for people to "tacitly adjust themselves to oppression" and "thereby become conditioned to it." King's frustration is reflected in his forceful language, as when he asserted, "The job of arousing manhood within a people that have been taught for so many centuries that they are nobody is not easy."[82] For all that is appealing in historiographical trends that stress a long civil rights movement and everyday forms of resistance among African Americans, observers of the movement must not lose sight of how difficult it sometimes was to mobilize black communities for protest. Barriers to activism included opposition by those who had a vested economic interest in segregation, a generational divide over participation in potentially dangerous direct action campaigns, divisions among local leaders and among those leaders and regional activists, and the lack in some areas of a strong tradition of participation in civic life, including voting.[83]

In order to overcome those barriers, civil rights activists needed to encourage a sense of what King termed "somebodiness." They also had to convince black southerners of the efficacy of nonviolent direct action. King wrote of the decades before the Montgomery bus boycott, "While there were always solo voices in the Negro community crying out against segregation, conditions of fear and apathy made it difficult to develop a mass chorus."[84] During those decades, however, a number of factors, including the world wars, increased rural to urban migration, and expanded economic and educational opportunities, had begun to cultivate a new sensibility among African Americans. King explained, "The Negro has now been driven to reevaluate himself. He has come to feel that he is somebody. With this new sense of somebodiness and self-respect, a new Negro has emerged with a new determination to achieve freedom and human dignity whatever the cost may be." The civil rights movement vastly accelerated this process of reevaluation, instilling African Americans with "a new sense of dignity and destiny." Much of that sense of destiny derived from the feeling that a method had been found that might actually work. King argued that part of the appeal of nonviolent direct action was the way in which "it brings to the point of action a great multitude who need the assurance that a technique exists which is suitable and practical for a minority confronting a majority." Through the success of nonviolent protests, the African American community, in King's words, "learned that its salvation lies in united action. When one Negro stands up, he is run out of town. But when a thousand stand up together the situation is drastically altered."[85]

The movement taught black southerners that segregation was not immutable or inevitable and that it was possible to launch a broad-based, public challenge to the system. In this way segregation became not a condition to be endured but a problem to be solved through collective action. An observation made by John Cell illustrates this point. Contemplating how individuals decide when injustice can be endured and when it must be challenged, Cell quoted Richard Wright's words about slavery in *Native Son:* "Injustice which lasts for three long centuries and which exists among millions of people over thousands of square miles of territory, is injustice no longer; it is an accomplished fact of life. Men adjust themselves."[86] Later Cell described the shock W.E.B. Du Bois felt when he learned that the remains of a lynched man named Sam Hose were for sale in a store window in Atlanta. Cell wrote of Du Bois's response to the system that sanctioned the lynching, "To reverse Richard Wright's sequence, it was no longer a fact, it was injustice."[87]

For many black southerners the civil rights movement served a similar jarring role in turning segregation from an accomplished fact of life into a personal, strongly felt injustice that required concerted action to rectify. Whereas psychologists often aspire to produce "well-adjusted" individuals who have learned to live within the confines of their society, King called on African Americans instead to become "maladjusted" to segregation. He intoned, "God grant that we will be so maladjusted that we will be able to go out and change our world and our civilization."[88] In explaining his own adjustment to the daily indignities of segregation, James Farmer once observed, "The nerves must become calloused to protect themselves from too much pain." He described how such calluses allowed him to perform the rituals of segregation without feeling or even thinking about the humiliation they were meant to inflict. He continued his metaphor to explain how the racial conditioning of a lifetime might be overcome: "We've got to remove those callouses, rub the nerves raw till they hurt more each time, till we can stand it no longer. Then we will turn and rend the system."[89] The civil rights movement served to rub the calluses formed by black southerners' racial conditioning raw while simultaneously providing an outlet for the acute sense of racial injustice produced in the process. Through their understanding of black and white southerners' racial conditioning and the types of experiences through which it might be overcome, civil rights leaders were indeed able to make the tolerable intolerable.

NOTES

INTRODUCTION

1. Katharine Du Pre Lumpkin, *The Making of a Southerner* (1946; Athens: University of Georgia Press, 1991), 189. Lumpkin was born on Dec. 22, 1897, in Macon, Ga. Her parents were from prewar planter families. Her father worked for a railroad, eventually moving the family to South Carolina. Lumpkin attended Brenau from 1912 to 1915 (177). For biographical information, see Jacquelyn Dowd Hall, "'You Must Remember This': Autobiography as Social Critique," *Journal of American History* 85, no. 2 (Sept. 1998): 446 and 459–60, on her commitment to the Social Gospel.

2. Lumpkin, *Making of a Southerner*, 192–93, 191, 189, 192.

3. For the story of Uzzah, see 2 Samuel 6:3–8; 1 Chronicles 13:7–11. Uzzah's transgression involved not only touching the ark but also violating restrictions about how and by whom it was to be carried. By referring to the "minutely prescribed rules and regulations" for handling the ark, Lumpkin invoked the complicated rules of segregation. Lumpkin, *Making of a Southerner*, 193.

4. Lumpkin, *Making of a Southerner*, 193.

5. James Farmer, *Lay Bare the Heart: An Autobiography of the Civil Rights Movement* (New York: Arbor House, 1985), 120, 31. Farmer was born on Jan. 12, 1920, and grew up in Holly Springs, Miss. He was fourteen years old when he entered Wiley College in Marshall, Tex. His father was a Methodist preacher and scholar who taught at Rust College in Holly Springs, at Samuel Huston College (later Huston-Tillotson University) in Austin, Tex., and at Wiley College. James Farmer cofounded the Congress of Racial Equality (CORE) in the 1940s and served as its national director during the 1961 Freedom Rides.

6. Ibid., 122.

7. The gradual decline in the number of reported lynchings occurred despite a rise in Ku Klux Klan activity in the early 1920s. Although the various sets of lynching statistics differ somewhat, they support the idea of a general decline in the number of lynchings throughout the decade of the 1920s. Tuskegee Institute statistics record the number of African Americans lynched during this period as follows: 1919—76, 1920—53, 1921—59, 1922—51, 1923—29, 1924—16, 1925—17, 1926—23, 1927—16, 1928—10, and 1929—7. Although the numbers rose briefly during the early years of the Depression, they had fallen off to single digit levels again by 1936. See Robert L. Zangrando, *The NAACP Crusade against Lynching, 1909–1950* (Philadelphia: Temple University Press, 1980), 6–7. In a later study that characterized the Tuskegee statistics, as well as those compiled by the National Association for the Advancement of Colored People (NAACP), as "flawed," the numbers are different, but the trend line is the same. This study gives the number of African Americans lynched by whites for the same period as: 1919—59, 1920—34, 1921—45, 1922—32, 1923—22, 1924—14, 1925—13, 1926—20, 1927—12, 1928—7, 1929—6. Stewart E. Tolnay and E. M. Beck, *A Festival of Violence: An Analysis of Southern Lynchings, 1882–1930* (Urbana: University of Illinois Press, 1995), 259, 272. See also Jacquelyn Dowd Hall, *Revolt against Chivalry: Jessie Daniel Ames and the Women's Campaign against Lynching*, rev. ed. (1979; New York: Columbia University Press, 1993), 133–34. Hall offered the important qualification that the number of attempted lynchings continued to be high in the 1920s and that many of those became "legal

lynchings" when the accused was subjected to a hasty trial and then executed under the auspices of the criminal justice system. W. Fitzhugh Brundage argued that lynching declined in different states at different times throughout the period depending on the specific social and economic conditions in that state. In Virginia, e.g., lynchings were increasingly rare by 1910, while in Georgia and Mississippi they occurred throughout the 1920s. Brundage, *Lynching in the New South: Georgia and Virginia, 1880–1930* (Urbana: University of Illinois Press, 1993), 141.

8. Neil R. McMillen made a similar point about the role of violence in maintaining segregation in Mississippi in the years following the racial "hot time" from 1889 to 1919: "If violence was the 'instrument in reserve'—the ultimate deterrent normally used only against the most recalcitrant—social ritual regulated day-to-day race relations." McMillen, *Dark Journey: Black Mississippians in the Age of Jim Crow* (Urbana: University of Illinois Press, 1989), 31, 28.

9. John W. Cell, *The Highest Stage of White Supremacy: The Origins of Segregation in South Africa and the American South* (Cambridge: Cambridge University Press, 1982), 17.

10. Jason Sokol, *There Goes My Everything: White Southerners in the Age of Civil Rights, 1945–1975* (New York: Knopf, 2006), 61.

11. Carl T. Rowan, *South of Freedom* (1952; Baton Rouge: Louisiana State University Press, 1997), 130. Rowan was born in Ravenscroft, Tenn., on Aug. 11, 1925, and grew up in nearby McMinnville. Rowan worked for the *Minneapolis Tribune* for many years and later secured a series of positions in the Kennedy and Johnson administrations before returning to journalism. See also Carl T. Rowan, *Breaking Barriers: A Memoir* (Boston: Little, Brown, 1991).

12. John Egerton, *Speak Now against the Day: The Generation before the Civil Rights Movement in the South* (1994; Chapel Hill: University of North Carolina Press, 1995), 19, 37, 76, 233, 289.

13. Eugene Patterson, interview by Howell Raines, in *My Soul Is Rested: Movement Days in the Deep South Remembered* (1977; New York: Penguin Books, 1983), 368. Patterson served in editorial positions at the *Atlanta Journal* and *Atlanta Constitution*, among other influential papers.

14. Lillian Smith to the Student Nonviolent Coordinating Committee staff, [Dec. 1962 or Jan. 1963], in *How Am I to Be Heard? Letters of Lillian Smith*, ed. Margaret Rose Gladney (Chapel Hill: University of North Carolina Press, 1993), 302.

15. Lillian Smith, "Growing Plays," *South Today* 8, no. 1 (Spring–Summer 1944): 50.

16. C. Vann Woodward, *The Strange Career of Jim Crow*, 3rd rev. ed. (1955; New York: Oxford University Press, 1974), xv. See 102–9, for Woodward's discussion of the "folkways" versus "stateways" controversy that arose from William Graham Sumner's *Folkways: A Study of the Sociological Importance of Usages, Manners, Customs, Mores, and Morals* (Boston: Ginn, 1906). "Folkways" were thought to be immutable; thus, any attempt to change such established societal traditions through "stateways," that is, through changes in the law, would be futile. See also James C. Cobb, *The Brown Decision, Jim Crow, and Southern Identity* (Athens: University of Georgia Press, 2005), 8–9.

17. Much of the resulting debate about Woodward's analysis in the works of scholars like Joel Williamson and Howard Rabinowitz has revolved around the issue of whether conditions had, indeed, "always been that way," at least since the end of the Civil War. See Joel Williamson, *After Slavery: The Negro in South Carolina during Reconstruction, 1861–1877* (Chapel Hill: University of North Carolina Press, 1965); Howard Rabinowitz, *Race Relations in the Urban South, 1865–1890* (New York: Oxford University Press, 1978). For a more recent critical assessment of Woodward's argument, see Cobb, *Brown Decision*, 7–30.

18. According to published reports of the testimony of Mamie Bradley, Till's mother, at the trial of

her son's murderers, Bradley had told Till before he left that "he was coming South and that he would have to adapt himself to the customs." When asked if she had instructed her son specifically about how to act toward white women, she responded, "I did not mention women when I referred to white people in general. Naturally coming from Chicago he wouldn't know how to act." Christopher Metress, ed., *The Lynching of Emmett Till: A Documentary Narrative* (Charlottesville: University of Virginia Press, 2002), 81.

19. Ibid., 2. For the most frequently noted example of the Till lynching having influenced later civil rights activism, see Anne Moody, *Coming of Age in Mississippi* (1968; New York: Laurel, 1976), 121–28. For other accounts of the impact of the Till lynching, see Metress, *Lynching of Emmett Till*, 247–88.

20. Cell, *Highest Stage of White Supremacy*, 18.

21. Jacquelyn Dowd Hall, "The Long Civil Rights Movement and the Political Uses of the Past," *Journal of American History* 91, no. 4 (Mar. 2005): 1233–63; Glenda Elizabeth Gilmore, *Defying Dixie: The Radical Roots of Civil Rights, 1919–1950* (New York: Norton, 2008), 1–12. See also Patricia Sullivan, *Days of Hope: Race and Democracy in the New Deal Era* (Chapel Hill: University of North Carolina Press, 1996).

22. Hall, "Long Civil Rights Movement," 1234.

23. McMillen wrote of activism in Mississippi during the interwar years, "black malcontentment and protest, though mounting steadily, necessarily either remained muted and underground or, when it surfaced, flowed in relatively safe and nonconfrontational channels." McMillen, *Dark Journey*, 317.

24. Cell argued that segregation worked by "deflecting, channeling, and absorbing opposition." Cell, *Highest Stage of White Supremacy*, 272.

25. Black southerners who did argue for an earlier start to the movement were generally those who were personally involved in activism prior to the mid-1950s. Ruby Hurley, who started an NAACP office in Birmingham in 1951, asserted, "I think young people need to know, and some older people need to know, that it didn't all begin in 1960." Howell Raines wrote of Hurley, "To her the Movement is old and its cost has been dear." Hurley, interview by Raines, in *My Soul Is Rested*, 137, 131.

26. Hartman Turnbow, quoted in Raines, *My Soul Is Rested*, 25.

27. Robin D. G. Kelley, "'We Are Not What We Seem': Rethinking Black Working-Class Opposition in the Jim Crow South," *Journal of American History* 80, no. 1 (June 1993): 77.

28. Ibid., 75–112. Kelley expanded his argument in *Race Rebels: Culture, Politics, and the Black Working Class* (New York: Free Press, 1994). See also James C. Scott, *Domination and the Arts of Resistance: Hidden Transcripts* (New Haven: Yale University Press, 1990), 70–85. Scott asserted the existence of an offstage, hidden transcript of resistance to domination that was a counterpart to the glimpses of resistance revealed in the onstage, public transcript. He argued that domination was seldom naturalized but instead was critiqued and resisted through the hidden transcript. The civil rights movement was a rare event in that it brought forth countless "hidden transcripts" in the form of autobiographies and oral histories that reveal the extent to which aspects of segregation had come to be seen as facts of southern life.

29. Kelley, "'We Are Not What We Seem,'" 76, 110, 111, 109–10.

30. John H. Volter, interview by Kate Ellis, New Iberia, La., Aug. 1, 1994, Behind the Veil: Documenting African-American Life in the Jim Crow South, Center for Documentary Studies at Duke University, David M. Rubenstein Rare Book & Manuscript Library, Duke University. Volter was born on July 30, 1929, in Weeks Island, La. His father was a salt miner, and his mother worked as a cook and a domestic. Volter worked in a variety of positions in the aircraft industry. Note that McMillen

detailed the activities of the NAACP in Mississippi at this time although he acknowledged that efforts to establish chapters there between the two world wars "nearly always failed." McMillen, *Dark Journey*, 314. The point here is that even when such organizations existed in the South prior to the civil rights era, many people were either not aware of their activities or all too aware of the danger of joining or even expressing an interest in such an organization.

31. Gladys Austin, interview by Kim Adams, Laurel, Miss., May 2, 1995, Mississippi Oral History Project, Center for Oral History and Cultural Heritage, University of Southern Mississippi. Austin was born in Laurel on Apr. 1, 1927. She recalled that opposition to conditions in her community started to mount when African American soldiers returned home from World War II.

32. Charles S. Johnson, *Patterns of Negro Segregation* (New York: Harper & Brothers, 1943), 244.

33. Jennifer Ritterhouse, *Growing Up Jim Crow: How Black and White Southern Children Learned Race* (Chapel Hill: University of North Carolina Press, 2006), 4–5; Kristina DuRocher, *Raising Racists: The Socialization of White Children in the Jim Crow South* (Lexington: University Press of Kentucky, 2011), 8–9.

34. Ritterhouse, *Growing Up Jim Crow*, 7.

35. Ibid., 47; DuRocher, *Raising Racists*, 7.

36. Ritterhouse, *Growing Up Jim Crow*, 56, 13, 34, 19, 55.

37. DuRocher, *Raising Racists*, 4–5, 7–8.

38. For another perspective on unthinking adherence to segregation, see Mark M. Smith, *How Race Is Made: Slavery, Segregation, and the Senses* (Chapel Hill: University of North Carolina Press, 2006). Smith wrote of white southerners, "People supported segregation without really thinking why. They simply 'felt' it was right. Feeling, not thinking, was segregation's best friend" (115). While I argue that young people were taught by trusted adults not to question segregation and, thus, developed an unexamined loyalty to the system, Smith focused on how white southerners' connection to segregation was based in the senses, especially the sense of smell.

39. Ritterhouse and DuRocher included the same 1935 photograph of a smiling white girl gazing up at a lynched black man while other white girls look on. Ritterhouse, *Growing Up Jim Crow*, 73; DuRocher, *Raising Racists*, 2.

40. DuRocher, *Raising Racists*, 102, 121. Drawing on Tolnay and Beck's *A Festival of Violence*, DuRocher cited "the statistic that a southern white mob lynched an African American, on average, once a week between 1882 and 1930." DuRocher, *Raising Racists*, 116. Tolnay and Beck went on to list the number of African Americans lynched by whites in 1882 as thirty-three, in 1892 as ninety-two, in 1920 as thirty-four, and in 1930 as twelve. See Tolnay and Beck, *Festival of Violence*, ix, 271–72. Lynching did not occur at a constant rate between 1882 and 1930; thus, exposure to lynching as a tool of race socialization and, therefore, as a means of maintaining the social order was not constant during that period.

41. DuRocher, *Raising Racists*, 106.

42. Ritterhouse, *Growing Up Jim Crow*, 14, 53–54. Both Ritterhouse and David Goldfield—who made the "etiquette of race" a central analytical focus of his study *Black, White, and Southern: Race Relations and Southern Culture, 1940 to the Present* (Baton Rouge: Louisiana State University Press, 1990)—drew on sociologist Bertram Wilbur Doyle's *The Etiquette of Race Relations in the South: A Study in Social Control* (1937; New York: Schocken Books, 1971). Ritterhouse and Goldfield followed Doyle in viewing etiquette as a holdover from slavery, and all three characterized etiquette as distinct from the legal system of segregation and from the practice of racial separation. That is, etiquette, in their view, was based in custom rather than law, and it regulated the interactions of black and white southerners who were in close physical proximity to one another. Note that although Doyle's conceptualization

of etiquette influenced Ritterhouse's work, she was critical of much of his analysis, which prioritized achieving racial peace even at the cost of continued racial hierarchy. See Ritterhouse, *Growing Up Jim Crow*, 49, 245 n. 22. On the issue of vertical versus horizontal systems of racial domination, see Cell, *Highest Stage of White Supremacy*, ix, 13. Cell conceptualized slavery as a top-down, that is, a vertical, means of domination that operated largely on a one-to-one basis from master to slave. He argued that segregation was a new system that sought to establish social control in a society in which black and white southerners of similar economic circumstances interacted on a day-to-day basis. In order to regulate the now horizontal race relations, white southerners created the system of segregation, which encompassed, according to Cell, "far more than mere physical separation. Segregation is at the same time an interlocking system of economic institutions, social practices and customs, political power, law, and ideology" (ix, 14). I follow Cell in viewing segregation as a new system as opposed to a continuation of the race relations that prevailed under slavery and in understanding segregation as involving more than legalized physical separation.

43. Ritterhouse, *Growing Up Jim Crow*, 14.

44. Ibid., 20.

45. Ibid., 23–24, 17.

46. While Ritterhouse concluded that white southerners had come to see segregation as normal, she argued that this was not the case for black southerners. She wrote of white children, "By the time they had learned to write, they had also learned to think of white supremacy as natural, simply the way the world worked, no more worthy of comment than salt in the sea." Later she quoted contemporary anthropologist Hortense Powdermaker's conclusion about black parents that "the 'usual response' to children's inevitable questions [about race relations] was 'I don't know, that's just the way it is.'" Ibid., 12, 101. Ritterhouse's evidence here—if not her analysis—suggests that black children were also learning to think of segregation as "just the way it is," that is, as a permanent part of the social landscape. See also sociologist Kristen M. Lavelle's study *Whitewashing the South: White Memories of Segregation and Civil Rights* (Lanham, Md.: Rowman & Littlefield, 2015), which is based on oral history interviews Lavelle conducted with white southerners who grew up in Greensboro, N.C. She noted that her informants repeatedly explained that segregation was "just the way it was" when they were growing up (51–85). She concluded that white southerners used this statement to assert their own racial innocence for maintaining segregation and to downplay institutional racism (77, 81, 183). I argue that both white and black southerners used this phrase and others like it to convey their day-to-day lived experience of segregation.

47. Hall, "'You Must Remember This,'" 440–41.

48. Georges Gusdorf, "Conditions and Limits of Autobiography" (1956), in *Autobiography: Essays Theoretical and Critical*, ed. James Olney (Princeton: Princeton University Press, 1980), 35.

49. Roy Pascal, *Design and Truth in Autobiography* (Cambridge: Harvard University Press, 1960), 195.

50. Jennifer Jensen Wallach, *"Closer to the Truth than Any Fact": Memoir, Memory, and Jim Crow* (Athens: University of Georgia Press, 2008), 5.

51. See also John C. Inscoe's study, *Writing the South through the Self: Explorations in Southern Autobiography* (Athens: University of Georgia Press, 2011), in which Inscoe argued that "autobiography and memoir offer an exceptional window into the southern past" (ix).

52. Pascal, *Design and Truth*, 10.

53. Ibid., 69, 16–17.

54. Timothy Dow Adams, *Telling Lies in Modern American Autobiography* (Chapel Hill: University of North Carolina Press, 1990), 34, 9.

55. Larry L. King, *Confessions of a White Racist* (1969; New York: Viking Press, 1971), xvii–xviii. King was born in Texas in 1929.

56. Adams, *Telling Lies,* ix.

57. Barrett J. Mandel, "Full of Life Now," in Olney, *Autobiography,* 66.

58. King, *Confessions of a White Racist,* xviii.

59. Benjamin E. Mays, *Born to Rebel: An Autobiography* (1971; Athens: University of Georgia Press, 2003), lvii, 21. Mays was born in South Carolina in 1894. His parents were farmers who had been born slaves.

60. Paul Hemphill, *Leaving Birmingham: Notes of a Native Son* (1993; Tuscaloosa: University of Alabama Press, 2000), 41–42. Hemphill was born in Birmingham, Ala., in 1936. His father worked as a truck driver for much of his career.

61. Pat Watters, *Down to Now: Reflections on the Southern Civil Rights Movement* (1971; Athens: University of Georgia Press, 1993), 24. Watters was born in Spartanburg, S.C., in 1927.

62. Vernon E. Jordan Jr., with Annette Gordon-Reed, *Vernon Can Read! A Memoir* (New York: PublicAffairs, 2001), 10. Jordan was born in Atlanta in 1935. His mother worked at a country club and later ran a successful catering business, and his father was a mailman.

63. Ibid., 11.

CHAPTER 1
"THE SOUTHERN NEVER-NEVER LAND"

The title of this chapter is drawn from the section of Sarah Patton Boyle's autobiography in which she discussed her life before she became critical of segregation. Boyle, *The Desegregated Heart: A Virginian's Stand in Time of Transition* (New York: Morrow, 1962), 1. Lillian Smith also referred to white southerners' "never-never land" in *Killers of the Dream,* rev. ed. (1949; 1961; New York: Norton, 1994), 219.

1. Anne Braden, *The Wall Between* (1958; Knoxville: University of Tennessee Press, 1999), 115. Braden was born in Louisville, Ky., in 1924. She spent her childhood in Jackson and Columbus, Miss., and Anniston, Ala. In 1954 Braden and her husband, Carl, agreed to buy a home in a white Louisville subdivision for an African American acquaintance, Andrew Wade, and his wife, Charlotte, and then transfer ownership to the Wades, who had been unable to find adequate housing in any of the city's segregated neighborhoods. Once the exchange was made public, segregationists harassed the Bradens and the Wades, and the house was eventually bombed. Instead of investigating the bombing, a grand jury indicted the Bradens and five other whites on charges of sedition, claiming that the Bradens had bought the house as part of a communist plot. Carl Braden was convicted and sentenced to fifteen years in prison but was released on bond pending appeal several months later. In 1956 the U.S. Supreme Court rendered a decision that nullified state sedition laws, and the conviction and the indictments were thrown out. Catherine Fosl, *Subversive Southerner: Anne Braden and the Struggle for Racial Justice in the Cold War South* (New York: Palgrave Macmillan, 2002), xvii.

2. Smith, *Killers of the Dream,* 90.

3. Ibid., 202. Smith was born the daughter of a successful businessman in 1897 in Jasper, Fla. When her father suffered a financial setback in 1915, the family moved to their summer home in

Clayton in the mountains of north Georgia. For more on Smith, see Margaret Rose Gladney, ed., *How Am I to Be Heard? Letters of Lillian Smith* (Chapel Hill: University of North Carolina Press, 1993), 1–16.

4. Fred Hobson, *But Now I See: The White Southern Racial Conversion Narrative* (Baton Rouge: Louisiana State University Press, 1999), 6.

5. Smith, *Killers of the Dream,* 21. She made this statement at the conclusion to "A Letter to My Publisher," which served as the foreword to the revised 1961 version of her work. Both black and white autobiographers have noted Smith's influence on their thinking. See, e.g., Melton A. McLaurin, *Separate Pasts: Growing Up White in the Segregated South* (1987; Athens: University of Georgia Press, 1998), 66. For Smith's influence on Pauli Murray, see Darlene O'Dell, *Sites of Southern Memory: The Autobiographies of Katharine Du Pre Lumpkin, Lillian Smith, and Pauli Murray* (Charlottesville: University Press of Virginia, 2001), 38–30, 126–28. In addition to explicit mentions of an intellectual debt to Smith, echoes of her language are found in the works of many subsequent observers of segregation, suggesting the extent of her influence. Smith was not unaware of her impact. She described being visited in the mid-1960s by an Italian crew filming a television show about Martin Luther King Jr. Although the crew was not familiar with Smith's work, someone in Atlanta had apparently advised them to make the trip to Clayton to meet her. She wrote of the group's leader, "He quoted several southerners and commented on their beautiful words, their phrases—and everyone [*sic*] of the phrases were from some of my books. This pleased me; after all, that is what I am doing: enriching our vocabulary of human relationships; but since he had never read me he did not realize that the ideas were first put down by me." Lillian Smith to Margaret Sullivan, Dec. 9, 1965, in Gladney, *How Am I to Be Heard,* 337.

6. Smith and Snelling ran the camp from 1925 until 1948, the year before *Killers of the Dream* was originally published. For more on the camp, see O'Dell, *Sites of Southern Memory,* 84, 93–96. Smith sought to undo the socialization her campers had experienced in their homes by teaching them alternatives to the racial and gender roles they had learned. This work gave her a perspective on child development that is not as evident when one focuses only on her roles as journal editor and novelist.

7. Published between 1936 and 1945, the journal was known as *Pseudopodia* and the *North Georgia Review,* in turn, before becoming *South Today* in 1942. For more on the controversy surrounding *Strange Fruit,* see Anne C. Loveland, *Lillian Smith: A Southerner Confronting the South, A Biography* (Baton Rouge: Louisiana State University Press, 1986), 63–79.

8. Smith, *Killers of the Dream,* 57, 72, 96.

9. Lillian Smith, "Addressed to Intelligent White Southerners: 'There Are Things to Do,'" *South Today* 7, no. 2 (Winter 1942–43): 42.

10. Smith, *Killers of the Dream,* 95; Jay Watson, "Uncovering the Body, Discovering Ideology: Segregation and Sexual Anxiety in Lillian Smith's *Killers of the Dream,*" *American Quarterly* 49, no. 3 (Sept. 1997): 477.

11. Watson, "Uncovering the Body," 477, 481.

12. Smith, *Killers of the Dream,* 96.

13. O'Dell, *Sites of Southern Memory,* 4.

14. Watson, "Uncovering the Body," 478.

15. Smith, *Killers of the Dream,* 96.

16. Ibid., 39.

17. Lillian Smith, "How to Work for Racial Equality," *New Republic,* July 2, 1945, 23.

18. Smith, *Killers of the Dream,* 92.

19. Ibid., 96.

20. Watson, "Uncovering the Body," 494–95. Watson drew on Marxist philosopher Louis Althusser's concept of "an authorless theatre."

21. Smith, *Killers of the Dream*, 72. Smith went so far as to suggest that southerners "obeyed this invisible power as meekly as if Hitler or Stalin had given the orders," explicitly linking the South to the authoritarian regimes of the recent past.

22. Ibid., 12–13, 176. Smith devoted an entire chapter to a searing critique of the South's economic and racial history entitled, "Two Men and a Bargain," an earlier version of which had appeared in her journal.

23. Note that in the philosophical reflections that form the final chapter of the revised edition of *Killers of the Dream*, Smith suggested another identity for the killers: "If only we could rise up against the killers of man's dream. But sometimes, that killer of dreams is in us and we do not know how to rid ourselves of it" (252).

24. Ibid., 201–2.

25. In his classic analysis of segregation in Mississippi, James W. Silver wrote of the white response to African American James Meredith's 1962 admission to the University of Mississippi, "The closed society was operating efficiently, almost automatically. A malicious Frankenstein was on a rampage." Silver, *The Closed Society*, rev. ed. (1964; New York: Harcourt, Brace & World, 1966), 118.

26. Carl T. Rowan, *South of Freedom* (1952; Baton Rouge: Louisiana State University Press, 1997), 132.

27. John W. Cell, *The Highest Stage of White Supremacy: The Origins of Segregation in South Africa and the American South* (Cambridge: Cambridge University Press, 1982), 19.

28. Andrew Young, *An Easy Burden: The Civil Rights Movement and the Transformation of America* (New York: HarperCollins, 1996), 100. Young was born on Mar. 12, 1932, in New Orleans. His father was a dentist, and his mother was a one-time schoolteacher and later homemaker. Young has served as a minister, executive director of the Southern Christian Leadership Conference, member of the U.S. House of Representatives from Georgia, U.S. ambassador to the United Nations, mayor of Atlanta, and professor.

29. Beverly Daniel Tatum, *"Why Are All the Black Kids Sitting Together in the Cafeteria?" And Other Conversations about Race* (New York: Basic Books, 1997), 11.

30. Smith, *Killers of the Dream*, 27, dedication, 66, 152.

31. Lillian Smith, "Putting Away Childish Things," *South Today* 8, no. 1 (Spring–Summer 1944): 64.

32. Margaret Jones Bolsterli, "Reflections on Lillian Smith and the Guilts of the Betrayer," *Southern Quarterly* 27, no. 4 (1989): 73–74.

33. Lindy Boggs, with Katherine Hatch, *Washington through a Purple Veil: Memoirs of a Southern Woman* (New York: Harcourt Brace & Co., 1994), 26. Boggs was born on her family's plantation in Louisiana in 1916.

34. Will D. Campbell, *Brother to a Dragonfly* (1977; New York: Continuum, 2000), 108. Campbell was born on July 18, 1924, and grew up in Liberty, Miss.

35. Willie Morris, *North toward Home* (1967; New York: Vintage Books, 2000), 78. Morris was born in 1934, and he was raised in Yazoo City, Miss. He was a longtime author and editor.

36. Jimmy Carter, *An Hour before Daylight: Memories of a Rural Boyhood* (New York: Simon & Schuster, 2001), 269, 96. Carter was born in 1924, and he was raised in Archery, Ga.

37. Joan C. Browning, "Shiloh Witness," in *Deep in Our Hearts: Nine White Women in the Freedom Movement* (Athens: University of Georgia Press, 2000), 51. Browning was born in July 1942, in Shiloh, Ga.

38. Vetta L. Sanders Thompson, "Socialization to Race and Its Relationship to Racial Identification among African Americans," *Journal of Black Psychology* 20, no. 2 (May 1994): 175.

39. Diane Hughes and Lisa Chen, "The Nature of Parents' Race-Related Communications to Children: A Developmental Perspective," in *Child Psychology: A Handbook of Contemporary Issues*, ed. Lawrence Balter and Catherine S. Tamis-LeMonda (Philadelphia: Psychology Press, 1999), 467.

40. Sanders Thompson, "Socialization to Race," 176.

41. For a perspective that conceptualized race socialization as unique to black families, see Marie Ferguson Peters, "Racial Socialization of Young Black Children," in *Black Children: Social, Educational, and Parental Environments*, ed. Harriette Pipes McAdoo and John Lewis McAdoo (Beverly Hills, Calif.: Sage Publications, 1985), 161. On race socialization as an activity that occurs in all families, see Tony N. Brown et al., "Child, Parent, and Situational Correlates of Familial Ethnic/Race Socialization," *Journal of Marriage and Family* 69, no. 1 (Feb. 2007): 15.

42. See Chase L. Lesane-Brown, "A Review of Race Socialization within Black Families," *Developmental Review* 26, no. 4 (Dec. 2006): 403–5; Hughes and Chen, "The Nature of Parents' Race-Related Communications to Children," 470–71.

43. Smith, *Killers of the Dream*, 90.

44. Tatum, *"Why Are All the Black Kids Sitting Together in the Cafeteria?,"* 196, 93, 7, 95, 36.

45. Joseph G. Ponterotto and Paul B. Pedersen, *Preventing Prejudice: A Guide for Counselors and Educators* (Newbury Park, Calif.: Sage Publications, 1993), 31.

46. Tatum, *"Why Are All the Black Kids Sitting Together in the Cafeteria?,"* 96, 203–4.

47. Martin Luther King Jr., "The Most Durable Power" (1957), in *A Testament of Hope: The Essential Writings and Speeches of Martin Luther King, Jr.*, ed. James M. Washington (San Francisco: Harper, 1986), 10; Martin Luther King Jr., "An Experiment in Love" (1958), in Washington, *Testament of Hope*, 19. One hears Lillian Smith's influence in King's words. In Dec. 1956, not long after King preached the sermon in which he declared that "the festering sore of segregation debilitates the white man as well as the Negro" and just as the Montgomery bus boycott was coming to a successful conclusion, the Montgomery Improvement Association invited Smith to speak at an occasion marking the one-year anniversary of the boycott's start. Although she was unable to attend because of illness, the speech, read in her absence, was well received. King occasionally praised Smith's writing and her stance against segregation in his own speeches and writings, including the "Letter from Birmingham Jail." For her part Smith was a strong supporter of King and his use of nonviolent direct action, especially early on in the movement. See Gladney, *How Am I to Be Heard*, 193–95, 202–4, 311–13; Washington, *Testament of Hope*, 93, 263, 298; Loveland, *Lillian Smith*, 155–57. Smith also played a role in one of King's more memorable arrests. One evening in the spring of 1960, Smith had dinner with King and his wife, Coretta Scott King, in Atlanta. As King was driving Smith back to Emory Hospital, where she was undergoing treatment for cancer, he was pulled over because the car he was driving had an expired license plate. The police officer who stopped him also discovered that King had neglected to acquire a Georgia driver's license after moving from Alabama. Both Coretta Scott King and Smith believed King was really pulled over because there was a white woman in his car. When King was arrested during the fall 1960 Atlanta sit-ins, he was sent to state prison for having violated his probation from the earlier incident involving Smith. John F. Kennedy, who was then running for president, called Coretta Scott King to express his concern, and his brother, Robert Kennedy, assisted in having King released on bail. See Gladney, *How Am I to Be Heard*, 301; Coretta Scott King, *My Life with Martin Luther King, Jr.*, rev. ed. (1969; New York: Henry Holt, 1993), 174–81; Edythe Scott Bagley, with Joe Hilley, *Desert Rose: The Life and Legacy of Coretta Scott King* (Tuscaloosa: University of Alabama Press, 2012), 154–55.

48. Jennifer Jensen Wallach, *"Closer to the Truth than Any Fact": Memoir, Memory, and Jim Crow* (Athens: University of Georgia Press, 2008), 149–50. Although critical of Smith, Wallach took the title of her study from *Killers of the Dream*. Wallach, *"Closer to the Truth than Any Fact,"* 120; Smith, *Killers of the Dream*, 13.

49. Wallach, *"Closer to the Truth than Any Fact,"* 115; Hobson, *But Now I See*, 33.

50. Wallach, *"Closer to the Truth than Any Fact,"* 116.

51. Watson, "Uncovering the Body," 478.

52. Jason Sokol, *There Goes My Everything: White Southerners in the Age of Civil Rights, 1945–1975* (New York: Knopf, 2006), 323.

53. In highlighting the cost to whites of participating in segregation, my approach is similar to that of Tatum and other scholars who promote an antiracist perspective through calculating the cost of institutional racism to whites as well as blacks. See Tatum, *"Why Are All the Black Kids Sitting Together in the Cafeteria?,"* 11–14. This approach is distinct from that of many "whiteness studies." Both serve as critiques of white privilege, but the former does so by emphasizing the cost to whites of maintaining the system while the latter focuses on the benefits whites gain from the system. Thus, David R. Roediger, drawing on W.E.B. Du Bois's concept of a "psychological wage" for whites, argued that "wages of whiteness" accrued to white workers. Roediger, *The Wages of Whiteness: Race and the Making of the American Working Class*, rev. ed. (1991; London: Verso, 1999), 12–13. For more on "whiteness studies," see Peter Kolchin, "Whiteness Studies: The New History of Race in America," *Journal of American History* 89, no. 1 (June 2002): 154–73.

54. The Clarks' work grew out of Mamie P. Clark's graduate research on children's self-concept at Howard University in Washington, D.C., where she was only allowed access to black children in the city's segregated schools and, thus, came to focus her research on the development of self-concept in black children. In addition to the dolls test, the Clarks used a coloring test—wherein black children had to color pictures of children both the color they themselves were and the color they liked other children to be—to demonstrate a pattern of white group preference in black children. For more on the Clarks' tests, see Kenneth B. Clark, *Prejudice and Your Child* (1955; Middletown, Conn.: Wesleyan University Press, 1988), 19–20, 22–24, 42–46; Kenneth B. Clark and Mamie P. Clark, "Racial Identification and Preference in Negro Children," in *Readings in Social Psychology*, ed. Theodore M. Newcomb and Eugene L. Hartley (New York: Henry Holt, 1947), 169–78; and Clark and Clark, "Emotional Factors in Racial Identification and Preference in Negro Children," in "The Negro Child in the American Social Order," special issue, *Journal of Negro Education* 19, no. 3 (Summer 1950): 341–50. For more on other aspects of the Clarks' work, see Gerald Markowitz and David Rosner, *Children, Race, and Power: Kenneth and Mamie Clark's Northside Center* (Charlottesville: University Press of Virginia, 1996).

Many scholars have been critical of the dolls test and the Clarks' research in general, and much of the scholarship on race socialization grew out of attempts to refute the claim that segregation "damaged" black children. W. Curtis Banks argued that the results of the Clarks' research on racial preference were rarely statistically significant. See Banks, "White Preference in Blacks: A Paradigm in Search of a Phenomenon," *Psychological Bulletin* 83, no. 6 (1976): 1179–86. Others have argued variously that group preference cannot be equated with individual self-concept; that because a positive in-group attitude develops as black children age, the Clarks' studies of very young children would naturally find that they had not yet acquired this positive group identity; that white children's extremely high rate of in-group preference actually suggested that it was they, and not black children, who were pathological; and even that black children selected the white doll because they were unfamiliar with black dolls.

See Algea O. Harrison, "The Black Family's Socializing Environment: Self-Esteem and Ethnic Attitude among Black Children," in McAdoo and McAdoo, *Black Children,* 174–93. On the issue of whether black dolls were unfamiliar to black children, see bell hooks's autobiography, *Bone Black: Memories of Girlhood* (New York: Henry Holt, 1996), 24, in which she recalled that her initial requests for a black baby doll—made when she was growing up in the 1950s—were met with complaints from her parents that such dolls were expensive and harder to find than white dolls. On the other hand, black denominational newspapers featured advertisements for black dolls in the 1920s. Numerous scholars have re-created the dolls test, often still finding some evidence of preference for the white doll among African American children. See, e.g., Michelle Fine and Cheryl Bowers, "Racial Self-Identification: The Effects of Social History and Gender," *Journal of Applied Social Psychology* 14, no. 2 (1984): 136–46; Curtis W. Branch and Nora Newcombe, "Racial Attitude Development among Young Black Children as a Function of Parental Attitudes: A Longitudinal and Cross-Sectional Study," *Child Development* 57, no. 3 (June 1986): 712–21. See also Robert Coles, *Children of Crisis: A Study of Courage and Fear* (Boston: Little, Brown, 1967), 37–71, in which Coles analyzed drawings made by children involved in the early stages of school desegregation. Black children tended to depict whites as larger and more lifelike and with all of their limbs intact, while they depicted African Americans as smaller and often as lacking an eye, an ear, or an entire limb.

Ultimately, scholars sought to account for the Clarks' findings by turning to an examination of what children were learning about themselves and their racial group from their parents. In an influential article, Margaret Beale Spencer posed "the important question of the relationship between parental child-rearing strategies and young black children's Eurocentric values" out of which much of the scholarship on race socialization has developed. Spencer, "Children's Cultural Values and Parental Child Rearing Strategies," *Developmental Review* 3, no. 4 (Dec. 1983): 355.

55. Stewart B. Cook, foreword to *Prejudice and Your Child,* x–xii; Clark, *Prejudice and Your Child,* xx–xxi. The controversy among historians surrounding the Clarks' work has primarily involved their use of "damage" imagery. Daryl Michael Scott characterized Kenneth Clark's work as "posing blacks as damaged for political purposes." According to Scott, Clark took "damage imagery" and "fashioned it into a psychiatric appeal for white consumption," and Clark and other black intellectuals "took images generated to underscore the inhumanity of the oppressor and manipulated them to gain his sympathy." Scott, *Contempt and Pity: Social Policy and the Image of the Damaged Black Psyche, 1880–1996* (Chapel Hill: University of North Carolina Press, 1997), 95–97. For his part Clark recalled a 1951 conversation with Robert L. Carter of the NAACP legal staff about how the organization proposed to make the case that school segregation violated the equal protection clause of the Fourteenth Amendment: "He pointed out that if they were to be successful in obtaining this objective, they would have to demonstrate to the courts that racial segregation in public schools damaged Negro children. Because they could not demonstrate that segregation inflicted concrete, overt, physical damage upon these children, they had to find evidence of psychological damage—that is, injuries to the personality, the self-esteem of the rejected children." Clark, *Prejudice and Your Child,* xx. In a nuanced critique of the Clarks' work, William E. Cross Jr. explained, "In its struggle to destroy legal segregation, the NAACP defense team did not need complexity or texture—it needed clear-cut evidence that Negroes were being damaged by racial segregation." Cross, *Shades of Black: Diversity in African-American Identity* (Philadelphia: Temple University Press, 1991), 137. Debate about the issue of "damage" has raged among historians regarding slavery as well, particularly in response to Stanley Elkins's study, *Slavery: A Problem in American Institutional and Intellectual Life* (1959; Chicago: University of Chicago Press, 1968). Elkins drew a

comparison between the experience of slavery and that of Nazi concentration camps and argued that slavery had fostered a "Sambo" personality among African Americans, which left them psychologically compromised. In an effort to refute his argument and the political uses to which it was put in the 1960s, historians produced a number of works that focused instead on the strength and resiliency of slave families and communities, among them John W. Blassingame's *The Slave Community: Plantation Life in the Antebellum South* (New York: Oxford University Press, 1972); Eugene D. Genovese's *Roll Jordan Roll: The World the Slaves Made* (New York: Pantheon Books, 1974); and Herbert G. Gutman's *The Black Family in Slavery and Freedom, 1750–1925* (New York: Pantheon Books, 1976). See Peter Kolchin, "Reevaluating the Antebellum Slave Community: A Comparative Perspective," *Journal of American History* 70, no. 3 (Dec. 1983): 579–601, for a review of this scholarship.

56. Daryl Michael Scott's work is a notable exception. He observed that Kenneth Clark and other likeminded intellectuals "believed that the racial situation in America was pathological and damaging to blacks and whites alike." Scott, *Contempt and Pity,* 86.

57. Lillian Smith's work can also be read as an attempt to convince white parents of the cost to their own children of continuing segregation. Note that Clark was conversant with Smith's work on race, writing, "She has arrived at conclusions strikingly similar to those of the social psychologists who have studied the problem more systematically. She contends that the major forces responsible for the development of prejudices in American children are the anxieties and pressure that parents impose on their children in order to foster the values of respectability and conformity." Clark, *Prejudice and Your Child,* 69.

58. Ibid., 4.

59. Ibid., 80–81.

60. Rutledge M. Dennis, "Socialization and Racism: The White Experience," in *Impacts of Racism on White Americans,* ed. Benjamin P. Bowser and Raymond G. Hunt (Beverly Hills, Calif.: Sage Publications, 1981), 72, 79–84. Dennis also drew on Kenneth Clark's work. See also Ponterotto and Pedersen, *Preventing Prejudice,* 21.

61. Dennis, "Socialization and Racism," 73–79; Ponterotto and Pedersen, *Preventing Prejudice,* 19–22.

62. Ponterotto and Pedersen, *Preventing Prejudice,* 23.

63. Clark, *Prejudice and Your Child,* 29, 36, 81.

64. See ibid., 27, for an example of a white mother who had consciously tried to instill a concern for social justice in her small children and who became distraught when her son came home using a racial epithet he had learned from friends at school.

65. Katharine Du Pre Lumpkin, *The Making of a Southerner* (1946; Athens: University of Georgia Press, 1991), 112–20.

66. Ibid., 113, 125, 136. For more on the Children of the Confederacy, see Karen L. Cox, *Dixie's Daughters: The United Daughters of the Confederacy and the Preservation of Confederate Culture* (Gainesville: University Press of Florida, 2003), 134–40.

67. Lumpkin, *Making of a Southerner,* 86–87.

68. Ibid., 130, 137. The debate was undertaken largely owing to the presence of a northern student in the class.

69. Lumpkin wrote of the post-Reconstruction "Redemption" period and the era of disfranchisement and segregation that followed, "Some of this we children understood, some not. In any case our fathers did." Lumpkin, *Making of a Southerner,* 138.

70. Hodding Carter, *Southern Legacy* (Baton Rouge: Louisiana State University Press, 1950), 24.

Hodding Carter II was born on Feb. 3, 1907, in Hammond, La. He was the longtime editor and publisher of the *Delta Democrat-Times* in Greenville, Miss.

71. Carter, *Southern Legacy,* 18–19, 17, 21.

72. Ibid., 21–23.

73. Morris, *North toward Home,* 18–19, 64, 13–14, 35, 62, 37.

74. Ibid., 62–63.

75. Boyle, *Desegregated Heart,* 21. Boyle was born in Virginia in 1906.

76. Ibid., 22, 26, 34–35.

77. Braden, *Wall Between,* 21.

78. Harry Crews, *A Childhood: The Biography of a Place* (Athens: University of Georgia Press, 1978, 1995), 62–63. Crews was born in 1935 in Bacon County, Ga.

79. Anne Braden's family was an exception. She wrote of using the term "Negro": "Today in the South many of the most die-hard segregationists have learned to say, albeit with some effort, 'Nigra.' That was not so when I was a child. No matter what the level of a person's education, in the circles in which I grew up the word was 'nigger'—although of course one always said 'colored' when talking to a Negro. I was well in my teens before I knew what the correct pronunciation was. For years after my social views on segregation were well established I still had an odd feeling of speaking in an affected way when I said the word 'Negro.'" Braden, *Wall Between,* 21.

80. Smith, *Killers of the Dream,* 28.

81. Paul Hemphill, *Leaving Birmingham: Notes of a Native Son* (1993; Tuscaloosa: University of Alabama Press, 2000), 61.

82. Hobson, *But Now I See,* 137.

83. Boyle, *Desegregated Heart,* 79.

84. Margaret Jones Bolsterli, *Born in the Delta: Reflections on the Making of a Southern White Sensibility* (Knoxville: University of Tennessee Press, 1991), 60. Bolsterli grew up in the Arkansas Delta in the 1930s.

85. McLaurin, *Separate Pasts,* 91, 93. McLaurin was born in 1941, and he was raised in Wade, N.C. A historian of the South and race, he served for many years as a professor and administrator at the University of North Carolina Wilmington.

86. Ibid., 71.

87. Morris, *North toward Home,* 86–87.

88. Hemphill, *Leaving Birmingham,* 37.

89. Bolsterli, *Born in the Delta,* 68, 73.

90. Crews, *Childhood,* 127, 74, 133–34.

91. Pat Watters, *Down to Now: Reflections on the Southern Civil Rights Movement* (1971; Athens: University of Georgia Press, 1993), 26.

92. Ibid., 27. John Egerton explained the complicated usage of these terms: "The most common and hated word was *nigger;* only slightly less cutting was *negro,* uncapitalized (and pronounced *nig-ra*), for it was a visible and explicit denial of any status as a person." Egerton, *Speak Now against the Day: The Generation before the Civil Rights Movement in the South* (1994; Chapel Hill: University of North Carolina Press, 1995), 31.

93. Lillian Quick Smith, interview by Sonya Ramsey, Wilmington, N.C., July 19, 1993, Behind the Veil: Documenting African-American Life in the Jim Crow South, Center for Documentary Studies at Duke University, David M. Rubenstein Rare Book & Manuscript Library, Duke University.

94. The term *alternative explanation* comes from JoAnne Banks-Wallace and Lennette Parks, "'So That Our Souls Don't Get Damaged': The Impact of Racism on Maternal Thinking and Practice Related to the Protection of Daughters," *Issues in Mental Health Nursing* 22, no. 1 (Jan. 2001): 89. Banks-Wallace and Parks used the term to describe efforts by African American mothers to protect their daughters from the effects of racism.

95. John Seigenthaler Sr., "Son of the South," in *When Race Becomes Real: Black and White Writers Confront Their Personal Histories,* ed. Bernestine Singley (Chicago: Lawrence Hill Books, 2002), 54. Seigenthaler was born in Nashville, Tenn., in 1927. He was a longtime journalist for the city's leading newspaper, the *Tennessean,* and he later served as editor, publisher, and CEO of the paper. John Lewis's description of the movie theaters in Nashville corroborates Seigenthaler's account. Lewis remembered of the theaters on Church Street, "Not only were we relegated to the balconies, but to get there, black customers in some instances actually had to walk outside, go into a dark alley and climb an exterior fire escape." Lewis, with Michael D'Orso, *Walking with the Wind: A Memoir of the Movement* (New York: Simon & Schuster, 1998), 129.

96. Seigenthaler, "Son of the South," 57–58.

97. Smith, *Killers of the Dream,* 36–37.

98. Morris, *North toward Home,* 17–18.

99. Braden, *Wall Between,* 25.

100. Clark, *Prejudice and Your Child,* 93–94.

101. Ibid., 5.

102. Braden, *Wall Between,* 75, 29.

103. Smith, *Killers of the Dream,* 51–52, 54. Smith wrote of this exchange, "I did not record that conversation but it has fixed itself in my mind so deeply that I do not think I shall distort its truth as I tell it now" (51).

104. Ibid., 55, 54.

CHAPTER 2

THE AFRICAN AMERICAN DILEMMA

1. Septima Poinsette Clark, with LeGette Blythe, *Echo in My Soul* (New York: Dutton, 1962), 237. Clark was born in Charleston, S.C., in 1898. Over the course of her life she served as a public school teacher, as director of workshops for the Highlander Folk School, and as a key organizer of citizenship schools for the Southern Christian Leadership Conference (SCLC). Her son, Nerie Clark, was born in 1925.

2. Martin Luther King Jr., "Letter from Birmingham City Jail" (1963), in *A Testament of Hope: The Essential Writings and Speeches of Martin Luther King, Jr.,* ed. James M. Washington (San Francisco: Harper, 1986), 292–93.

3. Carlton Winfrey, "Spelling Lesson," in *When Race Becomes Real: Black and White Writers Confront Their Personal Histories,* ed. Bernestine Singley (Chicago: Lawrence Hill Books, 2002), 306.

4. Studies on race socialization have often focused on classifying the various messages conveyed by African American parents. Based on their analysis of responses to the National Survey of Black Americans, conducted between 1979 and 1980, Tony N. Brown and Chase L. Lesane-Brown categorized black parents' race socialization messages thus: no messages, individual pride, racial group pride, deference

172

to or fear of whites, colorblind messages, and messages that stress white prejudice. See Brown and Lesane-Brown, "Race Socialization Messages across Historical Time," *Social Psychology Quarterly* 69, no. 2 (June 2006): 204. In an influential study A. Wade Boykin and Forrest D. Toms divided African American parents' race socialization messages into three categories: mainstream messages, those that emphasize hard work, equality, and a positive self-concept; minority messages, those that focus on racial barriers and coping strategies; and messages that stress an African American cultural experience and racial pride. See Boykin and Toms, "Black Child Socialization: A Conceptual Framework," in *Black Children: Social, Educational, and Parental Environments,* ed. Harriette Pipes McAdoo and John Lewis McAdoo (Beverly Hills, Calif.: Sage Publications, 1985), 39; Michael C. Thornton, "Strategies of Racial Socialization among Black Parents: Mainstream, Minority, and Cultural Messages," in *Family Life in Black America,* ed. Robert Joseph Taylor, James S. Jackson, and Linda M. Chatters (Thousand Oaks, Calif.: Sage Publications, 1997), 206–7. Diane Hughes and Lisa Chen generated four categories: cultural socialization, which includes messages on racial pride and black history; preparation for bias, which involves lessons about discrimination and coping strategies; promotion of mistrust, which entails discouraging interracial interaction and issuing warnings about racism but does not include coping strategies; and egalitarianism, which involves lessons about equality and appreciation for all racial and ethnic groups but can also include parental silence on matters of race. See Hughes and Chen, "The Nature of Parents' Race-Related Communications to Children: A Developmental Perspective," in *Child Psychology: A Handbook of Contemporary Issues,* ed. Lawrence Balter and Catherine S. Tamis-LeMonda (Philadelphia: Psychology Press, 1999), 473–78. Drawing on the model established by this scholarship, I am proposing a system of classification for the race socialization strategies that African American parents developed to teach their children about segregation. These strategies are as follows: development of internal resources, isolation from contact with whites, avoidance, promotion of acceptance, promotion of challenge, and silence on segregation and race. The terms "acceptance" and "challenge" are drawn from James S. Jackson et al., "Race Identity," in *Life in Black America,* ed. James S. Jackson (Newbury Park, Calif.: Sage Publications, 1991), 249. Several studies have displayed considerable ambiguity as to whether silence or "no messages" should be considered a separate strategy or taken to mean that parents who did not teach their children about race and discrimination did not have a race socialization strategy. I argue that black parents' silence in the form of either refusing to answer their children's questions about segregation or discouraging their children from discussing the system constituted a distinct strategy on their part, one that took into account their relative powerlessness within southern society.

5. Ralph David Abernathy, *And the Walls Came Tumbling Down: An Autobiography* (New York: Harper & Row, 1989), 182. Abernathy was born in Marengo County, Ala., in 1926. He served as Martin Luther King Jr.'s second-in-command in SCLC and assumed leadership of the organization after King's assassination.

6. Marian Wright Edelman, *Lanterns: A Memoir of Mentors* (Boston: Beacon Press, 1999), xiv. Edelman was born in Bennettsville, S.C., on June 6, 1939. She participated in the 1960 Atlanta sit-ins while she was a student at Spelman College, and she attended law school at Yale before moving to Mississippi to work as a lawyer for civil rights cases. Edelman went on to found the Children's Defense Fund.

7. Ibid., 16.

8. Ibid., 5–7. This was not Edelman's only exposure to the poetry of Langston Hughes. Traveling through South Carolina in the early 1940s and unable to find a place to stay because of segregation,

Hughes was directed to the principal of Edelman's elementary school. After staying the night at the principal's home, Hughes accepted an invitation to read his poetry at the school. Such firsthand contact with African American dignitaries did much to instill racial pride in young children.

9. Ibid., 16.

10. See, e.g., Harriette Pipes McAdoo and John Lewis McAdoo, preface, in McAdoo and McAdoo, *Black Children*, 9; Michael C. Thornton et al., "Sociodemographic and Environmental Correlates of Racial Socialization by Black Parents," in "Minority Children," special issue, *Child Development* 61, no. 2 (Apr. 1990): 401.

11. Pauli Murray, *Proud Shoes: The Story of an American Family* (1956; New York: Harper & Row, 1978), 152. Murray was born in 1910 in Baltimore, Md., but she grew up with extended family in Durham, N.C. She was a writer, lawyer, and activist, and she was later the first African American woman ordained as an Episcopal priest. For more on the life and work of Pauli Murray, see Glenda Elizabeth Gilmore, *Defying Dixie: The Radical Roots of Civil Rights, 1919–1950* (New York: Norton, 2008).

12. Murray, *Proud Shoes*, 33, 59.

13. Ibid., 246–47.

14. Benjamin E. Mays, *Born to Rebel: An Autobiography* (1971; Athens: University of Georgia Press, 2003), 2.

15. Coretta Scott King, *My Life with Martin Luther King, Jr.*, rev. ed. (1969; New York: Henry Holt, 1993), 79, 32.

16. Ibid., 198. King recalled that Funtown "quietly desegregated" in the spring of 1963, and the Kings took their three older children to the park. This would have been around the same time that Martin Luther King Jr. invoked Funtown in the "Letter from Birmingham Jail." See also Martin Luther King Jr., "*Playboy* Interview: Martin Luther King, Jr." (1965), in Washington, *Testament of Hope*, 342.

17. King, *My Life with Martin Luther King, Jr.*, 197.

18. Lanetha Branch, interview by Doris Dixon, Memphis, Tenn., June 16, 1995, Behind the Veil: Documenting African-American Life in the Jim Crow South, Center for Documentary Studies at Duke University, David M. Rubenstein Rare Book & Manuscript Library, Duke University. Branch was born in Memphis on Jan. 22, 1935. Her father worked as a laborer, and her mother was a taxi owner and beautician. Branch remembered having grown up in a fairly prosperous integrated neighborhood in Memphis. She went on to become a public school teacher.

19. Charlayne Hunter-Gault, *In My Place* (1992; New York: Vintage Books, 1993), 3. Hunter-Gault was born in Due West, S.C., on Feb. 27, 1942. She grew up in Covington and Atlanta, Ga., and spent one school year living in Alaska. Her father was an African Methodist Episcopal (AME) minister and an army chaplain, and her mother worked variously as a cook, homemaker, and clerical worker. Hunter-Gault and Hamilton Holmes desegregated the University of Georgia on Jan. 9, 1961. Hunter-Gault went on to pursue a successful career in journalism.

20. Abernathy, *And the Walls Came Tumbling Down*, 28.

21. James Farmer, *Lay Bare the Heart: An Autobiography of the Civil Rights Movement* (New York: Arbor House, 1985), 37, 52.

22. For more on Mississippi's segregationist order as having been qualitatively different from that of other southern states, see James W. Silver, *Mississippi: The Closed Society*, rev. ed. (1964; New York: Harcourt, Brace & World, 1966). See also Neil R. McMillen, *Dark Journey: Black Mississippians in the Age of Jim Crow* (Urbana: University of Illinois Press, 1989).

23. Clarie Collins Harvey, interview by John Dittmer and John Jones, Jackson, Miss., Apr. 21,

1981, Mississippi Department of Archives and History. Harvey was born on Nov. 27, 1916, in Meridian, Miss., and she grew up in Meridian and Jackson. She was running her family's funeral home at the time of her interview. Harvey had also been involved in various civil rights and organizing activities, including Womanpower Unlimited, a network of women who sent food, clothing, and other supplies to the Freedom Riders who were jailed in Jackson in 1961. See John Dittmer, *Local People: The Struggle for Civil Rights in Mississippi* (Urbana: University of Illinois Press, 1994), 98–99. For more on Harvey's work with Womanpower Unlimited, see Tiyi M. Morris, *Womanpower Unlimited and the Black Freedom Struggle in Mississippi* (Athens: University of Georgia Press, 2015).

24. Carolyn McKinstry, interview by Horace Huntley, Apr. 23, 1998, transcribed interview (vol. 35, sec. 1, 6–9). BCRI Oral History Project, Birmingham Civil Rights Institute, Birmingham, Ala. McKinstry was born in Clanton, Ala., in 1949, and she grew up in Birmingham. Her parents were teachers, and her father also worked as a waiter in Mountain Brook. McKinstry participated in the 1963 civil rights campaign in Birmingham, was inside Sixteenth Street Baptist Church when it was bombed in Sept. 1963, and knew the four girls who were killed. She went on to become a teacher and later pursued a career in the ministry. See also Carolyn Maull McKinstry, with Denise George, *While the World Watched: A Birmingham Bombing Survivor Comes of Age during the Civil Rights Movement* (Carol Stream, Ill.: Tyndale House Publishers, 2011).

25. Interview of John Wesley Hatch, in *Freedom on the Border: An Oral History of the Civil Rights Movement in Kentucky*, ed. Catherine Fosl and Tracy E. K'Meyer (Lexington: University Press of Kentucky, 2009), 19–20. Hatch was born in Louisville, Ky., in 1928. After a thwarted attempt to obtain a nonsegregated legal education in Kentucky in the late 1940s, he pursued a career in public health and became a distinguished professor at the University of North Carolina at Chapel Hill (271).

26. Murray, *Proud Shoes*, 265. Some scholarship on race socialization has focused on how the age of the child affects parents' strategies. Diane Hughes and Lisa Chen suggested that although children as young as three can recognize racial differences, they attach no meaning to those differences and do not develop a sophisticated understanding of race until they are seven to ten years old. Hughes and Chen concluded that parents delay teaching their children about racial discrimination until such time as they feel their children will be able to understand it. These scholars also suggested that what they termed "cultural socialization," which I classify as a strategy of building up internal resources through instilling racial pride, is *not* dependent on children's ages. See Hughes and Chen, "The Nature of Parents' Race-Related Communications to Children," 484–85. In contrast, Debra Van Ausdale and Joe R. Feagin have argued that children are able to develop a sophisticated understanding of race and use racial concepts in their own, unsupervised play well before most parents and teachers suspect, e.g., by three to five years old. See Van Ausdale and Feagin, *The First R: How Children Learn Race and Racism* (Lanham, Md.: Rowman & Littlefield, 2001).

27. John Hope Franklin, *Mirror to America: The Autobiography of John Hope Franklin* (New York: Farrar, Straus & Giroux, 2005), 162. John Whittington "Whit" Franklin was born on Aug. 24, 1952 (152–53).

28. King, *My Life with Martin Luther King, Jr.*, 197.

29. G. K., "People Write Us," *South Today* 8, no. 1 (Spring–Summer 1944): 92–94.

30. Shirley A. Hill, *African American Children: Socialization and Development in Families* (Thousand Oaks, Calif.: Sage Publications, 1999), 83.

31. G. K., "People Write Us," 92, 94.

32. Mays, *Born to Rebel*, 23.

33. Maya Angelou, *I Know Why the Caged Bird Sings* (1969; New York: Bantam Books, 1993), 47. Angelou was born on Apr. 4, 1928, in St. Louis, Mo., and spent much of her childhood in Stamps, Ark. She lived with her paternal grandmother, Annie Henderson, who owned a general store in Stamps. Angelou characterized her grandmother as someone who stood up to whites, and Henderson was known locally as the only black woman who had ever been referred to as "Mrs." by a white person. Angelou asserted, however, that her grandmother was a realist, and this quality is evident in the way she raised her grandchildren.

34. In her study of how black and white southern children "learned race," Jennifer Ritterhouse wrote, "Taking the middle ground—anticipating whites' behavior, adapting to whites' expectations, following racial etiquette—was always the safest course." She went on to argue, "Nevertheless, it is easy to overestimate how far this 'safety first' thinking went." Ritterhouse, *Growing Up Jim Crow: How Black and White Southern Children Learned Race* (Chapel Hill: University of North Carolina Press, 2006), 49. In contrast, I argue that the decision to prioritize safety was one that many African American parents made based on an assessment of the risks involved.

35. Robert Coles, *Children of Crisis: A Study of Courage and Fear* (Boston: Little, Brown, 1967), 66–67.

36. Henry Hooten, interview by Paul Ortiz, Tuskegee, Ala., July 11, 1994, Behind the Veil. Hooten was born on July 13, 1917, in Troy, Ala. His father was a foreman at a warehouse, and his mother was a homemaker and a domestic. Hooten spent the bulk of his professional career as a rehabilitation therapist at the Veterans Administration (VA) hospital in Tuskegee.

37. Ibid.

38. Ibid.

39. John Lewis, interview by Terry Gross, *Fresh Air*, National Public Radio (NPR), Jan. 19, 2009, www.npr.org/templates/story/story.php?storyId=99560979 (accessed Oct. 15, 2012). Lewis was born on Feb. 21, 1940, in rural Pike County, Ala., near Troy. His parents were sharecroppers. Lewis served as chairman of the Student Nonviolent Coordinating Committee (SNCC) from 1963 to 1966 and was elected to Congress from Georgia in 1986.

40. John Lewis, with Michael D'Orso, *Walking with the Wind: A Memoir of the Movement* (New York: Simon & Schuster, 1998), 58.

41. Cecil Brown, *Coming Up Down Home: A Memoir of a Southern Childhood* (Hopewell, N.J.: Ecco Press, 1993), 169–70. Brown was born in 1943, and he was raised in Bolton, N.C.

42. Angelou, *I Know Why the Caged Bird Sings*, 114.

43. Brown, *Coming Up Down Home*, 169; Angelou, *I Know Why the Caged Bird Sings*, 116–17.

44. Les Payne, "The Night I Stopped Being a Negro," in Singley, *When Race Becomes Real*, 37. Payne was born on July 12, 1941, in Tuscaloosa, Ala.

45. Ibid., 38.

46. Ibid., 39–40, 42–43.

47. Sadie G. Mays, quoted in Benjamin Mays, *Born to Rebel*, 32. Sadie Gray Mays was born on Aug. 5, 1900, and grew up in Georgia on her family's farm. She married Benjamin Mays in 1926.

48. Ibid., 33.

49. McKinstry, *While the World Watched*, 7, 47–48.

50. Annie Gavin, interview by Chris Stewart, James City, N.C., Aug. 3, 1993, Behind the Veil. Gavin was born on Oct. 28, 1911, in James City. After her father lost his foot working on the railroad, he opened a small business. Her mother was a homemaker. Gavin also owned a small business and had a longtime paper route.

51. Wilhelmina Jones, interview by Paul Ortiz, Tuskegee, Ala., July 18, 1994, Behind the Veil. Jones was born on Sept. 14, 1915, in Keysville, Ga. She came from a family of prosperous, landowning farmers. She was a clerical worker at Tuskegee Army Airfield and then at the VA hospital in Tuskegee.

52. Rosa Parks, with Jim Haskins, *Rosa Parks: My Story* (New York: Dial Books, 1992), 14–17, 30–32. Parks was born on Feb. 4, 1913, in Tuskegee, Ala. Her father was an itinerant builder, and her mother was a teacher. Parks lived in a number of towns in Alabama while she was growing up. She remembered thinking about her grandfather's courage as she waited on the bus to see what would happen after she refused to give up her seat (115–16).

53. Ibid., 22–23, 51.

54. Anne Moody, *Coming of Age in Mississippi* (1968; New York: Laurel, 1976), 31. Moody was born in Centreville, Miss., in 1940.

55. Ibid., 40.

56. Ibid., 145, 123.

57. Richard Wright, *Black Boy: A Record of Childhood and Youth* (1945; New York: Perennial Classics, 1998), 23–24. Wright was born near Natchez, Miss., on Sept. 4, 1908. He spent much of his childhood living in the homes of various relatives with his single mother after his father left the family.

58. Ibid., 47, 68. Note that Wright's autobiography must be used with more caution than some of the other autobiographies consulted here. Literary scholars have often noted the extent to which the "Richard" or "black boy" of the story differs from the historical person of the author Richard Wright, and, while the "I" of the text of an autobiography may always be distinct from the "I" of the author, the distance between the two is perhaps greater in this case. Scholars have argued that Wright intended for "black boy" to be a generic character who would capture the experience of the black, southern, particularly male child in general. For a discussion of Wright's autobiography, see Timothy Dow Adams, *Telling Lies in Modern American Autobiography* (Chapel Hill: University of North Carolina Press, 1990), 71–74.

59. Theresa Lyons, interview by Leslie Brown, Durham, N.C., Aug. 16, 1995, Behind the Veil. Lyons was born on Feb. 17, 1934, in Durham. Her mother worked in a shipyard during World War II and was later a farmer. Lyons held various clerical positions, including one as a corporate secretary at North Carolina Mutual, an African American life insurance company founded in Durham in 1898.

60. Alma Mitchell, interview by Mary Hebert, Norfolk, Va., July 20, 1995, Behind the Veil. Mitchell was born on Nov. 20, 1933, in South Hampton County, Va. Her father was a sharecropper, and her mother was a homemaker and a domestic. Mitchell was a homemaker and a dishwasher at a restaurant.

61. Edith Polk, interview by Kate Ellis, New Iberia, La., Aug. 2, 1994, Behind the Veil. Polk was born in New Iberia on Aug. 5, 1917. Her father was a carpenter, and her mother was a homemaker and a domestic. Polk was a nurse and later a teacher.

62. Alma Mitchell, interview by Mary Hebert, Norfolk, Va., July 20, 1995.

63. Edith Polk, interview by Kate Ellis, New Iberia, La., Aug. 2, 1994.

64. Scholars have argued that single parents, especially single mothers, are less likely to engage in race socialization. Hughes and Chen wrote, "Stressors such as poverty, single parenthood, and homelessness may preclude certain types of racial socialization . . . because they leave parents with little time or energy for socialization in general." Hughes and Chen, "When and What Parents Tell Children about Race: An Examination of Race-Related Socialization among African American Families," *Applied Developmental Science* 1, no. 4 (1997): 212.

65. Farmer, *Lay Bare the Heart*, 30, 37.

66. Abernathy, *And the Walls Came Tumbling Down,* 30–31.

67. Farmer, *Lay Bare the Heart,* 57–58.

68. Lil Hooten, interview by Paul Ortiz, Tuskegee, Ala., July 11, 1994, Behind the Veil. Hooten was born on Apr. 10, 1918, in Pensacola, Fla. Her father was a farmer who owned a small amount of land and rented additional acreage from a white landowner. Her mother was a homemaker and a farmer. Hooten spent her professional career as a public school teacher.

69. Brown, *Coming Up Down Home,* 199–201.

70. Ibid., 203–4, 155, 205, 206.

71. Anne Moody, interview by Debra Spencer, Jackson, Miss., Feb. 19, 1985. Mississippi Department of Archives and History, http://mdah.state.ms.us/arrec/digital_archives/vault/projects/OHtranscripts/AU076_096117.pdf (accessed Feb. 25, 2016).

72. Abernathy, *And the Walls Came Tumbling Down,* 33.

CHAPTER 3

SUPPLEMENTARY READING

1. Anne Braden, *The Wall Between* (1958; Knoxville: University of Tennessee Press, 1999), 34. Her son, James McCarty Braden, was born in Sept. 1951. See Catherine Fosl, *Subversive Southerner: Anne Braden and the Struggle for Racial Justice in the Cold War South* (New York: Palgrave Macmillan, 2002), 126.

2. Kenneth B. Clark, *Prejudice and Your Child* (1955; Middletown, Conn.: Wesleyan University Press, 1988), 31.

3. For another discussion of the lessons black children learned about race and segregation at school, see Leon F. Litwack, *Trouble in Mind: Black Southerners in the Age of Jim Crow* (1998; New York: Vintage Books, 1999), 71–78.

4. Vernon E. Jordan Jr., with Annette Gordon-Reed, *Vernon Can Read! A Memoir* (New York: PublicAffairs, 2001), 45. See also Adam Fairclough, *A Class of Their Own: Black Teachers in the Segregated South* (Cambridge: Belknap Press of Harvard University Press, 2007), 303, 305, in which Fairclough argued that early attempts to impose an exclusively industrial program on black schools had abated by the 1920s, by which time black parents and educators expressed a clear preference that the same curriculum be used in both white and black schools.

5. Clark wrote of racial prejudice, "When the effects of these forms of prejudice on the personalities of children are clearly understood, then the efforts to immunize our children from their virulence will be more effective." Clark, *Prejudice and Your Child,* 13.

6. Maurice Lucas, interview by Mausiki Stacey Scales, Renova, Miss., Aug. 7, 1995, Behind the Veil: Documenting African-American Life in the Jim Crow South, Center for Documentary Studies at Duke University, David M. Rubenstein Rare Book & Manuscript Library, Duke University. Lucas was born on Oct. 10, 1944, in Renova. His parents were landowning farmers. Lucas worked as an accountant and, at the time of his interview, was mayor of Renova.

7. See Herman James Sr., interview by Kate Ellis, New Iberia, La., Aug. 3, 1994; Amy Jones, interview by Mausiki Stacey Scales, Memphis, Tenn., June 28, 1995; Mildred Oakley Page, interview by Doris Dixon and Felicia Woods, Durham, N.C., June 1, 1995; and Hortense Williams, interview by Kisha Turner, Norfolk, Va., July 17, 1995, Behind the Veil.

8. Rosa Parks, with Jim Haskins, *Rosa Parks: My Story* (New York: Dial Books, 1992), 29.

9. Vermelle Ely, interview by Leslie Brown, Charlotte, N.C., June 17, 1993, Behind the Veil. Ely was born in Charlotte on Jan. 10, 1933. Her parents were both teachers, and her father was a principal.

10. Ferdie Walker, interview by Paul Ortiz, Tuskegee, Ala., July 17, 1994, Behind the Veil. Walker was born on Nov. 17, 1928, in Fort Worth, Tex. Her father was a railroad dining car waiter, and her mother was a registered nurse. Walker was also a nurse. Walker noted that the stoves, pots, and pans used in the home economics department also arrived used from the white school.

11. "Minutes of the State Board of Education," Aug. 12, 1937, Minutes July–Sept. 1937, 96, State Board of Education Minutes, Files, and Correspondence, Georgia Board of Education, 1870–1992, Georgia Department of Education, RG 12-1-28, Georgia Archives (GA).

12. Vermelle Ely, interview by Leslie Brown; Willie Morris, *North toward Home* (1967; New York: Vintage Books, 2000), 82.

13. "Minutes of the State Board of Education," Sept. 19, 1951, Minutes Sept. 1951–Oct. 1952, 14, State Board of Education Minutes, Files, and Correspondence, Georgia Board of Education, 1870–1992. GA.

14. Geraldine Davidson, interview by Paul Ortiz, Fargo, Ark., July 19, 1995, Behind the Veil. Davidson was born in Zent, Ark., on Apr. 30, 1927. Her parents were landowning farmers. Davidson worked variously as a factory worker and a museum curator.

15. Mary E. Mebane, *Mary* (New York: Viking Press, 1981), 54. Mebane was born on June 26, 1933, in the Wildwood community in Durham, N.C. Her father was a farmer, and her mother worked in a tobacco factory. Mebane eventually became a schoolteacher and a writer.

16. Anthony Farmer, interview by Sonya Ramsey, Enfield, N.C., July 25, 1993, Behind the Veil. Farmer was born on Sept. 26, 1929, in Danville, Va. His father was a Baptist preacher, and his mother was a homemaker and hairdresser. Farmer was later a school principal.

17. See, e.g., Pauli Murray's description of the stark differences between the black and white schools in her community in Durham, N.C. Murray, *Proud Shoes: The Story of an American Family* (1956; New York: Harper & Row, 1978), 269.

18. Clark, *Prejudice and Your Child*, 32.

19. Bruno Lasker, *Race Attitudes in Children* (New York: Henry Holt, 1929), 149–50, 159, 150.

20. "Textbook Omissions," *Interracial News Service*, Jan.–Feb. 1947, Una Roberts Lawrence Collection (URLC), AR 631, sec. 1, Professional Papers, Black Missions, box 3, folder 15, Southern Baptist Historical Library and Archives (SBHLA).

21. Clark, *Prejudice and Your Child*, 93.

22. Mark M. Krug, John B. Poster, and William B. Gillies III, *The New Social Studies: Analysis of Theory and Materials* (Itasca, Ill.: F. E. Peacock Publishers, 1970), 196.

23. Lawrence D. Reddick, "Racial Attitudes in American History Textbooks of the South," *Journal of Negro History* 19, no. 3 (July 1934): 235. While chair of the Alabama State College (later Alabama State University) history department in Montgomery during the late 1950s, Reddick befriended Martin Luther King Jr. and became his first biographer when *Crusader without Violence: A Biography of Martin Luther King, Jr.* (New York: Harper) was published in 1959. See Martin Luther King Jr., "My Trip to the Land of Gandhi" (1959), in *A Testament of Hope: The Essential Writings and Speeches of Martin Luther King, Jr.*, ed. James M. Washington (San Francisco: Harper, 1986), 23–24.

24. Reddick, "Racial Attitudes," 259, 245–46, 253.

25. Ibid., 258. In a 1941 study of textbooks used nationwide, Marie Elizabeth Carpenter found that books published from 1931 to 1939 had much more coverage of African Americans after Reconstruction

than did books published from 1901 to 1930. Carpenter, *The Treatment of the Negro in American History School Textbooks* (Menasha, Wisc.: George Banta Publishing Co., 1941), 91, 120. Carpenter offered a number of suggestions for further improvement, including more pictures of African Americans, treatment of "the Negro" as more than a "passive character," emphasis on the artistic and academic achievements of African Americans, and recognition of the effects of segregation and discrimination on African Americans (128–29). A 1972 study that explicitly considered the extent to which Carpenter's recommendations had been implemented found significant improvement in virtually every category. Irving Sloan, *The Negro in Modern American History Textbooks* (Washington, D.C.: American Federation of Teachers, 1972), 6–9.

26. Reddick, "Racial Attitudes," 261–62, 264.

27. Robert B. Eleazer, *School Books and Racial Antagonism: A Study of Omissions and Inclusions That Make for Misunderstanding*, 3rd ed. (1935; Atlanta: Commission on Interracial Cooperation, 1937), 1, URLC, box 2, folder 27, SBHLA.

28. Ibid., 1. See also James Overton Butler, "The Treatment of the Negro in Southern School Textbooks" (master's thesis, George Peabody College for Teachers, 1933).

29. Eleazer, *School Books and Racial Antagonism*, 1.

30. Ibid., 2, 3, 6, 7, 8.

31. Lawton B. Evans, *First Lessons in American History*, rev. ed. (1910; New York: Benjamin H. Sanborn & Co., 1922), 139; "Adopted Textbooks for the Elementary and High Schools of Alabama," State Board of Education, 1924, Department of Education, State of Alabama, Alabama Department of Archives and History (ADAH).

32. Evans, *First Lessons in American History*, 138.

33. Wilbur Fisk Gordy, *The History of the United States* (1922; New York: Charles Scribner's Sons, 1927), 300–301; "State Adoption, Elementary Field," Textbook Commission Minutes, 1929, Kentucky Department for Libraries and Archives.

34. Evans, *First Lessons in American History*, 257–85; Waddy Thompson, *The First Book in United States History* (Boston: D. C. Heath, 1921), 308–37; "A Brief Outline of Work for the Elementary Schools," State of Tennessee, State Department of Education, 1923, Tennessee State Library and Archives.

35. David Saville Muzzey, *An American History*, rev. ed. (1911; Boston: Ginn & Co., 1920), 383–84; Textbook Contract, Department of Public Instruction, Office of Superintendent, Textbook Correspondence, box 1, folder: "High School Textbook Contracts—1920," State Archives of North Carolina.

36. Muzzey, *American History*, 384.

37. Ibid., 388.

38. William H. Mace, *American History* (New York: Rand McNally, 1925), 214–15; "List of Textbooks for Grades 7–12 Adopted by the Textbook Purchasing Board, 1929," State of Alabama, Department of Education, ADAH.

39. Gordy, *History of the United States*, 380.

40. R. O. Hughes, *Problems of American Democracy* (Boston: Allyn & Bacon, 1922), 143.

41. Willis Mason West, *History of the American People*, rev. ed. (1918; Boston: Allyn & Bacon, 1922), 599; "The North Carolina State List of Approved High School Textbooks," State Superintendent of Public Instruction, 1924, Department of Public Instruction, Office of Superintendent, Textbook Correspondence, box 3, folder: "Approved High School Textbooks, 1924," State Archives of North Carolina.

42. Bessie Louise Pierce, *Public Opinion and the Teaching of History in the United States* (1926; New York: Da Capo Press, 1970), 136–46, 39, 66–67.

43. Fred Arthur Bailey, "The Textbooks of the 'Lost Cause': Censorship and the Creation of Southern State Histories," *Georgia Historical Quarterly* 75, no. 3 (Fall 1991): 508.

44. Karen L. Cox, *Dixie's Daughters: The United Daughters of the Confederacy and the Preservation of Confederate Culture* (Gainesville: University Press of Florida, 2003), 96, 157.

45. See Pierce, *Public Opinion and the Teaching of History*, 159–60, for her discussion of the controversy over Muzzey's work. See also Anastatia Sims, *The Power of Femininity in the New South: Women's Organizations and Politics in North Carolina, 1880–1930* (Columbia: University of South Carolina Press, 1997), 148.

46. Rutherford Committee, "Criticism of Muzzey's American History So Far as It Relates to Doing Justice to the South," n.d., 2, 4, Department of Public Instruction, Office of Superintendent, Textbook Correspondence, box 1, folder: "Controversy—'Muzzey's History,' 1921–1922," State Archives of North Carolina.

47. A collection of these letters can be found in Department of Public Instruction, Office of Superintendent, Textbook Correspondence, 'Muzzey's History,' 1921–1922," State Archives of North Carolina. For more on the work of Mildred Lewis Rutherford, see Cox, *Dixie's Daughters*, 96, 103.

48. "Minutes of the State Board of Education," Sept. 18, 1940, Minutes June 1939–Sept. 1940, 72, 83–84, 93, State Board of Education Minutes, Files, and Correspondence, Georgia Board of Education, 1870–1992. GA.

49. For more on the controversy surrounding Harold Rugg's books, see Julia L. Mickenberg, *Learning from the Left: Children's Literature, the Cold War, and Radical Politics in the United States* (New York: Oxford University Press, 2006), 96, 234.

50. "Subcommittee, Report A, Virginia History—Grade VII," Nov. 18, 1953, 3, Virginia History and Government Textbook Commission, Minutes, 1950–1956, accession no. 32492, State Government Records Collection, Library of Virginia (LVA).

51. D. A. Cannaday, "Comments on Revised Geography, History, and Government Text for the Seventh Grade," Apr. 20, 1955, Virginia History and Government Textbook Commission, Minutes, LVA.

52. D. A. Cannaday, "Comments on the Tentative Manuscript of Senior High School History," Feb. 17, 1954, 4, Virginia History and Government Textbook Commission, Minutes, LVA.

53. Ibid., 6.

54. Thomas P. Abernathy, "Comments on High School Manuscript for Virginia History and Government," July 26, 1956, 2, Virginia History and Government Textbook Commission, Minutes, LVA.

55. D. A. Cannaday, "Comments on the Tentative Manuscript of the Seventh Grade History Text," Mar. 25, 1954, 3, Virginia History and Government Textbook Commission, Minutes, LVA.

56. "Minutes, Joint Meeting of the Subcommittee to Prepare Textbook on Virginia History, Government, and Geography and Textbook Committee of the State Board of Education," Feb. 24, 1954, 4, Virginia History and Government Textbook Commission, Minutes, LVA.

57. "Revision in Dr. W. Edwin Hemphill's Virginia High School History, Agreed upon December 7, 1956," 3, Virginia History and Government Textbook Commission, Minutes, LVA.

58. Cannaday, "Comments on the Tentative Manuscript of Senior High School History," 7.

59. "Minutes, Meeting of the Subcommittee to Prepare Textbook on Virginia History, Government, and Geography," Apr. 20, 1955, 1, Virginia History and Government Textbook Commission, Minutes, LVA.

60. Cannaday, "Comments on the Tentative Manuscript of Senior High School History," 9.

61. "Revision in Dr. W. Edwin Hemphill's Virginia High School History," 6.

62. "Minutes, Joint Meeting of the Subcommittee to Prepare Textbook on Virginia History, Government, and Geography and Textbook Committee of the State Board of Education," 2.

63. A. G. Richardson, "Comments on the Seventh Grade Geography, History, and Government Text," Nov. 4, 1955, Virginia History and Government Textbook Commission, Minutes, LVA.

64. Natalie Blanton, "Comments on the History and Government High School Text," July 26 and Mar. 9, 1956, Virginia History and Government Textbook Commission, Minutes, LVA.

65. John Seigenthaler Sr., "Son of the South," in *When Race Becomes Real: Black and White Writers Confront Their Personal Histories,* ed. Bernestine Singley (Chicago: Lawrence Hill Books, 2002), 56.

66. Larry L. King, *Confessions of a White Racist* (1969; New York: Viking, 1971), 15–17.

67. Ibid., 14.

68. Raymond Andrews, *The Last Radio Baby: A Memoir* (Atlanta: Peachtree Publishers, 1990), 193. Andrews was born on June 6, 1934, and grew up in the community of Plainville, near Madison, Ga. His parents were sharecroppers. Andrews was an avid movie fan who was crestfallen when his mother reluctantly informed him that African Americans appeared in movies only "under 'certain' conditions," thus ending his dream of becoming a movie star (191).

69. Ibid., 193.

70. Roy Blount Jr., *Be Sweet: A Conditional Love Story* (New York: Knopf, 1998), 237. Blount was born in 1941 and grew up in Decatur, Ga.

71. Sue Thrasher, "Circle of Trust," in *Deep in Our Hearts: Nine White Women in the Freedom Movement* (Athens: University of Georgia Press, 2000), 214. Thrasher was born in 1941 and attended school in Savannah, Tenn.

72. Ibid., 214–15.

73. Edward Cohen, *The Peddler's Grandson: Growing Up Jewish in Mississippi* (Jackson: University Press of Mississippi, 1999), 53. Cohen was born on July 3, 1948, and was raised in Jackson, Miss. He came from a family of merchants.

74. Ibid., 54.

75. Andrew Young, *An Easy Burden: The Civil Rights Movement and the Transformation of America* (New York: HarperCollins, 1996), 32–33.

76. Marguirite DeLaine, interview by Kisha Turner, Summerton, S.C., July 8, 1995, Behind the Veil. DeLaine was born in Manning, S.C., on July 7, 1940. Her father was a landowning farmer, and her mother was a teacher. DeLaine was also a teacher. Her uncle, Rev. J. A. DeLaine, was a local NAACP leader and a key figure in the 1952 *Briggs v. Elliot* case, which became one of the cases involved in the *Brown v. Board of Education* decision. The Briggs case originated in Clarendon County, S.C., and began as a dispute over the county's unwillingness to provide buses to take black students to school even though it did provide buses for white students. See David R. Goldfield, *Black, White, and Southern: Race Relations and Southern Culture, 1940 to the Present* (Baton Rouge: Louisiana State University Press, 1990), 60–61.

77. Georgia Sutton, interview by Rhonda Manhood, New Bern, N.C., July 30, 1993, Behind the Veil. Sutton was born on June 14, 1929, in New Bern. After her father died, her mother supported the family by working as a domestic.

78. Young, *Easy Burden,* 32.

79. Lillian Quick Smith, interview by Sonya Ramsey, Wilmington, N.C., July 19, 1993, Behind the Veil. Smith was born on Oct. 5, 1931, in Wilmington. Her father was a chef at a hotel, and her mother worked as a domestic. Smith later lived with her grandparents, and she remembered her grandfather,

who drove a delivery truck for a white merchant in town, as having been a prominent man in the black community.

80. Mary E. Mebane, *Mary, Wayfarer* (1976; New York: Viking, 1983), 48–49.

81. See, e.g., Marian Wright Edelman, *Lanterns: A Memoir of Mentors* (Boston: Beacon Press, 1999), 6, 21; Mebane, *Mary,* 66–67; and Ira Lee Jones, interview by Paul Ortiz, Tuskegee, Ala., July 22, 1994, Behind the Veil.

82. Carter G. Woodson, *The Mis-Education of the Negro* (Washington, D.C.: Associated Publishers, 1933), xiii. Woodson was born on Dec. 19, 1875, in Buckingham County, Va. After a struggle to gain an education and a stint as a coal miner in West Virginia, he earned degrees from Berea College in Kentucky, the University of Chicago, and Harvard University, where he received his doctorate in history. In his professional career Woodson taught high school, served briefly on the faculty of Howard University, and published numerous works on African American history. He founded the Association for the Study of Negro Life and History (ASNLH) in 1915 and directed its activities until his death on Apr. 3, 1950. "Biographical Sketch," *Negro History Bulletin* 13, no. 8 (May 1950): 171–73. For more on Woodson's life and work, see Jacqueline Goggin, *Carter G. Woodson: A Life in Black History* (Baton Rouge: Louisiana State University Press, 1993).

83. Woodson, *Mis-Education of the Negro,* 23.

84. Ibid., 75, 101.

85. Fairclough, *Class of Their Own,* 20.

86. "What the Association for the Study of Negro Life and History Does to Promote Truth," *Negro History Bulletin* 3, no. 5 (Jan. 1940): 64.

87. Daryl Michael Scott, "Origins of Black History Month," Association for the Study of African American Life and History, https://asalh100.org/origins-of-black-history-month/ (accessed July 23, 2016). Woodson's organization first celebrated Black History Month in 1976, the fiftieth anniversary of Negro History Week.

88. "Negro History Week, February 11, 1940," *Negro History Bulletin* 3, no. 1 (Oct. 1939): 10.

89. Fairclough, *Class of Their Own,* 389.

90. "Activities for Negro History Week," *Negro History Bulletin* 6, no. 4 (Jan. 1943): 94.

91. "Usual suspects" from Fairclough, *Class of Their Own,* 389. See also Sloan, *Negro in Modern American History Textbooks,* in which the author, writing in 1972, surveyed a series of eighteen textbooks in order to determine what progress had been made toward incorporating black history. Sloan noted the presence or absence of Crispus Attucks's name for virtually every text he studied.

92. "Advocates of Social Justice," *Negro History Bulletin* 12, no. 2 (Nov. 1948): 46.

93. See, e.g., "The Fifteenth Celebration of Negro History Week," *Negro History Bulletin* 3, no. 6 (Mar. 1940): 88.

94. State Board of Education, Minutes and Attachments of the State Board of Education, vol. 6, Nov. 22, 1938, and vol. 8, Dec. 19, 1947; South Carolina Department of Archives and History.

95. Report of Beatrice H. Beaumont, Feb. 28, 1930; Report of Maude Mitchell Jeffers, Feb. 28, 1938; and Report of Clara B. Hicks, Feb. 28, 1949. Department of Public Instruction, Division of Negro Education, Special Subject File, box 2, folder: "Jeanes Schools: Monthly Reports," State Archives of North Carolina. Anna T. Jeanes was a wealthy Quaker who established a fund in 1907 to support black education in the South's rural schools. Jeanes Fund supervisors worked with white administrators to oversee the activities of these schools. For more on the work of Jeanes supervisors, see Fairclough, *Class of Their Own,* 248–63.

96. See, e.g., N. C. Newbold to Presidents of Colleges and to Jeanes Teachers, Jan. 11, 1937, Department of Public Instruction, Division of Publications, Mimeograph Material, box 2, vol. 8; N. C. Newbold to Jeanes Teachers and Principals, Jan. 10, 1938, Department of Public Instruction, Division of Publications, Mimeograph Material, box 3, vol. 13, State Archives of North Carolina.

97. See Lasker, *Race Attitudes in Children*, 154–55; Gunnar Myrdal, with the assistance of Richard Sterner and Arnold Rose, *An American Dilemma: The Negro Problem and Modern Democracy* (New York: Harper & Brothers, 1944), 752. Myrdal explained, "When we call the activities of the Negro History movement 'propaganda,' we do not mean to imply that there is any distortion in the facts presented. Excellent historical research has accompanied the efforts to publicize it. But there has been a definite distortion in the emphasis and the perspective given the facts: mediocrities have been expanded into 'great men'; cultural achievements which are no better—and no worse—than any others are placed on a pinnacle; minor historical events are magnified into crises. This seems entirely excusable, however, in view of the greater distortion and falsification of the facts in the writings of white historians" (752).

98. Daryl Michael Scott, *Contempt and Pity: Social Policy and the Image of the Damaged Black Psyche, 1880–1996* (Chapel Hill: University of North Carolina Press, 1997), 39. Scott has served in a variety of positions with the Association for the Study of African American Life and History (ASALH), as the ASNLH is now known.

99. Myrdal, *American Dilemma*, 752.

100. For more on teachers stressing the importance of voting see Andrews, *Last Radio Baby*, 198–99; Lola Hendricks, interview by Tywanna Whorley, Birmingham, Ala., June 22, 1994, Behind the Veil. See also Fairclough, *Class of Their Own*, 342, 387–88. Fairclough noted that a number of civil rights activists remembered a particular teacher who encouraged them to challenge the prevailing social order, but he found that in general "most black teachers did not impart lessons in protest and activism" (388). See also William H. Chafe's discussion of the lessons the black students who kicked off the 1960 sit-in movement learned from their teachers about not only racial pride but also the importance of asserting one's political rights. Chafe, *Civilities and Civil Rights: Greensboro, North Carolina, and the Black Struggle for Freedom* (1980; New York: Oxford University Press, 1981), 80–81.

101. Carolyn McKinstry, interview by Horace Huntley, Apr. 23, 1998, transcribed interview (vol. 35, sec. 1, 16). BCRI Oral History Project, Birmingham Civil Rights Institute, Birmingham, Ala.

102. Jordan, *Vernon Can Read*, 45–46.

103. John Hope Franklin, *Mirror to America: The Autobiography of John Hope Franklin* (New York: Farrar, Straus & Giroux, 2005), 25. Franklin was born on Jan. 2, 1915, in Rentiesville, Okla. He attended Booker T. Washington High School in Tulsa.

104. Edelman, *Lanterns*, 21, 20.

105. For more on the salary equalization campaign, see Fairclough, *Class of Their Own*, 309–10, 344–53. For an autobiographical account of the campaign, see Septima Poinsette Clark, with LeGette Blythe, *Echo in My Soul* (New York: Dutton, 1962). Although Edelman was critical of her own teachers, she praised Clark's work. She also noted Clark's disappointment that more of her colleagues did not support the equalization campaign. Edelman, *Lanterns*, 21.

106. Evelyn Brooks Higginbotham articulated the concept of "the politics of respectability" in her study *Righteous Discontent: The Women's Movement in the Black Baptist Church, 1880–1920* (Cambridge: Harvard University Press, 1993), 14.

107. Young, *Easy Burden*, 30, 36, 34, 40.

108. Adam Fairclough, *Teaching Equality: Black Schools in the Age of Jim Crow* (Athens: University of Georgia Press, 2001), 56.

109. In her discussion of efforts by "Cold Warriors" to use education to shield children from communism in the 1950s, Julia L. Mickenberg characterized this undertaking as an attempt "to inoculate children against Communism." Mickenberg, *Learning from the Left*, 262. Although different ideological considerations were at work in the efforts of African American teachers to protect their students, the strategy of using education as a preemptive means to insulate children from outside threats was the same.

110. Carl T. Rowan, *South of Freedom* (1952; Baton Rouge: Louisiana State University Press, 1997), 25.

CHAPTER 4

"RED AND YELLOW, BLACK AND WHITE"

The inspiration for the title of this chapter comes from Paul Hemphill, *Leaving Birmingham: Notes of a Native Son* (1993; Tuscaloosa: University of Alabama Press, 2000), 280.

1. "Jesus Loves the Little Children," in *The Broadman Hymnal*, ed. and comp. B. B. McKinney (Nashville: Broadman Press, 1940), hymn 311. Note that different versions of the song exist. Some children would have sung, "Red, brown, yellow, black, and white," while others would have sung, "Brown, red, yellow, black, and white." Note, too, that in a more recent version of the song, the specific colors have been eliminated altogether. The lyrics read, "Every color, every race, all are covered by his grace." Wesley L. Forbis, ed., *The Baptist Hymnal* (Nashville: Convention Press: 1991), hymn 592.

2. David L. Chappell described efforts by interracial organizations to improve race relations gradually within the confines of the segregated system as an attempt to "educate away" racial prejudice. Chappell, *Inside Agitators: White Southerners in the Civil Rights Movement* (Baltimore: Johns Hopkins University Press, 1994), 38.

3. Paul Harvey, *Redeeming the South: Religious Cultures and Racial Identities among Southern Baptists, 1865–1925* (Chapel Hill: University of North Carolina Press, 1997), 6; Peter C. Murray, *Methodists and the Crucible of Race, 1930–1975* (Columbia: University of Missouri Press, 2004), xiii–viv; and Joel L. Alvis Jr., *Religion and Race: Southern Presbyterians, 1946–1983* (Tuscaloosa: University of Alabama Press, 1994), 3–6.

4. Gardiner H. Shattuck Jr., *Episcopalians and Race: Civil War to Civil Rights* (Lexington: University Press of Kentucky, 2000), 9–10.

5. R. Bentley Anderson, *Black, White, and Catholic: New Orleans Interracialism, 1947–1956* (Nashville: Vanderbilt University Press, 2005), 1–2.

6. The PCUS established the segregated Snedecor Memorial Synod in 1916, and the General Assembly voted to begin phasing it out in 1951. Even after this process was begun, however, local congregations continued to operate on a largely segregated basis. Mark Newman, *Getting Right with God: Southern Baptists and Desegregation, 1945–1995* (Tuscaloosa: University of Alabama Press, 2001), 170, 173.

7. Shattuck, *Episcopalians and Race*, 28–29.

8. Anderson, *Black, White, and Catholic*, 2–3. Catholic churches, particularly those in Louisiana and Mississippi, reached out to African American children through their parochial schools. Black southerners who attended these schools remembered the education they received there as having been

the best available in their communities at the time, and they stressed the sense of self-worth that the frequently all-white faculties of nuns and priests instilled in them. For the most part, however, black southerners did not remember learning lessons about black history or racial pride in these schools, nor did they recall being encouraged to challenge segregation. See Jacqueline Jordan Irvine and Michèle Foster, eds., *Growing Up African American in Catholic Schools* (New York: Teachers College Press, 1996); Danny Duncan Collum, *Black and Catholic in the Jim Crow South: The Stuff That Makes Community* (New York: Paulist Press, 2006).

9. Murray, *Methodists and the Crucible of Race,* 19–20. The Colored Methodist Episcopal Church was rechristened the Christian Methodist Episcopal Church in 1954.

10. When northern and southern Methodists reunited in 1939 to create the Methodist Church, they organized the black congregations within their ranks into the segregated Central Jurisdiction, which overlapped with a series of five regional jurisdictions. The process of integrating the functions of the Central Jurisdiction into the various regional jurisdictions had largely been completed by the time the Methodist Church combined with the Evangelical United Brethren (EUB) in 1968 to form the United Methodist Church, though local congregations continued to operate on a largely segregated basis. Ibid., xiv.

11. C. Eric Lincoln and Lawrence H. Mamiya, *The Black Church in the African American Experience* (Durham: Duke University Press, 1990), 28–34.

12. The two denominations were the National Baptist Convention, USA, Inc., and the National Baptist Convention of America.

13. Lincoln and Mamiya, *Black Church,* 50–57. Growing out of a movement among black Methodists initiated by Richard Allen and Absalom Jones in Philadelphia in 1787, the AME Church was officially organized in 1816. Tracing its roots to a split from a white Methodist congregation, in this case in New York in 1796, the AMEZ Church was officially organized in 1821.

14. Ibid., 11–15. Note that Evelyn Brooks Higginbotham has sought to complicate Lincoln and Mamiya's dialectic model, arguing that experiences within black churches, especially among women, were characterized more by a "multiplicity" of "meanings and intentions" than by "a series of discrete polarities." See Higginbotham, *Righteous Discontent: The Women's Movement in the Black Baptist Church, 1880–1920* (Cambridge: Harvard University Press, 1993), 16–18.

15. Lincoln and Mamiya, *Black Church,* 12. The authors felt this other-worldly focus had been overemphasized in past histories of black churches.

16. Ibid., 14.

17. Benjamin E. Mays, *Born to Rebel: An Autobiography* (1971; Athens: University of Georgia Press, 2003), 15–16. Out of 118 interviews of other African Americans that Mays consulted in the process of writing his autobiography, only four individuals remembered their ministers having told them to "demand their rights" while half of those who could remember the nature of sermons from their childhood asserted that their preachers had taught them nothing about white people (16). Mays and coauthor Joseph W. Nicholson also explored other-worldly messages in their study of black churches. Of the 100 sermons by black ministers that they consulted for the study, over half were found to emphasize the concerns of the afterlife rather than the concerns of this life. Mays and Nicholson, *The Negro's Church* (1933; Salem, N.H.: Ayer, 1988), 70, 92–93.

18. John Lewis, with Michael D'Orso, *Walking with the Wind: A Memoir of the Movement* (New York: Simon & Schuster, 1998), 55.

19. Anne Moody, *Coming of Age in Mississippi* (1968; New York: Laurel, 1976), 303.

20. Maya Angelou, *I Know Why the Caged Bird Sings* (1969; New York: Bantam Books, 1993), 129. Although the revival was a joint venture by various black churches, Angelou usually attended a CME church.

21. Lewis, *Walking with the Wind,* 34–35.

22. Mays, *Born to Rebel,* 15–16.

23. Raymond Andrews, *The Last Radio Baby: A Memoir* (Atlanta: Peachtree Publishers, 1990), 140–41. Andrews remembered that when a white landowner did occasionally come to visit, the atmosphere inside the church would change automatically.

24. Ira Lee Jones, interview by Paul Ortiz, Tuskegee, Ala., July 22, 1994, Behind the Veil: Documenting African-American Life in the Jim Crow South, Center for Documentary Studies at Duke University, David M. Rubenstein Rare Book & Manuscript Library, Duke University. Jones was born on Aug. 16, 1919, in Birmingham. Her father worked at a coal company, and her mother was a laundress. Jones was a teacher.

25. See, e.g., Harold Roland, interview by Charles H. Houston Jr., Orangeburg, S.C., Aug. 4, 1994, Behind the Veil.

26. See, e.g., "A Grusome [sic] Record," *Southwestern Christian Advocate,* Jan. 29, 1920, 2; "The Anti-Lynching Bill," *Christian Index,* Jan. 27, 1938, 3, United Methodist Archives and History Center.

27. Coretta Scott King, *My Life with Martin Luther King, Jr.,* rev. ed. (1969; New York: Henry Holt, 1993), 28–29.

28. Bertha Todd, interview by Sonya Ramsey, Wilmington, N.C., July 15, 1993, Behind the Veil. Todd was born on Mar. 20, 1929, in Sampson County, N.C. She held a variety of positions throughout her professional career as an administrator, principal, and librarian.

29. See, e.g., Lillian Quick Smith, interview by Sonya Ramsey, Wilmington, N.C., July 19, 1993, Behind the Veil.

30. Mays, *Born to Rebel,* 17.

31. P. James Bryant, "A Brief of the Colored American's Case," *Journal of the Forty-First Annual Session of the National Baptist Convention,* Chicago, Sept. 1921, Southern Baptist Historical Library and Archives (SBHLA).

32. "Twenty-Ninth Annual Report of the Sunday School Publishing Board," *Journal of the Forty-Sixth Annual Session of the National Baptist Convention,* Fort Worth, Tex., Sept. 1926, SBHLA.

33. "Third Annual Richard Allen Youth Week, February 8–15, 1948," *AME Church Review* 59, no. 157 (Dec.–Mar. 1947–48): 174–76, African Methodist Episcopal Church (AMEC) Department of Research and Scholarship.

34. "Work of Our Founders We Extol," *AME Zion Hymnal* (Charlotte, N.C.: AME Zion Publishing House, 1957), hymn 283, United Methodist Archives and History Center; "Youth's Corner," *Star of Zion,* Feb. 14, 1935, 2, and Feb. 21, 1935, 2, AMEC Department of Research and Scholarship.

35. "Negroes Honoring Notables of Race," *Star of Zion,* Feb. 14, 1935, 5, AMEC Department of Research and Scholarship.

36. Eleanor F. Pease, "Family Altar: Black Gumdrops," *Star of Zion,* Jan. 23, 1941, 2–3, AMEC Department of Research and Scholarship.

37. Lavinia R. Davis, "Youth's Corner: A Surprise for Bobby," *Star of Zion,* Mar. 27, 1941, 2, AMEC Department of Research and Scholarship.

38. Bryant, "Brief of the Colored American's Case."

39. In the interest of featuring the language through which many congregants at the time would have been introduced to these ideas, I have drawn on the King James Version of the Bible.

40. Matthew 22:39; Luke 6:31.

41. John 4:1–26.

42. Luke 10:25–37.

43. Matthew 25:31–46.

44. Luke 12:13–21.

45. Luke 16:25.

46. Galatians 6:7.

47. "In Christ There Is No East or West," *AME Zion Hymnal*, hymn 543. This song was a staple in many black churches, but white churches sang it as well, especially in conjunction with lessons about missions. See *The Presbyterian Hymnal* (Richmond: Presbyterian Committee of Publication, 1927), hymn 375. See also *The Hymnal of the Protestant Episcopal Church* (New York: Church Pension Fund, 1940), hymn 263, which identified the song as a "Negro Melody." *The United Methodist Hymnal*, published in 1989, included a new version of the third stanza, which reads, "In Christ is neither Jew nor Greek, and neither slave nor free; both male and female heirs are made, and all are kin to me." The music of the hymn is identified as an "Afro-American spiritual." *The United Methodist Hymnal* (Nashville: United Methodist Publishing House, 1989), hymn 548.

48. "In Christ There Is No East or West."

49. "Christianity and the Races," *Star of Hope* (Nashville: Sunday School Publishing Board), Feb. 1938, 6–7, Una Roberts Lawrence Collection (URLC), AR 631, sec. 1, Professional Papers, Black Missions, box 5, folder 4, SBHLA.

50. Acts 10:34.

51. D. D. Martin, "Missionary Interpretation," *Southwestern Christian Advocate*, Feb. 5, 1920, 14, United Methodist Archives and History Center.

52. See, e.g., King, *My Life with Martin Luther King, Jr.*, 198.

53. Mays and Nicholson, *Negro's Church*, 256. For more on the increasing use of uniform lessons starting in the late nineteenth century as well as resistance to this development, see Sally G. McMillen, *To Raise Up the South: Sunday Schools in Black and White Churches, 1865–1915* (Baton Rouge: Louisiana State University Press, 2001), 134–38.

54. Harvey, *Redeeming the South*, 244.

55. See, e.g., Methodist Book Concern advertisement, *Southwestern Christian Advocate*, Feb. 5, 1920, 13, United Methodist Archives and History Center. The Methodist Episcopal Church was marketing its Sunday school literature to the African American readership of the paper.

56. See, e.g., "LaGrange Negro Vacation Bible School," *Western Recorder*, Oct. 10, 1940, URLC, box 2, folder 9; "Tompkinsville Has Vacation Schools for Whites and Negroes," *Western Recorder*, July 31, 1941, URLC, box 4, folder 22, SBHLA.

57. Verda Von Hagen Wood, "My Responsibility for Social Justice," *Sunday School Young People and Adults*, Apr. 1940, 25, URLC, box 4, folder 23, SBHLA.

58. Edgar Williamson, "Amos Pleads for Justice," *Sunday School Builder*, Apr. 1940, 33, URLC, box 4, folder 23, SBHLA.

59. G. S. Dobbins, "Adults Studying the Lesson," *Sunday School Young People and Adults*, Apr. 1940, 25, URLC, box 4, folder 23, SBHLA.

60. Harvey, *Redeeming the South,* 244.

61. "Twenty-Ninth Annual Report of the Sunday School Publishing Board."

62. "Shake Off Your Mental Shackles," *Star of Zion,* Apr. 4, 1929, 1, 5, AMEC Department of Research and Scholarship.

63. See McMillen, *To Raise Up the South,* 102. See also J. Francis Lee, "An Appeal to the Connectional Pride of the AME Zion Sunday Schools," *Star of Zion,* Oct. 21, 1920, 6, AMEC Department of Research and Scholarship.

64. See, e.g., the 1954, 1955, 1956, and 1958 fourth quarter issues of the *AME Church Review,* AMEC Department of Research and Scholarship.

65. See, e.g., Elizabeth McE. Shields, "Thanksgiving for God's Best Gift," *Beginners' Bible Stories* (Richmond, Va.: Presbyterian Committee of Publication), Dec. 27, 1925; Elizabeth McE. Shields, "Why We Celebrate Christmas," *Primary Bible Lessons* (Richmond, Va.: Presbyterian Committee of Publication), Dec. 8, 1940, Presbyterian Historical Society (PHS). See also Edward J. Blum and Paul Harvey, *The Color of Christ: The Son of God and the Saga of Race in America* (Chapel Hill: University of North Carolina Press, 2012), on changing understandings and depictions of the race of Jesus.

66. "Cradle Roll Charts," *Star of Zion,* May 29, 1919, 8, AMEC Department of Research and Scholarship.

67. See *Star of Zion,* Sept. 23, 1920, 3, for an example of an ad for a black doll. See also *Star of Zion,* Dec. 16, 1920, 8, AMEC Department of Research and Scholarship.

68. Harvey, *Redeeming the South,* 248.

69. Higginbotham, *Righteous Discontent,* 194.

70. See, e.g., "Sunday School and Missionary Convention," *Star of Zion,* June 19, 1919, 2, AMEC Department of Research and Scholarship.

71. See, e.g., *Star of Zion,* Jan. 10, 1918, 6, AMEC Department of Research and Scholarship; *Southwestern Christian Advocate,* Jan. 1, 1920, 15; *Christian Index,* Jan. 6, 1938, 15, United Methodist Archives and History Center; *Star of Zion,* Nov. 20, 1941, 8; *AME Church Review* 68, no. 173 (July–Sept. 1952): 68, AMEC Department of Research and Scholarship.

72. Dolores Aaron, interview by Michele Mitchell, New Orleans, June 30, 1994, Behind the Veil. Aaron was born on Jan. 14, 1924, in New Orleans. Her father was in sales while her mother ran a boardinghouse. Aaron worked as a teacher and school administrator.

73. Cecil Brown, *Coming Up Down Home: A Memoir of a Southern Childhood* (Hopewell, N.J.: Ecco Press, 1993), 76.

74. Daisy Bates, *The Long Shadow of Little Rock: A Memoir* (1962; Fayetteville: University of Arkansas Press, 1987), 20. Bates was born in Huttig, Ark., in 1914. In her capacity as a local NAACP leader, she served as an advisor to the "Little Rock Nine."

75. Not all black children were conflicted by white images of Jesus. Carolyn McKinstry remembered the comfort she received in the years before the bombing of Sixteenth Street Baptist Church from two stained glass windows in the church, both of which featured white depictions of Jesus. She recalled, "On both sides of the sanctuary, the stained-glass images of Jesus comforted me and brought me great peace and joy." She wrote of her favorite of these windows, which depicted Jesus knocking at a wooden door, "I had the stained-glass face of Jesus in the window looking down upon me with his love, approval, and assurance of protection against the hostile world outside." McKinstry, with Denise George, *While the World Watched: A Birmingham Bombing Survivor Comes of Age during the Civil Rights Movement* (Carol Stream, Ill.: Tyndale House Publishers, 2011), 14, 39. McKinstry's favorite window

was damaged during the bombing when the face of Jesus was knocked out. See Blum and Harvey, *Color of Christ*, 2, for a picture of the window after the bombing. Although Blum and Harvey indicated that the damaged image of Jesus was replaced by the so-called Wales window—which was funded by Welsh donors and created by a Welsh artist and featured a black figure that has often been characterized as a black Christ—the window that affected McKinstry so deeply was actually painstakingly restored after the bombing. The Wales window replaced a window on a different side of the church. See ibid., 23–24, 243, 276.

76. For more on the work of Nannie Burroughs, see Higginbotham, *Righteous Discontent*, 158–64, 211–29.

77. "Twenty-Second Annual Report of the Executive Board and Corresponding Secretary of the Woman's Convention," *Journal of the Twenty-Second Annual Session of the Woman's Convention, Auxiliary to the National Baptist Convention*, St. Louis, Mo., Dec. 1922, SBHLA.

78. "Twenty-Eighth Annual Report of the Executive Board and Corresponding Secretary of the Woman's Convention," *Journal of the Twenty-Eighth Annual Session of the Woman's Convention, Auxiliary to the National Baptist Convention*, Louisville, Ky., Sept. 1928, SBHLA.

79. "Twenty-Fourth Annual Report of the Executive Board and Corresponding Secretary of the Woman's Convention," *Journal of the Twenty-Fourth Annual Session of the Woman's Convention, Auxiliary to the National Baptist Convention*, Nashville, Tenn., Sept. 1924, SBHLA.

80. "Twenty-Third Annual Report of the Executive Board and Corresponding Secretary of the Woman's Convention," *Journal of the Twenty-Third Annual Session of the Woman's Convention, Auxiliary to the National Baptist Convention*, Los Angeles, Sept. 1923, SBHLA.

81. J. Harvey Anderson, "Negro Womanhood," *Star of Zion*, Dec. 11, 1919, 4, AMEC Department of Research and Scholarship.

82. W. J. Walls, "Saving the Boys," *Star of Zion*, May 20, 1920, 4, AMEC Department of Research and Scholarship.

83. Higginbotham, *Righteous Discontent*, 14, 193, 187–88, 227.

84. Andrew Young, *An Easy Burden: The Civil Rights Movement and the Transformation of America* (New York: HarperCollins, 1996), 31, 18.

85. Arthur D. Dukes to Gordon Persons, June 1954, Alabama Governor (1951–55: Persons), Administrative Files, 1954, folder 13: "Segregation in Public Schools," Government Records Collections, Alabama Department of Archives and History (ADAH).

86. Paul B. Trawick to Gordon Persons, Dec. 23, 1953, Alabama Governor (1951–55: Persons), Administrative Files, 1954, folder 5: "Segregation: Newspaper Editors and Writers," Government Records Collections, ADAH.

87. Hemphill, *Leaving Birmingham*, 280–81.

88. For several years John Rutland had espoused racial views that were not in line with the thinking of his congregation at Woodlawn United Methodist Church, of which notorious Commissioner of Public Safety Eugene "Bull" Connor was a member. Rutland's firing after giving the Christmas offering to a black family was "simply the last straw." Hemphill, *Leaving Birmingham*, 289. Such an act of charity by a white church would not have been uncommon. Willie Morris remembered of his white Methodist church group, "We would take Christmas baskets to poor Negro families living in shabby little cabins in the hills, and feel glad that our families were not in such bad straits." Morris, *North toward Home* (1967; New York: Vintage Books, 2000), 43.

89. Hemphill, *Leaving Birmingham*, 282, 284.

90. Luke 18:16.

91. The General Convention of the Episcopal Church, e.g., had a Joint Commission on Negro Work. See Shattuck, *Episcopalians and Race*, 32.

92. Melton A. McLaurin, *Separate Pasts: Growing Up White in the Segregated South* (1987; Athens: University of Georgia Press, 1998), 31.

93. Gunnar Myrdal, with the assistance of Richard Sterner and Arnold Rose, *An American Dilemma: The Negro Problem and Modern Democracy* (New York: Harper & Brothers, 1944), xlvii–xlviii.

94. S. Jonathan Bass, *Blessed Are the Peacemakers: Martin Luther King Jr., Eight White Religious Leaders, and the "Letter from Birmingham Jail"* (Baton Rouge: Louisiana State University Press, 2001), 12.

95. Anderson, *Black, White, and Catholic*, xiii.

96. Harvey, *Redeeming the South*, 230.

97. Anne Braden, *The Wall Between* (1958; Knoxville: University of Tennessee Press, 1999), 20.

98. Larry L. King, *Confessions of a White Racist* (1969; New York: Viking, 1971), 18.

99. Robert B. Eleazer, "'The Curse of Ham': A Conversation Concerning a Myth That Dies Hard," Department of General Church Social Work, General Board of Education, Methodist Church, n.d., URLC, box 4, folder 21, SBHLA. See also Genesis 9:18–27.

100. King, *Confessions of a White Racist*, 18–19.

101. McLaurin, *Separate Pasts*, 31.

102. David L. Chappell, *A Stone of Hope: Prophetic Religion and the Death of Jim Crow* (Chapel Hill: University of North Carolina Press, 2004), 112; Paul Harvey, "Religion, Race, and the Right in the South, 1945–1990," in *Politics and Religion in the White South*, ed. Glenn Feldman (Lexington: University Press of Kentucky, 2005), 107. Informed by Harvey's work, Chappell discussed the thought of "lay segregationists" in *Stone of Hope* (112, 254 n. 29).

103. Gertrude English to Richard B. Russell Jr., May 24 [1954], Richard B. Russell Jr. Collection, Subgroup C, ser. X: Civil Rights, box 165, folder 8: "School Segregation: Correspondence, May 25, 1954," Richard B. Russell Library for Political Research and Studies, University of Georgia Libraries.

104. Genesis 9:22, 25.

105. Sara A. Thompson to Gordon Persons, Aug. 14, 1954. Alabama Governor (1951–55: Persons), Administrative Files, 1954, folder 12: "Segregation in Public Schools," Government Records Collections, ADAH.

106. Edna Morris to Gordon Persons, Mar. 12, 1954. Alabama Governor (1951–55: Persons), Administrative Files, 1954, folder 15: "Segregation Letters-Misc.," Government Records Collections, ADAH.

107. Mrs. V. O. Warren to Gordon Persons, June 26, 1954. Alabama Governor (1951–55: Persons), Administrative Files, 1954, folder 13: "Segregation in Public Schools," Government Records Collections, ADAH.

108. T. E. Davenport, "Segregation Good for Colored and White Alike," Sept. 27, 1954. Alabama Governor (1951–55: Persons), Administrative Files, 1954, folder 12: "Segregation in Public Schools," Government Records Collections, ADAH.

109. See, e.g., Lillian Smith, *Killers of the Dream*, rev. ed. (1949; 1961; New York: Norton, 1994), 84; Sarah Patton Boyle, *The Desegregated Heart: A Virginian's Stand in Time of Transition* (New York: Morrow, 1962), 24.

110. Kenneth B. Clark, *Prejudice and Your Child* (1955; Middletown, Conn.: Wesleyan University Press, 1988), 34.

111. Smith, *Killers of the Dream*, 86.

112. Roy Blount Jr., *Be Sweet: A Conditional Love Story* (New York: Knopf, 1998), 45.

113. Dorothy Dawson Burlage, "Truths of the Heart," in *Deep in Our Hearts: Nine White Women in the Freedom Movement* (Athens: University of Georgia Press, 2000), 94. Burlage was born in San Antonio, Tex., in 1938.

114. Drew Gilpin Faust, "Living History," in *Shapers of Southern History: Autobiographical Reflections,* ed. John B. Boles (Athens: University of Georgia Press, 2004), 221–22. Faust was born in 1947, and she was raised in Virginia's Shenandoah Valley. She included her original account of the circumstances under which she wrote the letter to Eisenhower in *Mothers of Invention: Women of the Slaveholding South in the American Civil War* (1996; New York: Vintage Books, 1997), xi.

115. Faust, "Living History," 229–31.

116. Sue Thrasher, "Circle of Trust," in *Deep in Our Hearts,* 217–18.

117. Many female civil rights activists later developed a critique of southern and American society on the basis of gender. Female activists' use of language about "the brotherhood of man" appears to represent an earlier stage of their thinking, one not informed by second wave feminism.

118. Thrasher, "Circle of Trust," 218.

119. Joan C. Browning, "Shiloh Witness," in *Deep in Our Hearts,* 51.

120. Braden, *Wall Between,* 22–23.

121. Ibid., 230.

122. See Newman, *Getting Right with God,* 7–10, 12, on the SBC's Woman's Missionary Union and Home Mission Board as well as the increasingly active role in promoting positive racial attitudes taken by the SBC's Social Service Commission, which was succeeded by the Christian Life Commission. See also Murray, *Methodists and the Crucible of Race,* 64, for the effort by Methodist women in the Women's Division of Christian Service to highlight segregated conditions in the South by enlisting Pauli Murray to compile "the first comprehensive collection of state laws regarding race." See Murray, ed. and comp., *States' Laws on Race and Color* (1951; Athens: University of Georgia Press, 1997).

123. Taffey Hall, "Una Roberts Lawrence Collection: Biographical Note," www.sbhla.org/downloads/631.pdf (accessed Mar. 8, 2007).

124. See Una Roberts Lawrence, "Adult and Young People's Book: Patterns for Living," MS, n.d., URLC, box 4, folder 24; Una Roberts Lawrence to All State WMU Young People's Secretaries, Apr. 17, 1939, URLC, box 4, folder 19, SBHLA.

125. Nan F. Weeks, comp., "World Friendship," Interracial Missionary Department of Woman's Missionary Union of Virginia, n.d., 4–11, 26–30, URLC, box 1, folder 18, SBHLA

126. See, e.g., the Oct.–Dec. 1922 and Jan.–Mar. 1923 covers of *World Comrades* (Birmingham, Ala.: Woman's Missionary Union), SBHLA.

127. Frank Means, "Junior Royal Ambassador: America, the Rainbow Land," *World Comrades* (Birmingham, Ala.: Woman's Missionary Union), May 1946, 17, SBHLA.

128. Mrs. J. T. McRae, "Sunbeam Band: Second Meeting, God's Garden," *World Comrades* (Birmingham, Ala.: Woman's Missionary Union), May 1946, 28, SBHLA.

129. H. Cornell Goerner, "Intermediate Royal Ambassador: First Meeting," *World Comrades* (Birmingham, Ala.: Woman's Missionary Union), Aug. 1945, 15, SBHLA.

130. Alan Scot Willis, *All According to God's Plan: Southern Baptist Missions and Race, 1945–1970* (Lexington: University Press of Kentucky, 2005), 72, 4.

131. Sadie Mai Wilson, "Longer Missionary Program: Of One Blood," *The Workers' Council* (Nashville: Methodist Publishing House), June 28, 1931, 28, United Methodist Archives and History Center.

132. "Mary McLeod Bethune," Department of Education and Promotion, Woman's Section, Board of Missions, ME Church, South, n.d., URLC, box 3, folder 2, SBHLA.

133. Eleazer, "'Curse of Ham'"; Genesis 9:18–27.

134. "Good Will to People of Other Races," *Methodist Intermediate-Senior Quarterly* (Nashville: Methodist Publishing House), July 14, 1929, 8, United Methodist Archives and History Center.

135. "Surprises in Friendship," *Methodist Intermediate Quarterly* (Nashville: Methodist Publishing House), Dec. 1, 1935, 26–27, United Methodist Archives and History Center.

136. "Racial Readjustments," *Minutes of the Eighty-Fifth General Assembly of the Presbyterian Church in the United States* (Austin, Tex.: Press of Von Boeckmann-Jones Co.), Montreat, N.C., May 1945, 147, PHS.

137. "Dreamers of Destiny Review," *Senior Teacher's Quarterly* (Richmond, Va.: Presbyterian Committee of Publication), Mar. 31, 1935, 65, PHS.

138. "The Church Is for All People," *Senior Teacher's Guide* (Richmond, Va.: Presbyterian Committee of Publication), Nov. 9, 1947, 37, PHS.

139. "Let the Children Come," *Primary Leader's Guide* (Richmond, Va.: Presbyterian Committee of Publication), Feb. 20, 1944, 30–31; "Introduction to Unit V—God's Children Live in Many Lands," *Primary Leader's Guide* (Richmond, Va.: Presbyterian Committee of Publication), Feb. 13, 1944, 26, PHS.

140. Mrs. C. D. Creasman, "Royal Ambassador: First Meeting," *World Comrades* (Birmingham, Ala.: Woman's Missionary Union), Aug. 1924, 10, SBHLA.

141. Mrs. C. D. Creasman, "Girls' Auxiliary: First Meeting," *World Comrades* (Birmingham, Ala.: Woman's Missionary Union), Aug. 1924, 23, SBHLA.

142. Mary Entwistle, "At School in Many Lands: Quashie's Trouble," *Story Hour* (Richmond, Va.: Presbyterian Committee of Publication), Jan. 15, 1928, 3, PHS.

143. See, e.g., Mrs. C. D. Creasman, "Girls' Auxiliary: First Meeting, Crowning Our Southland," *World Comrades* (Birmingham, Ala.: Woman's Missionary Union), Mar. 1924, 24, SBHLA; "You and Other People," *Senior Teacher's Quarterly* (Richmond, Va.: Presbyterian Committee of Publication), Sept. 20, 1936, 60, PHS.

144. "Jonah's Lesson in World Friendship," *Methodist Intermediate Quarterly* (Nashville: Methodist Publishing House), Sept. 8, 1935, 29, United Methodist Archives and History Center.

145. "The Centenary for Children," *Young Christian Worker* (Nashville: Woman's Missionary Council), Apr. 1919, 111, United Methodist Archives and History Center.

146. "The Medicine Man," *Young Christian Worker* (Nashville: Woman's Missionary Council), Feb. 1919, 79, United Methodist Archives and History Center. See, e.g., Mrs. C. D. Creasman, "Royal Ambassador: First Meeting, Religion of the Negro," *World Comrades* (Birmingham, Ala.: Woman's Missionary Union), Aug. 1924, 11, SBHLA.

147. "A Letter to an African Friend," *Story Hour* (Richmond, Va.: Presbyterian Committee of Publication), June 16, 1929, 4, PHS.

148. Mrs. C. S. Marks, "Sunbeams: Second Meeting," *World Comrades* (Birmingham, Ala.: Woman's Missionary Union), May 1933, 46, SBHLA.

149. Mabel V. K. Ballard, "Sharing the Story of Jesus," *Primary Bible Lessons* (Richmond, Va.: Presbyterian Committee of Publication), Aug. 18, 1940, PHS.

150. See, e.g., Elizabeth McE. Shields, "Mothers Bringing Their Children to Jesus," *Beginners' Bible Stories* (Richmond, Va.: Presbyterian Committee of Publication), May 14, 1933; Elizabeth McE. Shields

and Eleanor R. Millard, "Children Jesus Knew," *Primary Bible Lessons* (Richmond, Va.: Presbyterian Committee of Publication), May 12, 1940; Elizabeth McE. Shields and Eleanor R. Millard, "Children of One Father," *Primary Bible Lessons* (Richmond, Va.: Presbyterian Committee of Publication), June 30, 1940, PHS.

151. See Elizabeth McE. Shields, "Jesus Loving All Children," *Beginners' Bible Stories* (Richmond, Va.: Presbyterian Committee of Publication), June 11, 1933, PHS. See also Blum and Harvey, *Color of Christ*, 160, for more on Harold Copping's depiction.

152. Elizabeth McE. Shields, "God, Our Father," *Primary Bible Lessons* (Richmond, Va.: Presbyterian Committee of Publication), Nov. 5, 1933, PHS.

153. Elizabeth McE. Shields, "Friends Who Help Me," *Beginners' Bible Stories* (Richmond, Va.: Presbyterian Committee of Publication), July 28, 1940; Mabel V. K. Ballard, "Working for a Healthy Neighborhood," *Primary Bible Lessons* (Richmond, Va.: Presbyterian Committee of Publication), Mar. 3, 1940, PHS. The rights to many of the images used in PCUS literature were owned by the Providence Lithograph Company, one of the leading publishers of religious imagery in the country. That is, the PCUS and other denominations chose many of the illustrations from a stock group of images rather than producing them in-house.

154. Weeks, "World Friendship," 8–10.

155. Mary L. Mason, "Jesus Loving Children All Over the World," *Primary Bible Lessons* (Richmond, Va.: Presbyterian Committee of Publication), Jan. 29, 1933, PHS. This lesson also featured Harold Copping's depiction of Jesus with children of many lands.

156. "The Boy Who Didn't Know His Own Family," *Story Hour* (Richmond, Va.: Presbyterian Committee of Publication), June 4, 1939, 3–4, PHS.

157. Lois Marshall, "Open My Eyes That I May See," *World Comrades* (Birmingham, Ala.: Woman's Missionary Union), Sept. 1948, 6, SBHLA.

158. Kellie Hix, "A Pattern for an Angel," *World Comrades* (Birmingham, Ala.: Woman's Missionary Union), Dec. 1943, 8, SBHLA.

159. See, e.g., *Minutes of the Eighty-Fifth General Assembly of the Presbyterian Church in the United States,* 131, which articulated the "missionary obligation" and "Christian responsibility" of the church in regard to African Americans.

160. Bruno Lasker, *Race Attitudes in Children* (New York: Henry Holt, 1929), 344.

161. "Forces That Are Shaping My Community," *Senior Bible Studies* (Richmond, Va.: Presbyterian Committee of Publication), Mar. 20, 1949, 27; Marjorie Glenn, "Young People Help Build Swimming Pool," *Senior Bible Studies* (Richmond, Va.: Presbyterian Committee of Publication), Mar. 20, 1949, 29, PHS.

162. Sadie Mai Wilson, "Missionary Education," MS, n.d., United Methodist Archives and History Center.

163. Hemphill, *Leaving Birmingham,* 323.

164. Edwin King, "Growing Up in Mississippi in a Time of Change," in *Mississippi Writers: Reflections of Childhood and Youth, Volume 2: Nonfiction,* ed. Dorothy Abbott (Jackson: University Press of Mississippi, 1986), 379.

165. Harry B. Coker to the Christian Life Commission, Feb. 25, 1958, Christian Life Commission Administrative Files, box 21.3: "Race Relations—Letters of Opposition—1958," SBHLA.

166. P. S. Hightower and R. C. Peacock to James L. Sullivan, n.d., Christian Life Commission Administrative Files, box 21.3: "Race Relations—Letters of Opposition—1958," SBHLA.

167. See, e.g., E. Bunyan Collins to A. C. Miller, Nov. 5, 1957; D. E. Henderson to the Christian Life Commission, Mar. 13, 1957, Christian Life Commission Administrative Files, box 21.1: "Race Relations—Letters Expressing Alarm or Opposition—1957," SBHLA.

168. A. H. Reid to A. C. Miller, June 28, 1957, Christian Life Commission Administrative Files, box 21.1: "Race Relations—Letters Expressing Alarm or Opposition—1957," SBHLA.

169. Willis, *All According to God's Plan*, 149.

170. "Report of the Committee on Christian Relations: States' Rights and Human Rights," *Minutes of the Eighty-Ninth General Assembly of the Presbyterian Church in the United States* (Austin, Tex.: Press of Von Boeckmann-Jones Co.), Montreat, N.C., May–June 1949, 189, PHS.

171. Smith, *Killers of the Dream*, 51. Elsewhere Smith described the plays at her camp: "My children's theater where we (I with their help) grew plays, each play taking three or four summers to grow out of our group talks, our constant examination of the unanswerable questions and our own personal experiences." Lillian Smith to Arthur L. Klein, May 8, 1965, in *How Am I to Be Heard? Letters of Lillian Smith*, ed. Margaret Rose Gladney (Chapel Hill: University of North Carolina Press, 1993), 321. Smith's description suggests that the play in question should be taken as something more than allegory.

172. Smith, *Killers of the Dream*, 43–48.

173. See Anderson, *Black, White, and Catholic*, 72–73.

CHAPTER 5

TO MAKE THE TOLERABLE INTOLERABLE

1. David L. Cohn, quoted in James C. Cobb, afterword to *The Mississippi Delta and the World*, by David L. Cohn (Baton Rouge: Louisiana State University Press, 1995), 187.

2. Ibid.

3. Leon F. Litwack, *Trouble in Mind: Black Southerners in the Age of Jim Crow* (1998; New York: Vintage Books, 1999), 16.

4. John W. Cell, *The Highest Stage of White Supremacy: The Origins of Segregation in South Africa and the American South* (Cambridge: Cambridge University Press, 1982), 239.

5. Fred Hobson, *But Now I See: The White Southern Racial Conversion Narrative* (Baton Rouge: Louisiana State University Press, 1999).

6. See Willie Morris, *North toward Home* (1967; New York: Vintage Books, 2000), 90, on the "unthinking sadism" characteristic of his relationship with African Americans in his hometown of Yazoo City, Miss. See also Hobson, *But Now I See*, 92.

7. Hobson conceded this point in his discussion of Lillian Smith, writing, "To a black reader of *Killers of the Dream*—as, indeed, of most white racial conversion narratives—the author's thinking might have seemed somewhat self-indulgent. That is, attaining psychic wholeness for whites sometimes seemed for Smith to be at least as important as attaining equal rights for blacks." Hobson, *But Now I See*, 33. Many of those whites who became critical of segregation did so not because they felt guilty about their treatment of African Americans but rather because they became aware of the negative impact the system had on themselves and other white southerners.

8. Kristina DuRocher, *Raising Racists: The Socialization of White Children in the Jim Crow South* (Lexington: University Press of Kentucky, 2011), 95. Although DuRocher also focused on whites, her term, "racial awakening narratives," is applicable to the works of both black and white southerners in a way *racial conversion narratives* is not.

9. Lynn Z. Bloom, "Coming of Age in the Segregated South: Autobiographies of Twentieth-Century Childhoods, Black and White," in *Home Ground: Southern Autobiography,* ed. J. Bill Berry (Columbia: University of Missouri Press, 1991), 113. Bloom noted that there are exceptions to the rule that all southern coming-of-age narratives from the twentieth century discuss segregation; among the autobiographers she named were Russell Baker, Florence King, and Harry Crews. She attributed these exceptions to geographical and class considerations. Other narratives are exceptions not on the basis of class or geography but because, having lived otherwise normal, segregated childhoods, their authors failed to note the impact of segregation on their lives. Eudora Welty's *One Writer's Beginnings* (Cambridge: Harvard University Press, 1984) is a notable example.

10. Elnora Hayslette, interview by Mary Hebert, Norfolk, Va., Aug. 5, 1995, Behind the Veil: Documenting African-American Life in the Jim Crow South, Center for Documentary Studies at Duke University, David M. Rubenstein Rare Book & Manuscript Library, Duke University. Hayslette was born on Jan. 6, 1928, in Virginia. Her father was a farmer, and her mother was a homemaker. Hayslette was a teacher.

11. Margaret Jones Bolsterli, *Born in the Delta: Reflections on the Making of a Southern White Sensibility* (Knoxville: University of Tennessee Press, 1991), 73.

12. J. Waties Waring, quoted in Carl T. Rowan, *South of Freedom* (1952; Baton Rouge: Louisiana State University Press, 1997), 98. Waring was born in Charleston, S.C., in 1880.

13. James Farmer, *Lay Bare the Heart: An Autobiography of the Civil Rights Movement* (New York: Arbor House, 1985), 30. By the 1960s, according to Farmer, segregation had become a "splintering door."

14. Darlene Clark Hine, foreword to *The Making of a Southerner,* by Katharine Du Pre Lumpkin (1946; Athens: University of Georgia Press, 1991), xv.

15. Lillian Smith, *Killers of the Dream,* rev. ed. (1949; 1961; New York: Norton, 1994), 29–30.

16. Sarah Patton Boyle, *The Desegregated Heart: A Virginian's Stand in Time of Transition* (New York: Morrow, 1962), 43, 50. This "tidal wave" surfaced in July 1950, when her husband, a professor at the University of Virginia, told her that a young African American student had initiated a suit to gain admission to the university's law school. Sarah Patton Boyle's support of this student's admission was the beginning of a long, painful reeducation process for her.

17. Farmer, *Lay Bare the Heart,* 37.

18. Bruno Lasker noted that while the acquisition of new attitudes about race can occur through "violent conversions," in general the development of new attitudes is "cumulative," not "substitutive." Lasker, *Race Attitudes in Children* (New York: Henry Holt, 1929), 369. Hobson also noted the gradual nature of the process, writing, "Most southern racial conversions have come not in a single impulse, as religious conversions, often induced by religious revivals, tend to." Hobson, *But Now I See,* 5. As Hobson's concept of the "racial conversion narrative" has come to dominate scholarly understanding of white southern autobiographies of this era, however, the nuance of this aspect of his argument has been lost.

19. Farmer, *Lay Bare the Heart,* 32. Farmer served as national director of CORE during the Freedom Rides, and he and other activists from CORE and SNCC were arrested in Jackson, Miss. (194).

20. Daisy Bates, *The Long Shadow of Little Rock: A Memoir* (1962; Fayetteville: University of Arkansas Press, 1987), 8.

21. Ibid., 7, 9.

22. Ibid., 7, 11–12, 14–15, 18, 23, 20, 29–31.

23. Le Ester Jones, interview by Paul Ortiz, Brinkley, Ark., July 12, 1995, Behind the Veil. Jones was born in Lee County, Ark., in 1930. Her father was a farmer, and her mother was a homemaker and a laundress. Jones was also a farmer.

24. Ibid. Jones described an incident that showed the risks involved when one did not stay within the boundaries defined by whites. When walking home from school, black children in the neighborhood had been in the habit of moving aside when white children approached. One day Jones's brother decided they should refuse to move when pressured by whites. Some of the white boys retaliated by telling their parents that Jones's brother had been "messing with their sisters." The white parents responded by coming to the Jones home and threatening violence against her brother. Jones's parents, in turn, kept their son at home until the situation quieted down.

25. Pauli Murray, *Proud Shoes: The Story of an American Family* (1956; New York: Harper & Row, 1978), 56–57.

26. Mary E. Mebane, *Mary* (New York: Viking, 1981), 52.

27. Benjamin Adams, interview by Charles H. Houston Jr., Orangeburg, S.C., July 20, 1994, Behind the Veil. Adams was born in Edgefield, S.C., on July 19, 1933. His father was a sharecropper but was later able to buy his own land, and his mother worked as a domestic. Adams held a variety of positions, including court official, real estate agent, and fireman.

28. Ibid.

29. Xernona Clayton, with Hal Gulliver, *I've Been Marching All the Time: An Autobiography* (Atlanta: Longstreet Press, 1991), 7. Clayton was born in Muskogee, Okla., on Aug. 30, 1930. Her husband, Ed Clayton, handled public relations for SCLC in the early 1960s. The Claytons were close to the Kings, and Xernona Clayton helped Coretta Scott King make arrangements in the hours and days after Martin Luther King Jr. was assassinated. Clayton later worked as a television host and held a number of other positions with Turner Broadcasting System.

30. Ibid., 42.

31. Ibid., 42–45. Clayton later learned that the store, having suffered no ill effects from allowing her to try on hats, had begun to allow other black women to try on not only hats but dresses and shoes as well.

32. Ibid., 46.

33. Emogene Wilson, interview by Mausiki Stacey Scales, Memphis, Tenn., June 5, 1995, Behind the Veil. Wilson was born in Memphis on Apr. 15, 1924. Her father was a physician, and her mother was a teacher. Wilson worked as a government clerk in Washington, D.C., in the 1940s and later as a teacher in Memphis. Her husband, Alex Wilson, was a journalist who reported on both the Emmett Till lynching and the 1957 Little Rock desegregation crisis, during which he was beaten. Carl Rowan's account of traveling through the South in early 1951 confirms that, although many aspects of life in Washington, D.C., were segregated, the city's public buses were not. Rowan, *South of Freedom*, 68.

34. Emogene Wilson, interview by Mausiki Stacey Scales, Memphis, June 5, 1995.

35. On barriers to traveling, see, e.g., Audrey Grevious, interview, in *Freedom on the Border: An Oral History of the Civil Rights Movement in Kentucky*, ed. Catherine Fosl and Tracy E. K'Meyer (Lexington: University Press of Kentucky, 2009), 28–29.

36. Marian Wright Edelman, *Lanterns: A Memoir of Mentors* (Boston: Beacon Press, 1999), 24–36, 43.

37. Anne Braden, *The Wall Between* (1958; Knoxville: University of Tennessee Press, 1999), 8–9.

38. Andrew Wade, interview by Catherine Fosl, Louisville, Ky., Nov. 8, 1989. Anne Braden Oral History Project, Louie B. Nunn Center for Oral History, University of Kentucky Libraries, https://

kentuckyoralhistory.org/catalog/xt7mcv4bpp1t (accessed July 23, 2016). Wade grew up in Louisville in the 1920s.

39. Braden, *Wall Between,* 8. Few African Americans who fought in World War II would have described their experience in such positive terms. In addition, most did not serve in integrated settings. Many informants in the Behind the Veil project did, however, describe a pattern by which they were segregated en route overseas and on the return trip but experienced some degree of integration for the duration of their service, especially in the Pacific theater. For a consideration of these issues as well as other examples of African Americans who experienced contact with whites while serving in World War II, see Neil R. McMillen, "Fighting for What We Didn't Have: How Mississippi's Black Veterans Remember World War II," in *Remaking Dixie: The Impact of World War II on the American South,* ed. Neil R. McMillen (Jackson: University Press of Mississippi, 1997), 99–101.

40. Braden, *Wall Between,* 9.

41. Although the wartime experiences of several high-profile African Americans, including slain Mississippi civil rights leader Medgar Evers, have reinforced the notion that World War II produced a widespread change in outlook among black southerners, some oral history evidence suggests that this change was less widespread than has been thought. See, e.g., McMillen, "Fighting for What We Didn't Have," 103–10. McMillen presented considerable evidence from black veterans who suggested that the conditions they returned to after the war were much the same as those they had left behind before the war and that a way out seemed just as elusive. In one particularly compelling account, a black veteran explained that he had not even been aware of the "Double V" campaign—the much-heralded idea that African Americans saw themselves as fighting for victory over racism at home even as they fought for victory over fascism abroad—until he studied histories of the war years later. McMillen confessed that he had not found what he expected to find in the testimony of these black veterans when he began the project, and he asserted that the memories of these veterans should not be allowed to undermine the narrative of World War II as an important milestone along the road to the civil rights movement.

42. Rowan, *South of Freedom,* 10.

43. Carl T. Rowan, *Breaking Barriers: A Memoir* (Boston: Little, Brown, 1991), 53.

44. Rowan, *South of Freedom,* 132–33.

45. Ibid., 11. Fulfilling his promise to Brannon, Rowan began traveling around the South on Jan. 11, 1951, as a reporter for the *Minneapolis Morning Tribune.* The result was a series of articles and his book, *South of Freedom* (12–13).

46. Ibid., 11–12.

47. Edward Cohen, *The Peddler's Grandson: Growing Up Jewish in Mississippi* (Jackson: University Press of Mississippi, 1999), 144–45.

48. Bolsterli, *Born in the Delta,* 73–74.

49. Ibid., 128–29.

50. Virginia Foster Durr, *Outside the Magic Circle: The Autobiography of Virginia Foster Durr,* ed. Hollinger F. Barnard (Tuscaloosa: University of Alabama Press, 1985), 56. Durr was born in 1903 and grew up in Birmingham, Ala.

51. Ibid., 56, 58–59.

52. Will D. Campbell, *Brother to a Dragonfly* (1977; New York: Continuum, 2000), 96.

53. A prolific author, Howard Fast wrote *Freedom Road* in the early 1940s while working for the U.S. Office of War Information and the Voice of America. In 1944, the year the novel was published, Fast resigned his position amid charges that he harbored communist sympathies, and he went on

to join the Communist Party later that year. Tried and convicted for contempt of Congress in 1947 surrounding testimony given before the House Un-American Activities Committee, Fast served a three-month prison sentence in 1950. He left the Communist Party in 1957. Although many of his books were banned at various points, Fast went on to have a long career as an author, often writing under pseudonyms. Andrew Macdonald, *Howard Fast: A Critical Companion* (Westport, Conn.: Greenwood Press, 1996), 13–22, 27. See also Howard Fast, *Freedom Road* (New York: Duell, Sloan & Pearce, 1944). Operating from 1942 to 1946, the Council on Books in Wartime took as its motto "Books Are Weapons in the War of Ideas." The council produced pocket-sized Armed Services Editions of various books for U.S. service members, as well as a series of Overseas Editions that were translated into several languages and distributed for use in European and Asian countries once they had been liberated. The council also produced a series of films and radio programs in support of the war effort. For more on the council's activities, see Robert O. Ballou, with Irene Rakosky, *A History of the Council on Books in Wartime, 1942–1946* (New York: Country Life Press, 1946).

54. Campbell, *Brother to a Dragonfly*, 96.

55. Ibid., 97–98.

56. Although wartime experiences caused some white southerners to question segregation, historians have cautioned that such reactions, while not isolated, are not representative either. See James C. Cobb, "World War II and the Mind of the Modern South," in McMillen, *Remaking Dixie*, 6–7. Cobb and later Jason Sokol argued that fighting for freedom in World War II actually had the opposite effect on some white southerners; that is, it inspired them to be that much more ready to defend segregation because they saw the system as a means of ensuring their own freedom to choose with whom they would associate. See Sokol, *There Goes My Everything: White Southerners in the Age of Civil Rights, 1945–1975* (New York: Knopf, 2006), 23.

57. Larry L. King, *Confessions of a White Racist* (1969; New York: Viking, 1971), 24, 39–55, 68.

58. Farmer, *Lay Bare the Heart*, 129–30. Although Farmer recalled that this trip took place in 1938, he was likely referring to the first Southern Negro Youth Conference held in Richmond, Virginia, in 1937. The 1938 conference was held in Chattanooga, Tenn. For more on the National Negro Congress and the Southern Negro Youth Congress (SNYC) and the conferences it held, see C. Alvin Hughes, "We Demand Our Rights: The Southern Negro Youth Congress, 1937–1949," *Phylon* 48, no. 1 (1987): 38–50. Among the concerns of the SNYC was the lack of attention paid to African American history in the nation's public schools.

59. Farmer, *Lay Bare the Heart*, 131–32.

60. Ibid., 133.

61. Tim McLaurin, *Keeper of the Moon: A Southern Boyhood* (New York: Norton, 1991), 125. McLaurin was born in the early 1950s and grew up in Beard Station, N.C.

62. Ibid., 124.

63. Bobo's full name was James Robert Fuller Jr. Melton A. McLaurin, *Separate Pasts: Growing Up White in the Segregated South* (1987; Athens: University of Georgia Press, 1998), 27.

64. Ibid., 37.

65. Mark M. Smith, *How Race Is Made: Slavery, Segregation, and the Senses* (Chapel Hill: University of North Carolina Press, 2006), 123.

66. McLaurin, *Separate Pasts*, 27, 41.

67. Dorothy Dawson Burlage, "Truths of the Heart," in *Deep in Our Hearts: Nine White Women in the Freedom Movement* (Athens: University of Georgia Press, 2000), 96.

68. Ibid.

69. Smith, *Killers of the Dream,* 39.

70. Braden, *Wall Between,* 22.

71. Ibid., 24. One frequently hears echoes of Lillian Smith in Braden's text, as is the case here. Braden directed her readers to *Killers of the Dream,* deeming it "an excellent study of the psychological roots of race prejudice" (290). Braden's biographer, Catherine Fosl, observed that Braden "admired" Smith's work. Fosl, *Subversive Southerner: Anne Braden and the Struggle for Racial Justice in the Cold War South* (New York: Palgrave Macmillan, 2002), 102. The admiration may not have been mutual. Smith's biographers have noted her criticism of the left-leaning Southern Conference Educational Fund (SCEF), of which Braden was an integral part. Anne C. Loveland, *Lillian Smith: A Southerner Confronting the South, A Biography* (Baton Rouge: Louisiana State University Press, 1986), 224, 287–88 n. 19; Margaret Rose Gladney, ed., *How Am I to Be Heard? Letters of Lillian Smith* (Chapel Hill: University of North Carolina Press, 1993), 259.

72. In Braden's author's note to the 1999 edition of *Wall Between,* she explained that the title was suggested by the Bradens' friend and fellow civil liberties activist Harvey O'Connor after the book went to press, which may explain the discrepancy between the book's title and Braden's references to multiple walls (xv).

73. Ibid., 25, 331.

74. Ibid., 27.

75. Ibid., 30.

76. Ibid., 24.

77. Ibid., 11.

CONCLUSION

1. John Lewis, with Michael D'Orso, *Walking with the Wind: A Memoir of the Movement* (New York: Simon & Schuster, 1998), 105.

2. Martin Luther King Jr., "The Social Organization of Nonviolence" (1959), in *A Testament of Hope: The Essential Writings and Speeches of Martin Luther King, Jr.,* ed. James M. Washington (San Francisco: Harper, 1986), 33.

3. Martin Luther King Jr., "Black Power Defined" (1967), in Washington, *Testament of Hope,* 305.

4. Andrew Young, *An Easy Burden: The Civil Rights Movement and the Transformation of America* (New York: HarperCollins, 1996), 210.

5. For more on the varied approaches of these organizations, see John Egerton, *Speak Now against the Day: The Generation before the Civil Rights Movement in the South* (1994; Chapel Hill: University of North Carolina Press, 1995), 47–50, 177–97, 307–16, 355–56.

6. Morton Sosna, *In Search of the Silent South: Southern Liberals and the Race Issue* (New York: Columbia University Press, 1977), 165.

7. David L. Chappell, *Inside Agitators: White Southerners in the Civil Rights Movement* (Baltimore: Johns Hopkins University Press, 1994), 38, 46.

8. Harry S. Ashmore, *An Epitaph for Dixie* (New York: Norton, 1958), 70–71.

9. Anne Braden, *The Wall Between* (1958; Knoxville: University of Tennessee Press, 1999), 77.

10. Gunnar Myrdal, with the assistance of Richard Sterner and Arnold Rose, *An American Dilemma: The Negro Problem and Modern Democracy* (New York: Harper & Brothers, 1944), 49.

11. Ibid., xlvii–xlviii, 48.

12. David M. Kennedy, *Freedom from Fear: The American People in Depression and War, 1929–1945* (New York: Oxford University Press, 1999), 762.

13. Myrdal, *American Dilemma*, 1009.

14. Kennedy, *Freedom from Fear*, 762.

15. Myrdal, *American Dilemma*, 1031.

16. Ibid., 585, 1022.

17. Sosna, *In Search of the Silent South*, 6, 203, 198. While Lillian Smith was a chief proponent of the idea that segregation harmed white southerners, she was not a gradualist, so she cannot properly be classified as among the white liberals under consideration here. Smith was more radical on the issue of segregation than her contemporaries.

18. Ibid., 8.

19. Michael J. Klarman, "*Brown*, Racial Change, and the Civil Rights Movement," in "Twentieth-Century Constitutional History," special issue, *Virginia Law Review* 80, no. 1 (Feb. 1994): 51–52. Various elements of Klarman's larger argument have been critiqued elsewhere. See David J. Garrow, "Hopelessly Hollow History: Revisionist Devaluing of *Brown v. Board of Education*," in "Twentieth-Century Constitutional History," special issue, *Virginia Law Review* 80, no. 1 (Feb. 1994): 151–60; James C. Cobb, *The* Brown *Decision, Jim Crow, and Southern Identity* (Athens: University of Georgia Press, 2005), 31–55.

20. Egerton, *Speak Now against the Day*, 10–11. For another consideration of the "moment of opportunity" thesis, see Tony Badger, "Closet Moderates: Why White Liberals Failed, 1940–1970," in *The Role of Ideas in the Civil Rights South*, ed. Ted Ownby (Jackson: University Press of Mississippi, 2002), 83–112.

21. Myrdal, *American Dilemma*, 1009. Klarman likewise argued that World War II served to "accelerate preexisting trends towards racial equality," and he identified a number of "byproducts of World War II," such as the increasing migration of African Americans out of the South and the Cold War context, that he believed had "proved conducive to racial change." Klarman, "*Brown*, Racial Change, and the Civil Rights Movement," 14–15.

22. Myrdal, *American Dilemma*, 1003.

23. See John Cell's argument that segregation was actually "closely associated with what we commonly regard as indexes of modernization: with cities and towns, with the early stages of industrialization, with class and state (or party) formation." Cell, *The Highest Stage of White Supremacy: The Origins of Segregation in South Africa and the American South* (Cambridge: Cambridge University Press, 1982), x. Rejecting the notion that segregation was a remnant of the South's past that would eventually give way to the ameliorative forces of industrialization, modernization, and urbanization, Cell argued that the system had been *created in response to* the pressures those new forces put on race relations in the region. It was designed in part to circumvent the very real threat of economic competition posed by African Americans in a modernizing economy (xi).

24. Egerton, *Speak Now against the Day*, 624.

25. Sosna, *In Search of the Silent South*, 206.

26. Ibid., 209.

27. Egerton, *Speak Now against the Day*, 460–61.

28. Ibid., 548.

29. Ibid., 549.

30. Sarah Patton Boyle, quoted in John Egerton, *A Mind to Stay Here: Profiles from the South* (New York: Macmillan, 1970), 135.

31. Martin Luther King Jr., "Give Us the Ballot—We Will Transform the South" (1957), "Letter from Birmingham City Jail" (1963), both in Washington, *Testament of Hope*, 199, 295–96. For a sympathetic analysis of the challenges facing white religious leaders in the South, particularly those to whom King's Birmingham letter was ostensibly addressed, see S. Jonathan Bass, *Blessed Are the Peacemakers: Martin Luther King Jr., Eight White Religious Leaders, and the "Letter from Birmingham Jail"* (Baton Rouge: Louisiana State University Press, 2001).

32. Sosna, *In Search of the Silent South*, 171.

33. Egerton, *Speak Now against the Day*, 357.

34. Myrdal, *American Dilemma*, 1002–3, 592, 48.

35. Myrdal had asserted, "The popular beliefs rationalizing caste in America are no longer intellectually respectable." Ibid., 1003.

36. Mark M. Smith, *How Race Is Made: Slavery, Segregation, and the Senses* (Chapel Hill: University of North Carolina Press, 2006), 94–95.

37. Braden, *Wall Between*, 51.

38. Jason Sokol, *There Goes My Everything: White Southerners in the Age of Civil Rights, 1945–1975* (New York: Knopf, 2006), 63, 92.

39. Sokol characterized "those whites who opposed segregation" as "a largely silent minority." Ibid., 82. Sosna asserted that white liberals recognized "themselves for the small minority they were." Sosna, *In Search of the Silent South*, 166.

40. Chappell, *Inside Agitators*, 49.

41. Virginia Durr to Clark Foreman, Nov. 20, 1956, in *Freedom Writer: Virginia Foster Durr, Letters from the Civil Rights Years*, ed. Patricia Sullivan (2003; Athens: University of Georgia Press, 2006), 129.

42. Lillian Smith, "Laurel Leaf for Parents," summer 1946, in *How Am I to Be Heard? Letters of Lillian Smith*, ed. Margaret Rose Gladney (Chapel Hill: University of North Carolina Press, 1993), 106.

43. Bob Zellner, with Constance Curry, *The Wrong Side of Murder Creek: A White Southerner in the Freedom Movement* (Montgomery, Ala.: NewSouth Books, 2008), 123, 293.

44. Constance Curry, "Wild Geese to the Past," in *Deep in Our Hearts: Nine White Women in the Freedom Movement* (Athens: University of Georgia Press, 2000), 9.

45. Martin Luther King Jr., *Stride toward Freedom* (1958), "Bold Design for a New South" (1963), "The Ethical Demands for Integration" (1963), "*Playboy* Interview: Martin Luther King, Jr." (1965), all in Washington, *Testament of Hope*, 477, 114, 117, 377.

46. Young, *Easy Burden*, 95, 249.

47. Bob Zellner, interview, Mar. 2006, in *Anne Braden: Southern Patriot*, dir. Anne Lewis and Mimi Pickering (Appalshop, 2012), DVD.

48. Martin Luther King Jr., "The Burning Truth in the South" (1960), in Washington, *Testament of Hope*, 98.

49. Young, *Easy Burden*, 252.

50. Ibid., 299.

51. Adam Fairclough, *To Redeem the Soul of America: The Southern Christian Leadership Conference and Martin Luther King, Jr.* (Athens: University of Georgia Press, 1987), 52.

52. David L. Chappell, "Niebuhrisms and Myrdaleries: The Intellectual Roots of the Civil Rights Movement Reconsidered," in Ownby, *Role of Ideas in the Civil Rights South*, 15, 18. Chappell expanded

his discussion of King's approach in *A Stone of Hope: Prophetic Religion and the Death of Jim Crow* (Chapel Hill: University of North Carolina Press, 2004).

53. Lewis, *Walking with the Wind*, 181.

54. King, "*Playboy* Interview," 349.

55. Ibid.

56. Sokol, *There Goes My Everything*, 347, 100.

57. Ibid., 118.

58. Mark Newman, *Getting Right with God: Southern Baptists and Desegregation, 1945–1995* (Tuscaloosa: University of Alabama Press, 2001), ix.

59. Elizabeth Jacoway, "An Introduction: Civil Rights and the Changing South," in *Southern Businessmen and Desegregation*, ed. Elizabeth Jacoway and David R. Colburn (Baton Rouge: Louisiana State University Press, 1982), 7.

60. Chappell, *Inside Agitators*, 127.

61. Myrdal, *American Dilemma*, 1034.

62. Martin Luther King Jr., "The American Dream" (1961), in Washington, *Testament of Hope*, 208–9; King, *Stride toward Freedom*, 468; Martin Luther King Jr., "Showdown for Nonviolence" (1968), in Washington, *Testament of Hope*, 71.

63. Martin Luther King Jr., "Facing the Challenge of a New Age" (1957), in Washington, *Testament of Hope*, 140.

64. Ibid., 144.

65. For another discussion of the distinction between shame and guilt in southern life, see Fred Hobson, *But Now I See: The Southern White Racial Conversion Narrative* (Baton Rouge: Louisiana State University Press, 1999), 11. Drawing on Bertram Wyatt-Brown's work on honor, Hobson argued that shame was more characteristic of the Old South while "the southern party of guilt," particularly as it was expressed through white southern autobiography, gained prominence in the 1940s (15).

66. Lillian Smith, "How to Work for Racial Equality," *New Republic*, July 2, 1945, 23–24. Smith's biographer, Anne C. Loveland, drew on this quote in arguing of Smith, "Unlike so many other liberals she did not feel guilty about segregation and, significantly, did not try to persuade whites to abolish it by arousing guilt feelings in them. Emphasizing the harm segregation did to whites, she urged them to eliminate it in their own and their children's interest." Loveland, *Lillian Smith: A Southerner Confronting the South, A Biography* (Baton Rouge: Louisiana State University Press, 1986), 262. I would argue that the most consistent theme in Smith's work is that of guilt, both personal and regional. Although she declared the South guilty of the sin of segregation, she understood that an appeal to self-interest would be much more effective than an appeal to conscience.

67. Sokol, *There Goes My Everything*, 137.

68. Numan V. Bartley, *The Rise of Massive Resistance: Race and Politics in the South during the 1950's* (1969; Baton Rouge: Louisiana State University Press, 1999), 27.

69. Martin Luther King Jr., *Where Do We Go from Here: Chaos or Community?* (1967), in Washington, *Testament of Hope*, 568.

70. Sokol, *There Goes My Everything*, 321.

71. Hobson, *But Now I See*, 59.

72. Martin Luther King Jr., "A Time to Break Silence" (1967), in Washington, *Testament of Hope*, 233; Fairclough, *To Redeem the Soul of America*, 32.

73. Chappell, *Inside Agitators*, 81.

74. Young, *Easy Burden*, 219.

75. Sokol, *There Goes My Everything*, 309–13; Fannie Lou Hamer, quoted in ibid., 180.

76. Lewis, *Walking with the Wind*, 250.

77. Pauli Murray, *Song in a Weary Throat: An American Pilgrimage* (New York: Harper & Row, 1987), 128.

78. Braden, *Wall Between*, 9.

79. Young, *Easy Burden*, 150.

80. Ibid., 253; King, *Where Do We Go from Here?*, 582.

81. Young, *Easy Burden*, 172.

82. Martin Luther King Jr., *Stride toward Freedom*, 482; "Where Do We Go from Here?" (1972), in Washington, *Testament of Hope*, 245.

83. For a consideration of black southerners who had a vested interest in maintaining segregation, see Lauren F. Winner, "Doubtless Sincere: New Characters in the Civil Rights Cast," in Ownby, *Role of Ideas in the Civil Rights South*, 157–69. On the subject of voting, Raymond Andrews explained of his Georgia community in the 1940s, "Voting was just not a part of the community's tradition. Voting to these folks always meant trouble." Andrews, *The Last Radio Baby: A Memoir* (Atlanta: Peachtree Publishers, 1990), 199. Likewise, Anne Moody recalled the frustration she and other young activists felt trying to register voters in rural Mississippi in the early 1960s: "It didn't take me long to find out that the Negroes in Madison County were just the same as those in most of the other counties. They were just as apathetic or indifferent about voting." She also believed many parents in the community disapproved of their children participating in the voter registration drive, mostly out of concern for their safety. Moody, *Coming of Age in Mississippi* (1968; New York: Laurel, 1976), 292–93.

84. Martin Luther King Jr., "An Address before the National Press Club" (1962), in Washington, *Testament of Hope*, 101.

85. Ibid.; King, "Burning Truth in the South," 97; Martin Luther King Jr., "Civil Right No. 1: The Right to Vote" (1965), in Washington, *Testament of Hope*, 184.

86. Richard Wright, quoted in Cell, *Highest Stage of White Supremacy*, 246. See also Richard Wright, *Native Son* (1940; New York: Harper & Row, 1966), 360.

87. Cell, *Highest Stage of White Supremacy*, 273.

88. Martin Luther King Jr., "The Current Crisis in Race Relations" (1958), "The Power of Nonviolence" (1958), both in Washington, *Testament of Hope*, 89, 15.

89. James Farmer, *Lay Bare the Heart: An Autobiography of the Civil Rights Movement* (New York: Arbor House, 1985), 122.

BIBLIOGRAPHY

ARCHIVAL AND MANUSCRIPT SOURCES

African Methodist Episcopal Church Department of Research and Scholarship. Nashville, Tenn.

Alabama Department of Archives and History. Governor Gordon Persons Administrative Files. Montgomery.

David M. Rubenstein Rare Book & Manuscript Library, Duke University. Behind the Veil: Documenting African-American Life in the Jim Crow South. Durham, N.C.

Georgia Archives. Morrow.

Kentucky Department for Libraries and Archives. Frankfort.

Library of Virginia. Richmond.

Mississippi Department of Archives and History. Jackson.

Presbyterian Historical Society. Philadelphia, Pa.

Richard B. Russell Library for Political Research and Studies. Richard B. Russell Jr. Collection. Athens, Ga.

South Carolina Department of Archives and History. Columbia.

Southern Baptist Historical Library and Archives. Christian Life Commission Administrative Files and Una Roberts Lawrence Collection. Nashville, Tenn.

State Archives of North Carolina. Raleigh.

Tennessee State Library and Archives. Nashville.

United Methodist Archives and History Center. Madison, N.J.

PRIMARY SOURCES

Abernathy, Ralph David. *And the Walls Came Tumbling Down: An Autobiography.* New York: Harper & Row, 1989.

AME Zion Hymnal. Charlotte, N.C.: AME Zion Publishing House, 1957.

Andrews, Raymond. *The Last Radio Baby: A Memoir.* Atlanta: Peachtree Publishers, 1990.

Angelou, Maya. *I Know Why the Caged Bird Sings.* 1969. New York: Bantam Books, 1993.

Ashmore, Harry S. *An Epitaph for Dixie.* New York: Norton, 1958.

Bagley, Edythe Scott, with Joe Hilley. *Desert Rose: The Life and Legacy of Coretta Scott King.* Tuscaloosa: University of Alabama Press, 2012.

Bates, Daisy. *The Long Shadow of Little Rock: A Memoir.* 1962. Fayetteville: University of Arkansas Press, 1987.

Blount, Roy, Jr. *Be Sweet: A Conditional Love Story.* New York: Knopf, 1998.

Boggs, Lindy, with Katherine Hatch. *Washington through a Purple Veil: Memoirs of a Southern Woman*. New York: Harcourt Brace & Co., 1994.

Bolsterli, Margaret Jones. *Born in the Delta: Reflections on the Making of a Southern White Sensibility*. Knoxville: University of Tennessee Press, 1991.

Boyle, Sarah Patton. *The Desegregated Heart: A Virginian's Stand in Time of Transition*. New York: Morrow, 1962.

Braden, Anne. *The Wall Between*. 1958. Knoxville: University of Tennessee Press, 1999.

Brown, Cecil. *Coming Up Down Home: A Memoir of a Southern Childhood*. Hopewell, N.J.: Ecco Press, 1993.

Campbell, Will D. *Brother to a Dragonfly*. 1977. New York: Continuum, 2000.

Carter, Hodding. *Southern Legacy*. Baton Rouge: Louisiana State University Press, 1950.

Carter, Jimmy. *An Hour before Daylight: Memories of a Rural Boyhood*. New York: Simon & Schuster, 2001.

Clark, Septima Poinsette, with LeGette Blythe, *Echo in My Soul*. New York: Dutton, 1962.

Clayton, Xernona, with Hal Gulliver. *I've Been Marching All the Time: An Autobiography*. Atlanta: Longstreet Press, 1991.

Cohen, Edward. *The Peddler's Grandson: Growing Up Jewish in Mississippi*. Jackson: University Press of Mississippi, 1999.

Cohn, David L. *The Mississippi Delta and the World*. Edited by James C. Cobb. Baton Rouge: Louisiana State University Press, 1995.

Crews, Harry. *A Childhood: The Biography of a Place*. 1978. Athens: University of Georgia Press, 1995.

Curry, Constance, Joan C. Browning, Dorothy Dawson Burlage, Penny Patch, Theresa Del Pozzo, Sue Thrasher, Elaine Delott Baker, Emmie Schrader Adams, and Casey Hayden. *Deep in Our Hearts: Nine White Women in the Freedom Movement*. Athens: University of Georgia Press, 2000.

Durr, Virginia Foster. *Outside the Magic Circle: The Autobiography of Virginia Foster Durr*. Edited by Hollinger F. Barnard. Tuscaloosa: University of Alabama Press, 1985.

Edelman, Marian Wright. *Lanterns: A Memoir of Mentors*. Boston: Beacon Press, 1999.

Evans, Lawton B. *First Lessons in American History*. Rev. ed. 1910. New York: Benjamin H. Sanborn & Co., 1922.

Farmer, James. *Lay Bare the Heart: An Autobiography of the Civil Rights Movement*. New York: Arbor House, 1985.

Fast, Howard. *Freedom Road*. New York: Duell, Sloan & Pearce, 1944.

Faust, Drew Gilpin. "Living History." In *Shapers of Southern History: Autobiographical Reflections*, edited by John B. Boles. Athens: University of Georgia Press, 2004.

———. *Mothers of Invention: Women of the Slaveholding South in the American Civil War*. 1996. New York: Vintage Books, 1997.

Forbis, Wesley L., ed. *The Baptist Hymnal*. Nashville: Convention Press, 1991.

Franklin, John Hope. *Mirror to America: The Autobiography of John Hope Franklin*. New York: Farrar, Straus & Giroux, 2005.

Gladney, Margaret Rose, ed. *How Am I to Be Heard? Letters of Lillian Smith*. Chapel Hill: University of North Carolina Press, 1993.

Gordy, Wilbur Fisk. *The History of the United States*. 1922. New York: Charles Scribner's Sons, 1927.

Hemphill, Paul. *Leaving Birmingham: Notes of a Native Son*. 1993. Tuscaloosa: University of Alabama Press, 2000.

hooks, bell. *Bone Black: Memories of Girlhood*. New York: Henry Holt, 1996.

Hughes, R. O. *Problems of American Democracy*. Boston: Allyn & Bacon, 1922.

Hunter-Gault, Charlayne. *In My Place*. 1992. New York: Vintage Books, 1993.

The Hymnal of the Protestant Episcopal Church. New York: Church Pension Fund, 1940.

Jordan, Vernon E., Jr., with Annette Gordon-Reed. *Vernon Can Read! A Memoir*. New York: PublicAffairs, 2001.

King, Coretta Scott. *My Life with Martin Luther King, Jr.* Rev. ed. 1969. New York: Henry Holt, 1993.

King, Edwin. "Growing Up in Mississippi in a Time of Change." In *Mississippi Writers: Reflections of Childhood and Youth, Volume 2: Nonfiction*, edited by Dorothy Abbott. Jackson: University Press of Mississippi, 1986.

King, Larry L. *Confessions of a White Racist*. 1969. New York: Viking Press, 1971.

King, Martin Luther, Jr. *A Testament of Hope: The Essential Writings and Speeches of Martin Luther King, Jr.* Edited by James M. Washington. San Francisco: Harper, 1986.

Lewis, John, with Michael D'Orso. *Walking with the Wind: A Memoir of the Movement*. New York: Simon & Schuster, 1998.

Lumpkin, Katharine Du Pre. *The Making of a Southerner*. 1946. Athens: University of Georgia Press, 1991.

Mace, William H. *American History*. New York: Rand McNally, 1925.

Mays, Benjamin E. *Born to Rebel: An Autobiography*. 1971. Athens: University of Georgia Press, 2003.

McKinney, B. B., ed. and comp. *The Broadman Hymnal*. Nashville: Broadman Press, 1940.

McKinstry, Carolyn Maull, with Denise George. *While the World Watched: A Birmingham Bombing Survivor Comes of Age during the Civil Rights Movement*. Carol Stream, Ill.: Tyndale House Publishers, 2011.

McLaurin, Melton A. *Separate Pasts: Growing Up White in the Segregated South*. 1987. Athens: University of Georgia Press, 1998.

McLaurin, Tim. *Keeper of the Moon: A Southern Boyhood*. New York: Norton, 1991.

Mebane, Mary E. *Mary*. New York: Viking Press, 1981.

———. *Mary, Wayfarer*. 1976. New York: Viking Press, 1983.

Moody, Anne. *Coming of Age in Mississippi*. 1968. New York: Laurel, 1976.

Morris, Willie. *North toward Home*. 1967. New York: Vintage Books, 2000.

Murray, Pauli. *Proud Shoes: The Story of an American Family*. 1956. New York: Harper & Row, 1978.

———. *Song in a Weary Throat: An American Pilgrimage*. New York: Harper & Row, 1987.

Muzzey, David Saville. *An American History*. Rev. ed. 1911. Boston: Ginn & Co., 1920.

Parks, Rosa, with Jim Haskins. *Rosa Parks: My Story*. New York: Dial Books, 1992.

Payne, Les. "The Night I Stopped Being a Negro." In *When Race Becomes Real: Black and White Writers Confront Their Personal Histories*, edited by Bernestine Singley. Chicago: Lawrence Hill Books, 2002.

The Presbyterian Hymnal. Richmond: Presbyterian Committee of Publication, 1927.

Raines, Howell. *My Soul Is Rested: Movement Days in the Deep South Remembered*. 1977. New York: Penguin Books, 1983.

Rowan, Carl T. *Breaking Barriers: A Memoir*. Boston: Little, Brown, 1991.

———. *South of Freedom*. 1952. Baton Rouge: Louisiana State University Press, 1997.

Seigenthaler, John, Sr. "Son of the South." In *When Race Becomes Real: Black and White Writers Confront Their Personal Histories*, edited by Bernestine Singley. Chicago: Lawrence Hill Books, 2002.

Smith, Lillian. *Killers of the Dream*. Rev. ed. 1949. 1961. New York: Norton, 1994.

Sullivan, Patricia, ed. *Freedom Writer: Virginia Foster Durr, Letters from the Civil Rights Years*. 2003. Athens: University of Georgia Press, 2006.

Thompson, Waddy. *The First Book in United States History*. Boston: D. C. Heath, 1921.

The United Methodist Hymnal. Nashville: United Methodist Publishing House, 1989.

Watters, Pat. *Down to Now: Reflections on the Southern Civil Rights Movement*. 1971. Athens: University of Georgia Press, 1993.

Welty, Eudora. *One Writer's Beginnings*. Cambridge: Harvard University Press, 1984.

West, Willis Mason. *History of the American People*. Rev. ed. 1918. Boston: Allyn & Bacon, 1922.

Winfrey, Carlton. "Spelling Lesson." In *When Race Becomes Real: Black and White Writers Confront Their Personal Histories*, edited by Bernestine Singley. Chicago: Lawrence Hill Books, 2002.

Woodson, Carter G. *The Mis-Education of the Negro*. Washington, D.C.: Associated Publishers, 1933.

Wright, Richard. *Black Boy: A Record of Childhood and Youth*. 1945. New York: Perennial Classics, 1998.

———. *Native Son*. 1940. New York: Harper & Row, 1966.

Zellner, Bob, with Constance Curry. *The Wrong Side of Murder Creek: A White Southerner in the Freedom Movement*. Montgomery, Ala.: NewSouth Books, 2008.

SECONDARY SOURCES

Adams, Timothy Dow. *Telling Lies in Modern American Autobiography*. Chapel Hill: University of North Carolina Press, 1990.

Alvis, Joel L., Jr. *Religion and Race: Southern Presbyterians, 1946–1983*. Tuscaloosa: University of Alabama Press, 1994.

Anderson, R. Bentley. *Black, White, and Catholic: New Orleans Interracialism, 1947–1956*. Nashville: Vanderbilt University Press, 2005.

Anne Braden: Southern Patriot. DVD. Directed by Anne Lewis and Mimi Pickering. Whitesburg, Ky.: Appalshop, 2012.

Badger, Tony. "Closet Moderates: Why White Liberals Failed, 1940–1970." In *The Role of Ideas in the Civil Rights South,* edited by Ted Ownby. Jackson: University Press of Mississippi, 2002.

Bailey, Fred Arthur. "The Textbooks of the 'Lost Cause': Censorship and the Creation of Southern State Histories." *Georgia Historical Quarterly* 75, no. 3 (Fall 1991): 507–33.

Ballou, Robert O., with Irene Rakosky. *A History of the Council on Books in Wartime, 1942–1946.* New York: Country Life Press, 1946.

Banks, W. Curtis. "White Preference in Blacks: A Paradigm in Search of a Phenomenon." *Psychological Bulletin* 83, no. 6 (1976): 1179–86.

Banks-Wallace, JoAnne, and Lennette Parks. "'So That Our Souls Don't Get Damaged': The Impact of Racism on Maternal Thinking and Practice Related to the Protection of Daughters." *Issues in Mental Health Nursing* 22, no. 1 (Jan. 2001): 77–98.

Bartley, Numan V. *The Rise of Massive Resistance: Race and Politics in the South during the 1950's.* 1969. Baton Rouge: Louisiana State University Press, 1999.

Bass, S. Jonathan. *Blessed Are the Peacemakers: Martin Luther King Jr., Eight White Religious Leaders, and the "Letter from Birmingham Jail."* Baton Rouge: Louisiana State University Press, 2001.

Blassingame, John W. *The Slave Community: Plantation Life in the Antebellum South.* New York: Oxford University Press, 1972.

Bloom, Lynn Z. "Coming of Age in the Segregated South: Autobiographies of Twentieth-Century Childhoods, Black and White." In *Home Ground: Southern Autobiography,* edited by J. Bill Berry. Columbia: University of Missouri Press, 1991.

Blum, Edward J., and Paul Harvey. *The Color of Christ: The Son of God and the Saga of Race in America.* Chapel Hill: University of North Carolina Press, 2012.

Bolsterli, Margaret Jones. "Reflections on Lillian Smith and the Guilts of the Betrayer." *Southern Quarterly* 27, no. 4 (1989): 71–78.

Boykin, A. Wade, and Forrest D. Toms. "Black Child Socialization: A Conceptual Framework." In *Black Children: Social, Educational, and Parental Environments,* edited by Harriette Pipes McAdoo and John Lewis McAdoo. Beverly Hills, Calif.: Sage Publications, 1985.

Branch, Curtis W., and Nora Newcombe. "Racial Attitude Development among Young Black Children as a Function of Parental Attitudes: A Longitudinal and Cross-Sectional Study." *Child Development* 57, no. 3 (June 1986): 712–21.

Brown, Tony N., and Chase L. Lesane-Brown. "Race Socialization Messages across Historical Time." *Social Psychology Quarterly* 69, no. 2 (June 2006): 201–13.

Brown, Tony N., Emily E. Tanner-Smith, Chase L. Lesane-Brown, and Michael E. Ezell. "Child, Parent, and Situational Correlates of Familial Ethnic/Race Socialization." *Journal of Marriage and Family* 69, no. 1 (Feb. 2007): 14–25.

Brundage, W. Fitzhugh. *Lynching in the New South: Georgia and Virginia, 1880–1930.* Urbana: University of Illinois Press, 1993.

Butler, James Overton. "The Treatment of the Negro in Southern School Textbooks." Master's thesis, George Peabody College for Teachers, 1933.

Carpenter, Marie Elizabeth. *The Treatment of the Negro in American History School Textbooks.* Menasha, Wisc.: George Banta Publishing Co., 1941.

Cell, John W. *The Highest Stage of White Supremacy: The Origins of Segregation in South Africa and the American South.* Cambridge: Cambridge University Press, 1982.

Chafe, William H. *Civilities and Civil Rights: Greensboro, North Carolina, and the Black Struggle for Freedom.* 1980. New York: Oxford University Press, 1981.

Chappell, David L. *Inside Agitators: White Southerners in the Civil Rights Movement.* Baltimore: Johns Hopkins University Press, 1994.

———. "Niebuhrisms and Myrdaleries: The Intellectual Roots of the Civil Rights Movement Reconsidered." In *The Role of Ideas in the Civil Rights South,* edited by Ted Ownby. Jackson: University Press of Mississippi, 2002.

———. *A Stone of Hope: Prophetic Religion and the Death of Jim Crow.* Chapel Hill: University of North Carolina Press, 2004.

Clark, Kenneth B. *Prejudice and Your Child.* 1955. Middletown, Conn.: Wesleyan University Press, 1988.

Clark, Kenneth B., and Mamie P. Clark. "Emotional Factors in Racial Identification and Preference in Negro Children." In "The Negro Child in the American Social Order." Special issue, *Journal of Negro Education* 19, no. 3 (Summer 1950): 341–50.

———. "Racial Identification and Preference in Negro Children." In *Readings in Social Psychology,* edited by Theodore M. Newcomb and Eugene L. Hartley. New York: Henry Holt, 1947.

Cobb, James C. *The* Brown *Decision, Jim Crow, and Southern Identity.* Athens: University of Georgia Press, 2005.

———. "World War II and the Mind of the Modern South." In *Remaking Dixie: The Impact of World War II on the American South,* edited by Neil R. McMillen. Jackson: University Press of Mississippi, 1997.

Coles, Robert. *Children of Crisis: A Study of Courage and Fear.* Boston: Little, Brown, 1967.

Collum, Danny Duncan. *Black and Catholic in the Jim Crow South: The Stuff That Makes Community.* New York: Paulist Press, 2006.

Cox, Karen L. *Dixie's Daughters: The United Daughters of the Confederacy and the Preservation of Confederate Culture.* Gainesville: University Press of Florida, 2003.

Cross, William E., Jr. *Shades of Black: Diversity in African-American Identity.* Philadelphia: Temple University Press, 1991.

Dennis, Rutledge M. "Socialization and Racism: The White Experience." In *Impacts of Racism on White Americans,* edited by Benjamin P. Bowser and Raymond G. Hunt. Beverly Hills, Calif.: Sage Publications, 1981.

Dittmer, John. *Local People: The Struggle for Civil Rights in Mississippi.* Urbana: University of Illinois Press, 1994.

Doyle, Bertram Wilbur. *The Etiquette of Race Relations in the South: A Study in Social Control.* 1937. New York: Schocken Books, 1971.

DuRocher, Kristina. *Raising Racists: The Socialization of White Children in the Jim Crow South.* Lexington: University Press of Kentucky, 2011.

Egerton, John. *A Mind to Stay Here: Profiles from the South.* New York: Macmillan, 1970.

———. *Speak Now against the Day: The Generation before the Civil Rights Movement in the South.* 1994. Chapel Hill: University of North Carolina Press, 1995.

Elkins, Stanley. *Slavery: A Problem in American Institutional and Intellectual Life.* 1959. Chicago: University of Chicago Press, 1968.

Fairclough, Adam. *A Class of Their Own: Black Teachers in the Segregated South.* Cambridge: Belknap Press of Harvard University Press, 2007.

———. *Teaching Equality: Black Schools in the Age of Jim Crow.* Athens: University of Georgia Press, 2001.

———. *To Redeem the Soul of America: The Southern Christian Leadership Conference and Martin Luther King, Jr.* Athens: University of Georgia Press, 1987.

Fine, Michelle, and Cheryl Bowers. "Racial Self-Identification: The Effects of Social History and Gender." *Journal of Applied Social Psychology* 14, no. 2 (1984): 136–46.

Fosl, Catherine. *Subversive Southerner: Anne Braden and the Struggle for Racial Justice in the Cold War South.* New York: Palgrave Macmillan, 2002.

Fosl, Catherine, and Tracy E. K'Meyer, eds. *Freedom on the Border: An Oral History of the Civil Rights Movement in Kentucky.* Lexington: University Press of Kentucky, 2009.

Garrow, David J. "Hopelessly Hollow History: Revisionist Devaluing of *Brown v. Board of Education.*" In "Twentieth-Century Constitutional History." Special issue, *Virginia Law Review* 80, no. 1 (Feb. 1994): 151–60.

Genovese, Eugene D. *Roll Jordan Roll: The World the Slaves Made.* New York: Pantheon Books, 1974.

Gilmore, Glenda Elizabeth. *Defying Dixie: The Radical Roots of Civil Rights, 1919–1950.* New York: Norton, 2008.

Goggin, Jacqueline. *Carter G. Woodson: A Life in Black History.* Baton Rouge: Louisiana State University Press, 1993.

Goldfield, David R. *Black, White, and Southern: Race Relations and Southern Culture, 1940 to the Present.* Baton Rouge: Louisiana State University Press, 1990.

Gusdorf, Georges. "Conditions and Limits of Autobiography" (1956). In *Autobiography: Essays Theoretical and Critical,* edited by James Olney. Princeton: Princeton University Press, 1980.

Gutman, Herbert G. *The Black Family in Slavery and Freedom, 1750–1925.* New York: Pantheon Books, 1976.

Hall, Jacquelyn Dowd. "The Long Civil Rights Movement and the Political Uses of the Past." *Journal of American History* 91, no. 4 (Mar. 2005): 1233–63.

———. *Revolt against Chivalry: Jessie Daniel Ames and the Women's Campaign against Lynching.* Rev. ed. 1979. New York: Columbia University Press, 1993.

———. "'You Must Remember This': Autobiography as Social Critique." *Journal of American History* 85, no. 2 (Sept. 1998): 439–65.

Harrison, Algea O. "The Black Family's Socializing Environment: Self-Esteem and Ethnic Attitude among Black Children." In *Black Children: Social, Educational, and Parental Environments,* edited by Harriette Pipes McAdoo and John Lewis McAdoo. Beverly Hills, Calif.: Sage Publications, 1985.

Harvey, Paul. *Redeeming the South: Religious Cultures and Racial Identities among Southern Baptists, 1865–1925.* Chapel Hill: University of North Carolina Press, 1997.

———. "Religion, Race, and the Right in the South, 1945–1990." In *Politics and Religion in the White South,* edited by Glenn Feldman. Lexington: University Press of Kentucky, 2005.

Higginbotham, Evelyn Brooks. *Righteous Discontent: The Women's Movement in the Black Baptist Church, 1880–1920.* Cambridge: Harvard University Press, 1993.

Hill, Shirley A. *African American Children: Socialization and Development in Families.* Thousand Oaks, Calif.: Sage Publications, 1999.

Hobson, Fred. *But Now I See: The Southern White Racial Conversion Narrative.* Baton Rouge: Louisiana State University Press, 1999.

Hughes, C. Alvin. "We Demand Our Rights: The Southern Negro Youth Congress, 1937–1949." *Phylon* 48, no. 1 (1987): 38–50.

Hughes, Diane, and Lisa Chen. "The Nature of Parents' Race-Related Communications to Children: A Developmental Perspective." In *Child Psychology: A Handbook of Contemporary Issues,* edited by Lawrence Balter and Catherine S. Tamis-LeMonda. Philadelphia: Psychology Press, 1999.

———. "When and What Parents Tell Children about Race: An Examination of Race-Related Socialization among African American Families." *Applied Developmental Science* 1, no. 4 (1997): 200–214.

Inscoe, John C. *Writing the South through the Self: Explorations in Southern Autobiography.* Athens: University of Georgia Press, 2011.

Irvine, Jacqueline Jordan, and Michèle Foster, eds. *Growing Up African American in Catholic Schools.* New York: Teachers College Press, 1996.

Jackson, James S., Wayne R. McCullough, Gerald Gurin, and Clifford L. Broman. "Race Identity." In *Life in Black America,* edited by James S. Jackson. Newbury Park, Calif.: Sage Publications, 1991.

Jacoway, Elizabeth, and David R. Colburn, eds. *Southern Businessmen and Desegregation.* Baton Rouge: Louisiana State University Press, 1982.

Johnson, Charles S. *Patterns of Negro Segregation.* New York: Harper & Brothers, 1943.

Kelley, Robin D. G. *Race Rebels: Culture, Politics, and the Black Working Class.* New York: Free Press, 1994.

———. "'We Are Not What We Seem': Rethinking Black Working-Class Opposition in the Jim Crow South." *Journal of American History* 80, no. 1 (June 1993): 75–112.

Kennedy, David M. *Freedom from Fear: The American People in Depression and War, 1929–1945.* New York: Oxford University Press, 1999.

Klarman, Michael J. "*Brown,* Racial Change, and the Civil Rights Movement." In "Twentieth-Century Constitutional History." Special issue, *Virginia Law Review* 80, no. 1 (Feb. 1994): 7–150.

Kolchin, Peter. "Reevaluating the Antebellum Slave Community: A Comparative Perspective." *Journal of American History* 70, no. 3 (Dec. 1983): 579–601.

———. "Whiteness Studies: The New History of Race in America." *Journal of American History* 89, no. 1 (June 2002): 154–73.

Krug, Mark M., John B. Poster, and William B. Gillies III. *The New Social Studies: Analysis of Theory and Materials.* Itasca, Ill.: F. E. Peacock Publishers, 1970.

Lasker, Bruno. *Race Attitudes in Children.* New York: Henry Holt, 1929.

Lavelle, Kristen M. *Whitewashing the South: White Memories of Segregation and Civil Rights.* Lanham, Md.: Rowman & Littlefield, 2015.

Lesane-Brown, Chase L. "A Review of Race Socialization within Black Families." *Developmental Review* 26, no. 4 (Dec. 2006): 400–426.

Lincoln, C. Eric, and Lawrence H. Mamiya. *The Black Church in the African American Experience.* Durham, N.C.: Duke University Press, 1990.

Litwack, Leon F. *Trouble in Mind: Black Southerners in the Age of Jim Crow.* 1998. New York: Vintage Books, 1999.

Loveland, Anne C. *Lillian Smith: A Southerner Confronting the South, A Biography.* Baton Rouge: Louisiana State University Press, 1986.

Macdonald, Andrew. *Howard Fast: A Critical Companion.* Westport, Conn.: Greenwood Press, 1996.

Mandel, Barrett J. "Full of Life Now." In *Autobiography: Essays Theoretical and Critical,* edited by James Olney. Princeton: Princeton University Press, 1980.

Markowitz, Gerald, and David Rosner. *Children, Race, and Power: Kenneth and Mamie Clark's Northside Center.* Charlottesville: University Press of Virginia, 1996.

Mays, Benjamin E., and Joseph W. Nicholson. *The Negro's Church.* 1933. Salem, N.H.: Ayer, 1988.

McAdoo, Harriette Pipes, and John Lewis McAdoo. "Preface." In *Black Children: Social, Educational, and Parental Environments,* edited by Harriette Pipes McAdoo and John Lewis McAdoo. Beverly Hills, Calif.: Sage Publications, 1985.

McMillen, Neil R. *Dark Journey: Black Mississippians in the Age of Jim Crow.* Urbana: University of Illinois Press, 1989.

———. "Fighting for What We Didn't Have: How Mississippi's Black Veterans Remember World War II." In *Remaking Dixie: The Impact of World War II on the American South,* edited by Neil R. McMillen. Jackson: University Press of Mississippi, 1997.

McMillen, Sally G. *To Raise Up the South: Sunday Schools in Black and White Churches, 1865–1915.* Baton Rouge: Louisiana State University Press, 2001.

Metress, Christopher, ed. *The Lynching of Emmett Till: A Documentary Narrative.* Charlottesville: University of Virginia Press, 2002.

Mickenberg, Julia L. *Learning from the Left: Children's Literature, the Cold War, and Radical Politics in the United States.* New York: Oxford University Press, 2006.

Morris, Tiyi M. *Womanpower Unlimited and the Black Freedom Struggle in Mississippi.* Athens: University of Georgia Press, 2015.

Murray, Pauli, ed. and comp. *States' Laws on Race and Color.* 1951. Athens: University of Georgia Press, 1997.

Murray, Peter C. *Methodists and the Crucible of Race, 1930–1975.* Columbia: University of Missouri Press, 2004.

Myrdal, Gunnar, with the assistance of Richard Sterner and Arnold Rose. *An American Dilemma: The Negro Problem and Modern Democracy.* New York: Harper & Brothers, 1944.

Newman, Mark. *Getting Right with God: Southern Baptists and Desegregation, 1945–1995.* Tuscaloosa: University of Alabama Press, 2001.

O'Dell, Darlene. *Sites of Southern Memory: The Autobiographies of Katharine Du Pre Lumpkin, Lillian Smith, and Pauli Murray.* Charlottesville: University Press of Virginia, 2001.

Pascal, Roy. *Design and Truth in Autobiography.* Cambridge: Harvard University Press, 1960.

Peters, Marie Ferguson. "Racial Socialization of Young Black Children." In *Black Children: Social, Educational, and Parental Environments,* edited by Harriette Pipes McAdoo and John Lewis McAdoo. Beverly Hills, Calif.: Sage Publications, 1985.

Pierce, Bessie Louise. *Public Opinion and the Teaching of History in the United States.* 1926. New York: Da Capo Press, 1970.

Ponterotto, Joseph G., and Paul B. Pedersen. *Preventing Prejudice: A Guide for Counselors and Educators.* Newbury Park, Calif.: Sage Publications, 1993.

Rabinowitz, Howard. *Race Relations in the Urban South, 1865–1890.* New York: Oxford University Press, 1978.

Reddick, Lawrence D. "Racial Attitudes in American History Textbooks of the South." *Journal of Negro History* 19, no. 3 (July 1934): 225–65.

Ritterhouse, Jennifer. *Growing Up Jim Crow: How Black and White Southern Children Learned Race.* Chapel Hill: University of North Carolina Press, 2006.

Roediger, David R. *The Wages of Whiteness: Race and the Making of the American Working Class.* Rev. ed. 1991. London: Verso, 1999.

Sanders Thompson, Vetta L. "Socialization to Race and Its Relationship to Racial Identification among African Americans." *Journal of Black Psychology* 20, no. 2 (May 1994): 175–88.

Scott, Daryl Michael. *Contempt and Pity: Social Policy and the Image of the Damaged Black Psyche, 1880–1996.* Chapel Hill: University of North Carolina Press, 1997.

Scott, James C. *Domination and the Arts of Resistance: Hidden Transcripts.* New Haven: Yale University Press, 1990.

Shattuck, Gardiner H., Jr. *Episcopalians and Race: Civil War to Civil Rights.* Lexington: University Press of Kentucky, 2000.

Silver, James W. *The Closed Society.* Rev. ed. 1964. New York: Harcourt, Brace & World, 1966.

Sims, Anastatia. *The Power of Femininity in the New South: Women's Organizations and Politics in North Carolina, 1880–1930.* Columbia: University of South Carolina Press, 1997.

Sloan, Irving. *The Negro in Modern American History Textbooks.* Washington, D.C.: American Federation of Teachers, 1972.

Smith, Mark M. *How Race Is Made: Slavery, Segregation, and the Senses.* Chapel Hill: University of North Carolina Press, 2006.

Sokol, Jason. *There Goes My Everything: White Southerners in the Age of Civil Rights, 1945–1975.* New York: Knopf, 2006.

Sosna, Morton. *In Search of the Silent South: Southern Liberals and the Race Issue.* New York: Columbia University Press, 1977.

Spencer, Margaret Beale. "Children's Cultural Values and Parental Child Rearing Strategies." *Developmental Review* 3, no. 4 (Dec. 1983): 351–70.

Sullivan, Patricia. *Days of Hope: Race and Democracy in the New Deal Era.* Chapel Hill: University of North Carolina Press, 1996.

Sumner, William Graham. *Folkways: A Study of the Sociological Importance of Usages, Manners, Customs, Mores, and Morals.* Boston: Ginn, 1906.

Tatum, Beverly Daniel. *"Why Are All the Black Kids Sitting Together in the Cafeteria?" And Other Conversations about Race.* New York: Basic Books, 1997.

Thornton, Michael C. "Strategies of Racial Socialization among Black Parents: Mainstream, Minority, and Cultural Messages." In *Family Life in Black America,* edited by Robert Joseph Taylor, James S. Jackson, and Linda M. Chatters. Thousand Oaks, Calif.: Sage Publications, 1997.

Thornton, Michael C., Linda M. Chatters, Robert Joseph Taylor, and Walter R. Allen. "Sociodemographic and Environmental Correlates of Racial Socialization by Black Parents." In "Minority Children." Special issue, *Child Development* 61, no. 2 (Apr. 1990): 401–9.

Tolnay, Stewart E., and E. M. Beck. *A Festival of Violence: An Analysis of Southern Lynchings, 1882–1930.* Urbana: University of Illinois Press, 1995.

Van Ausdale, Debra, and Joe R. Feagin. *The First R: How Children Learn Race and Racism.* Lanham, Md.: Rowman & Littlefield, 2001.

Wallach, Jennifer Jensen. *"Closer to the Truth than Any Fact": Memoir, Memory, and Jim Crow.* Athens: University of Georgia Press, 2008.

Watson, Jay. "Uncovering the Body, Discovering Ideology: Segregation and Sexual Anxiety in Lillian Smith's *Killers of the Dream.*" *American Quarterly* 49, no. 3 (Sept. 1997): 470–503.

Williamson, Joel. *After Slavery: The Negro in South Carolina during Reconstruction, 1861–1877.* Chapel Hill: University of North Carolina Press, 1965.

Willis, Alan Scot. *All According to God's Plan: Southern Baptist Missions and Race, 1945–1970.* Lexington: University Press of Kentucky, 2005.

Winner, Lauren F. "Doubtless Sincere: New Characters in the Civil Rights Cast." In *The Role of Ideas in the Civil Rights South,* edited by Ted Ownby. Jackson: University Press of Mississippi, 2002.

Woodward, C. Vann. *The Strange Career of Jim Crow.* 3rd rev. ed. 1955. New York: Oxford University Press, 1974.

Zangrando, Robert L. *The NAACP Crusade against Lynching, 1909–1950.* Philadelphia: Temple University Press, 1980.

INDEX